New Jersey Historical Classics

# MURDER DID PAY

*Published with Funds from
Friends of the Society,
the Estate of Edward J. Grassmann,
and an Anonymous Gift
Dedicated to the Memory of
Delia Brinkerhoff Koster*

# MURDER DID PAY

## 19TH-CENTURY NEW JERSEY MURDERS

Introduced by

JOHN T. CUNNINGHAM

With a Bibliography by

DONALD A. SINCLAIR

NEWARK 1982
New Jersey Historical Society

*Acknowledgment*

THE FOUR PAMPHLETS reprinted in this book were each filmed from two complete copies, their text sizes photographically altered when necessary to achieve greater uniformity. The publisher wishes to thank Special Collections, the Rutgers University Libraries, for permission to reprint the bulk of the four pamphlets from copies in its collections, and the Joint Free Public Library of Morristown and Morris Township, Local History Department, for permission to film and reprint selected pages in its copy of *S. P. Hull's Report of the Trial and Conviction of Antoine Le Blanc* . . . . The New Jersey Historical Society itself provided a copy of the *Life, Trial, Execution and Dying Confession of John Erpenstein* . . . and most of the pictorial materials outside the pamphlets.

© 1981 by The New Jersey Historical Society
Library of Congress catalog card number 81-83978
ISBN: 0-911020-04-7


Printed in the U.S.A. by the
Harvard Printing Company,
Orange, New Jersey

# TABLE OF CONTENTS

John M. Armstrong "finishes the awful work," from the *Hunter-Armstrong Tragedy* . . . (Philadelphia: Barclay & Company, 1878).

# THE RIGHTEOUS PROFIT

MURDER IS UGLY, insane, and as anti-social as any action can be. Murder also has been profitable for those who would inform the public about dastardly deeds—whether the informers be newspaper editors, television sponsors, or the authors and publishers of such pamphlets as the four being presented here.

On the pages that follow are the cases of:

• Antoine Le Blanc, a French immigrant accused of the murders of Samuel and Sarah Sayre and their serving girl Phebe at Morristown in the spring of 1833. As the coup de grâce, Le Blanc stowed the Sayres under a manure heap before stealing their horse in a booty-laden mad dash toward New York.

• John Erpenstein, a German immigrant who in the summer of 1852 found a way out of his dilemma of being lover to a mistress, the mistress's mother, and his wife. He fed his wife an arsenic sandwich.

• Bridget Dergan, an Irish immigrant serving girl who in the winter of 1867 felt the pangs of love when she heard (or thought she heard) a New Market doctor say that he wished his wife were "out of the way." Bridget tried to fulfill his wish by stabbing the doctor's wife sixty times.

• Jacob Rosenzweig, alias Ascher, a New York doctor of considerably dubious repute whose specialty was illegal abortions. Beautiful Alice Bowlsby, of Paterson, decidedly pregnant, visited him on August 23, 1871, and was found dead three days later, stuffed into a trunk bound for Chicago.

Re-publication of the crimes, trials, and convictions of four of New Jersey's most notorious murder cases serves more than a twentieth-century sales potential. These pamphlets cast a penetrating light on their times and as such are solid, if colorful, sources of American history.

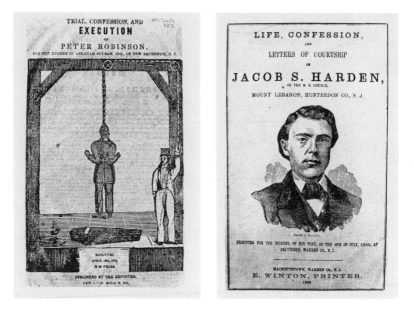

How a society deals with crime and criminals says much about its manners and morals. Puritans, God-loving all, thought nothing of putting witches to death, nor were communities disturbed that a small, self-appointed inner group was the sole judge of witchdom.

Much of nineteenth-century America was still quite puritanical in spirit, highly moralistic and self-righteous. Witches had gone out of style. But there were other possibilities, and too often murder pamphlets demonstrated not so much guilt or innocence as the insurmountable chasm between the pious and the heathen, between good and evil.

Antoine Le Blanc, John Erpenstein, Bridget Dergan, and Jacob Rosenzweig had some characteristics that fitted many nineteenth-century murderers. All of them were immigrants. Three were Catholic, the fourth was Jewish. One was Irish, two were German, and the fourth was French.

Those characteristics were important. To be a foreigner was bad enough. But being a Catholic or a Jew raised a person on any nineteenth-century hate list. Vicious attacks on Catholic churches in Newark and Jersey City in the 1840s were not considered out of the ordinary. John Erpenstein, one of the murderers about to be considered, won at least editorial absolution because on the gallows he delivered a confession presumably wrought since he had seen the light of Protestantism.

That is not to say that New Jerseyans of British ancestry were any less capable of murder. Donald A. Sinclair's bibliography shows that

Printed images of murderers: from left to right, Peter Robinson, 1841; Jacob S. Harden, 1860; and James P. Donnelly, 1858.

PORTRAIT OF JAMES P. DONNELLY,

"old-stock" murderers were in no short supply. But it was certainly easy for nineteenth-century New Jerseyans to believe in the total guilt of the likes of Le Blanc, Erpenstein, Dergan, and Rosenzweig. Reading the pamphlets makes it even easier to believe in their guilt—there is little question that all but the last were murderers.

Murder pamphlets served at least one other important function in purportedly innocent nineteenth-century days. They were a way to reveal ("modestly," one pamphlet said) unmentionable things such as pregnancy, abortion, illicit love, insane rage, alcoholic excess, and general anti-social behavior. It was possible, for example, to show a scantily clad female body in the guise of enlightening the public—she was, after all, dead and in a trunk bound for Chicago. Before the days of pulp murder novels, these murder pamphlets served as much to entertain and titilate as to give moral instruction.

The four pamphlets reprinted in this volume are just a modest sampling of the extensive non-fiction crime literature offered up to an eager nineteenth-century public. Thomas McDade, in his splendid book, *The Annals of Murder*, lists 1,126 murder titles published in this country between the 1620s and 1900. Thirty of the titles involved New Jersey. And Donald A. Sinclair lists many more New Jersey murder titles in this volume.

Certainly, there were many more murders committed in the United States than those listed by McDade and Sinclair. But "pamphlet murders" had some special quality that made them worthy of being enshrined in print, even if the special quality might be nothing more than the vanity of the preacher who felt that his long sermon to the condemned murderer (and the assembled throng) deserved immortality.

They were celebrated cases, whether they were published by local newspaper printing offices or by national crime publishers such as Barclay & Company, in Philadelphia. Many cases occasioned rival pamphlets, second editions, and translations. While the unquestionable commercial success of these pamphlets weighed heavily on their minds, most publishers professed the pious hope that their pamphlets would deter would-be slayers.

But Le Blanc's fate, vivid in printed form, did not keep John Erpenstein from lacing his wife's sandwich with arsenic in 1852. Nor did it keep Bridget Dergan from repeatedly stabbing her employer's wife in 1867. In Bridget's case, a thousand or ten thousand moralistic pamphlets would have availed nothing. Bridget could not read. And even if she could there is doubt that she would have been turned away, for hers was a crime of passion. So was Erpenstein's, albeit far more sordid and premeditated.

Highly moralistic nineteenth-century readers could take grim satisfaction as they read about Bridget and John. They might also have gained some indirect and secret insight into the ways of illicit love, a matter then strictly forbidden in polite conversation or reading. Such publications as the *National Police Gazette*, published in New York City from 1845 to 1932, made a great deal of money from such matters, particularly if someone driven by "unbridled passion" was brought to the noose.

The trials and executions themselves tell much about nineteenth-century law and attitudes. The wheels of "Jersey justice" were reputed to be swift and efficient. Based solely on the pamphlets, there was an effort to insure a reasonably fair trial. That took good legal discipline.

Court-appointed defense lawyers worked hard, in print at least, to present the best possible case for their clients. Theirs was not an easy task. Crowds gathered outside of many courthouses would have cheerfully lynched an acquitted murderer and all who worked in his or her defense.

Prosecutors had few restrictions on their statements against the accused, often bordering on outrageous half-truths. Judges, in turn, could scarcely have been accused of impartiality as they summed up what the jurors might find. They presented legal options to jurors, true enough, but their judicial embroidery often was both colorful and prejudicial.

The hangman's noose was all but unavoidable for the convicted murderer, for capital punishment was accepted with little opposition in nineteenth-century America as being blessed with divine authority and biblical injunction. Theodore Frelinghuysen, the New Jersey jurist and Henry Clay's running mate for Vice President, praised capital punishment in 1843 in his introduction to the Reverend George B. Cheever's book *Punishment by Death: Its Authority and Expedience.* "It is an almost universal sentiment that the crime of murder deserves to be punished with death," Frelinghuysen wrote, and "the culprit is doomed to suffer, because *he deserves to suffer.*"

The spectacle of public execution had its occasional critics. "One of the most unpleasant sights I think I ever witnessed," wrote Newark reporter Thomas T. Kinney, was the execution of Peter W. Parke and Joseph Carter, Jr., in Belvidere for the murder of the Castner family in 1843. "To see two men stand there shaking hands and conversing like the rest of us one moment, and the next, dangling like dead dogs from ropes, was well calculated to impress one with [life's] uncertainty and the ease with which it is done. It appeared to be a show for the whole neighborhood. . . ." (Note here Kinney's sketch of the gallows and his ticket to the execution, from the manuscript journal of Thomas T. Kinney, NJHS.)

All too often, executions took on all the characteristics of sporting events. When Joel Clough was hanged in Mount Holly on July 26, 1833, a contemporary observer declared, "the day of the hanging was made a holiday—a festive occasion—by 10,000 people who came to the sport from all the countryside and even from neighboring states. Along the road were tents and booths in which liquor was sold and in which gamblers plied their tricks. Around the gallows were several companies of militia drawn up in a hollow square. At the appointed time the murderer arrived in a carriage, escorted by a troop of cavalry and accompanied by six ministers of as many sects, and sat down on the raised platform while one of the ministers read his confession to the gaping crowd."

Six weeks later, when Antoine Le Blanc was executed in Morristown, "it was calculated that no less than 12,000 persons were present, of which a majority were females."

And so, while thousands cheered and thousands more bought the ensuing pamphlets, justice was done, society was served, and official good triumphed temporarily over forbidden evil.

# TANNING HIS HIDE

ANTOINE LE BLANC never had a chance to escape the hangman's noose—but whether his lifeless body should have been subjected to what happened after the hanging is another matter.

Le Blanc was arrested on May 12, 1833, as he sat sipping cider in the Mosquito Tavern in the Hackensack Meadows. Close to his chair was a sack filled with things belonging to Samuel and Sarah Sayre, of Morristown. Le Blanc readily admitted that he had stolen the Sayre possessions and that he was fleeing to New York, but he swore he knew nothing of any other crimes.

Unfortunately for Le Blanc (if he had been as innocent as he claimed), the lifeless bodies of the Sayres had been found in Morristown the same morning under a manure heap in the Sayre yard. They had been brutally slain the night before, along with "Phebe, a colored servant," whose murdered corpse was in the house.

No one actually saw Le Blanc wield the shovel that had bashed in the skulls of the Sayres. No one saw him tuck them under the manure pile. No one saw him slay Phebe. No one saw him escape, on Sayre's horse, in the early morning darkness.

However, the weight of evidence against Le Blanc was overwhelming. There never has been much reasonable doubt about his guilt. Even now, reading the account of his trial, there is ample reason to admire the careful case that the prosecution built against him. The only flaw was that Le Blanc stoutly insisted throughout the trial that he had not been the murderer.

The trial opened in the Morris County courthouse on August 13. It stirred tremendous passions, for the Sayres had been highly-respected and the servant Phebe was remembered as loyal. Most important, from the standpoint of seething anger, Le Blanc was a French immigrant who had landed in New York only seventeen days before the Sayres were murdered.

There he was—an immigrant, a Frenchman, and worst of all a Roman Catholic in a Protestant town. One witness at the trial said Le Blanc was "filthy in his manners; never saw him wash his feet on going to bed, although working barefoot."

His court-appointed lawyers presented a respectable defense — give them credit. A court-appointed translator, Amadee Boisaubin, a resident of Madison, apparently served Le Blanc well.

The trial took nine days, including a Sunday off, before the jury started deliberations at 5:10 P.M. on August 21. A verdict of guilty was reached in twenty minutes.

The next day, Judge Gabriel H. Ford sentenced Le Blanc to "be hung up by the neck until you are dead" on Friday, September 6. Then the judge set in motion a series of events that, from the splendid hindsight of 150 years, never should have happened. He decreed that Le Blanc's body would "be delivered to Dr. Isaac Canfield, a surgeon, for dissection." As for Le Blanc's soul, Judge Ford hoped that God would have mercy on it.

Two weeks until the hanging. There was much to do. First Le Blanc confessed, grudgingly declaring to translator Amadee Boisaubin that he might as well admit the murders. His confession was translated on August 29, in time for a pamphlet on the trial to be prepared by Samuel P. Hull, who undoubtedly was rushing his pamphlet into print, probably even hoping to have it ready for the throngs of people expected for the hanging. Sales would be fine.

Morris County had to erect a proper hanging device on the colonial green in Morristown, the pleasant little county seat. It was decided to use the "modern" device that jerked the criminal upward rather than letting him drop into a hole.

The town merchants put in extra stock; spectacle watchers are good buyers. Inns added to their supplies of food. Broadsides were spread for miles around urging people not to drive into town on the execution day.

Stephen Vail, a venerable citizen, went into town at 6 A.M. on September 6 to test the hanging device. He looked about until he found a "piece of old iron," exactly the right weight to lift "the culprit" off the ground.

Crowds estimated to be well upwards of ten thousand souls were on hand as Le Blanc marched down Washington Street from the jail to the gallows. Militiamen in resplendent uniforms held off the threaten-

THE

## TRIAL, SENTENCE AND CONFESSION

OF

# ANTOINE LE BLANC,

WHO WAS EXECUTED AT

*Morristown, N. J. on Friday the 6th Sept. 1833,*

FOR THE

# MURDER

OF

# MR. SAYRE AND FAMILY.

THE EXECUTION TOOK PLACE ON THE GREEN IN THE PRESENCE OF A CROWD OF SPECTATORS. IT WAS CALCULATED THAT NO LESS THAE TWELVE THOUSAND PERSONS WERE PRESENT, OF WHICH THE MAJORITY WERE FEMALES.

[This will be found one of the most interesting works of the kind.]

SECOND EDITION.

## MORRISTON, N. Y. PRINTED.

1833

The execution of Antoine Le Blanc, from the cover of *The Trial, Sentence and Confession of Antoine Le Blanc . . .* (Morristown, N.J., 1833).

ing crowd. A "Venerable Roman Catholic Clergyman" (as Vail wrote) gave a short service. The rope was adjusted on Le Blanc's neck, the "old piece of iron" did its job, and at twenty minutes past noon "the weight dropped and he went up eight feet."

Le Blanc "struggled two minutes" (by Vail's stop watch). Thirty-five minutes later Dr. Canfield took the body to his office across the street. The happy crowd jammed its way out of town, supposedly dissuaded forever from lives of crime.

Then the strange post-hanging rites began. Dr. Canfield and friends had been given the body for dissection, not uncommon in a time when cadavers were hard for physicians to get legally. They would get to the dissection, eventually. First, there were pre-arranged experiments by the esteemed Dr. Joseph Henry, a Princeton University professor who pioneered in basic studies of electrical currents.

Henry and several Princeton associates, scientists all, passed electric currents through Le Blanc's body to see whether electricity could resurrect a lifeless body. They were able to make the eyes roll, the legs and arms contract, and the mouth grin on the corpse.

Next a person or persons unknown, presumably ethical and licensed surgeons, pared the skin off Le Blanc and sent it to the Atno Tannery, where the skin was tanned to be made into such pleasant souvenirs as wallets, pouches, and book covers. It was no secret; several contemporary accounts told of the skin tanning. Assorted pieces of the Le Blanc tanned hide have survived in private collections.

And so it went, until Le Blanc was reduced to a skeleton, possibly for hanging in a surgeon's office to instruct young medical students — or, who knows, as a memento of a ghoulish afternoon's work.

May God have mercy on *all* their souls.

# S. P. HULL'S
### REPORT OF THE
# TRIAL AND CONVICTION
### OF
# ANTOINE LE BLANC,
### FOR THE
# MURDER
### OF THE
# SAYRE FAMILY,
## AT MORRISTOWN, N. J.
### ON THE NIGHT OF THE ELEVENTH OF MAY, 1833.

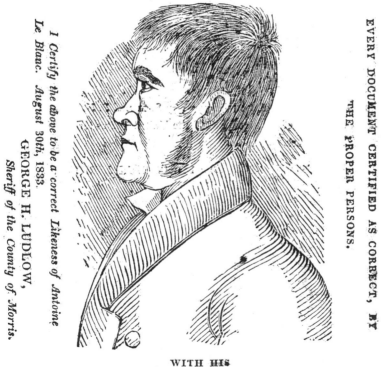

*I Certify the above to be a correct Likeness of Antoine Le Blanc. August 30th, 1833.*
**GEORGE H. LUDLOW,**
*Sheriff of the County of Morris.*

EVERY DOCUMENT CERTIFIED AS CORRECT, BY THE PROPER PERSONS.

### WITH HIS
# CONFESSION,
## AS GIVEN TO MR. A. BOISAUBIN, THE INTERPRETER.

LEWIS NICHOLS, *Printer,*
Corner of Pearl and Beekman streets, New York.

# TRIAL, &c.

State of New Jersey,
*vs.*
ANTOINE LE BLANC.
} MURDER.

Morris Oyer and Terminer,
*Special Term, August* 13, 1833.

Present—GABRIEL H. FORD Esq. Associate Justice.

Council for the State—HENRY A. FORD, Esq. Prosecutor of the PLEAS, associated with JOHN R. BROWN and JACOB W. MILLER, Esqrs.

Council for the Prisoner—FRANCIS R. M'CULLOCH, WILLIAM HALSEY, and N. W. WEISE, Esqrs., who were appointed by the Court to defend the Prisoner.

The following Oath was administered to Mr. Louis Theodore Snyder, the Interpreter :—

You shall well and truly interpret the questions and demands made by the court to the prisoner at the bar, and his answers made to them, according to the best of your skill and understanding. So help you God.

THE prisoner was indicted at the July term for the murder of Samuel Sayre, Esq., Mrs. Sarah S. Sayre, his wife, and Phebe, a colored servant woman belonging to Mr. Sayre, on the night of the 11th of May last past. The present term was appointed for the trial of the prisoner. After the opening of the court, Mr. Halsey entered a plea, that the present court had no jurisdiction to try the prisoner, principally upon the grounds, that said court had not been legally called. Mr. H. continued his remarks until the adjournment of the court.

Aug. 14—10 o'clock court met. Mr. Halsey continued his remarks, followed by Mr. M'Culloch. At 11 o'clock, Mr. Brown rose in reply to those gentlemen, followed by Mr. Miller.—Mr. Halsey rejoined. At 1 P. M., Judge Ford delivered the opinion of the court on the various points :—1st, That there is a *right* by the statutes of the state to call special terms. 2d, That he, (Judge F.) has a right to hold a special term of Oyer and Terminer, although he held the previous regular term. 3d, The notice calling the board of Freeholders *does* contain the proper reasons for calling the board to request a special term.  4th, That personal service of the notice on the freeholders is legal, and, in the eye of the law, a superior service than leaving it at the residence of the freeholder.  5th, The act says, the notice must be left 14 days previous to the meeting ; the notices were served on the 6th, and the board met on the 20th.  It is proper that one day be considered as *inclusive*, and one *exclusive*, either the day on which the notice was served, or on which the meeting was held.  The Court, therefore, is of opinion, that that body is legally empowered to proceed to the trial of the prisoner.

3 o'clock court met.  Mr. Halsey moved the court, that a jury be called consisting of equal numbers of foreigners, the remainder, citizens of New Jersey, alias " a jury de *mediatate linguæ.*"  Mr. Ford replied, after Mr. H.'s argument. *By the court*—The party must claim it either by common law or by statute ; in either case, we have no case on record in our courts. On this decision Mr. Halsey objected to further proceedings, as defendant had no copy of indictment served, as he had a right by statute.  Mr. Ford, in reply, stated, that such copy has been furnished, properly certified by the county clerk.  The caption to the indictment appears to be the principal point of difference. *By the court*—Many capital cases have been decided in New Jersey, but the court does not recollect of a single instance wherein the caption to the indictment was demanded.  In cases of *certiorari* it is proper the caption should be given.  The prisoner *may* have considerable interest in the caption, as it is a part of the history of the case.  The court, therefore, order that two entire days be given for the amendment of the indictment, by giving a copy of the *caption.*  Council for prisoner are willing to waive that right.  The court informed them that the prisoner himself might use that privilege ; after a conference with the prisoner, through the interpreter, prisoner says he will take no measures in the premises.  Mr. Ford wished the prisoner arraigned, that a copy of the panel may be rendered him two days previous to the trial.  Mr. Halsey objected—after some desultory conversation between the bench and the members of the bar, court adjourned for one hour to examine authorities.

6 o'clock P. M. court met.  The motion on the part of the state to arraign prisoner was objected to on the account that the caption was not attached to the copy of the indictment given prisoner : Mr. Halsey rose and commenced reading authorities, accompanied with his own observations ; Mr. Ford, in reply, read from Hale's Pleas, p. 189, that the caption is no part of the indictment ; Mr. H. again gave his opinions to the court. *By the court*—The prisoner can have a copy of the caption of the in-

dictment if he calls for it, but the state's council is not obliged to give it him ; Mr. Halsey again objected to the arraignment, and contended, that the prisoner was entitled to a copy of the indictment and a list of the jurors two entire days after the commencement of the court, and that the service of the copy of the indictment and panel before the sitting of the court, was not sufficient ; Mr. Ford, in reply, read an extract from our statute, as also from Chitty's Criminal Laws, vol. i, p. 517—which, after a few remarks, was followed by Mr. Miller, who contended, that a copy of the indictment and a list of the jury and witnesses might be legally furnished to the prisoner before the sitting of the court to try him, and that the statute had been fully complied with, if it appeared that they had been furnished to the prisoner two days before his arraigment for trial. Mr. Halsey again rose in defence of his former position—the court overruled the objection, and decided, that a copy of the indictment and of the panel of the jurors, were each duly served according to the statute. Adjourned to 9 o'clock to-morrow morning.

Thursday, Aug. 15, 9 o'clock court met. Prisoner was arraigned, and the indictment, read by Mr. Ford, in the English language. Mr. Amadee Boisaubin was directed by the court to explain to prisoner the contents of the indictments in the French language, (Mr. Boisaubin having been sworn as interpreter in the place of Mr. Snyder, who could not attend). After which the prisoner was asked, whether he was guilty or not. —He answered not guilty. The court ordered the jury to be called, when Mr. Halsey raised an objection as to the manner in which the panel was served. After his remarks, Mr. Brown read from Chitty's Criminal Laws the same extracts which he did last evening. The court overruled Mr. Halsey's objections, and ordered the trial to proceed. Mr. Halsey moved a postponement of the trial, on the ground that the recent time in which the crime was committed, and in which the indictment was found, a great excitement exists with the people prejudicial to the prisoner : Furthermore, that there are persons somewhere in the United States, he believes, who was acquainted with him in Europe. Also, that the money found in a belt around his body he obtained at a broker's in New York. Prisoner's counsel then presented an affidavit to the above effect, followed by remarks from Mr. M'Culloch. Mr. Brown answered, and read from 1st Chitty, p. 482—1st Massachusetts Reports, p. 6— Wheeler's Criminal Cases, vol. 2, p. 224—2d Halsted's Reports, p. 220. Mr. M'Culloch read in answer to Mr. Brown, from 1st Chitty, p. 493. Mr. Ford made a few remarks in addition to Mr. Brown, in opposition to a postponement of the

cause. Mr. Halsey followed in behalf of a postponement, and
continued until the adjournment of the court.

2 o'clock P. M. court met. The court overruled the objections of the prisoner's counsel, and ordered the trial to proceed.
The following jurors were sworn:—William Sayre,* Robert
Hand, David Bruen. James M. Flemming, John P. Cook, William N. Hennion, Freeman Wood, David T. Cooper, Robert
Caskey, Andrew Bay. The panel being here expended, the
court ordered a tales of twelve freeholders, from which number
Moses A. Brockfield was sworn. The tales being expended, a
second was ordered, and the court adjourned for one hour.

At the opening of the court, the second tales was called, from
which no one was sworn, all being rejected. A third tales of
twelve was then called, to be composed of persons in the court
room. The doors were immediately closed, and the sheriff proceeded to summon the jurors. On the third tales, Abraham B.
Walker was sworn as a juror, which completed the panel. Adjourned to 9 o'clock to-morrow morning.

Aug. 16—9 o'clock, court met. Mr. Ford opened the cause
in behalf of the state, in a speech of one hour and forty minutes,
and read from 1st Starkey on Evidence, p. 19, sec. 19.

Mr. Ford stated in substance the following Examination, which
is here given at length, as certified by the Clerk of the Court:

State of New Jersey, Morris county, to wit.

The examination of Antoine Le Blanc, late of the Township of Morris,
in the county of Morris aforesaid, taken before me Robert K. Tuttle, one
of the Justices of the Peace in and for said county, this 18th day May,
in the year of our Lord eighteen hundred and thirty-three, in pursance of
the statute in such case made and provided. The said Antoine Le Blanc
being charged before me with feloniously, wilfully, and with malice afore-
thought, murdered Samuel Sayre and Sarah his wife, and Phebe, a servant of the said Samuel Sayre, at the township of Morris aforesaid, on
the night of the eleventh day of this present month of May, A.D. eighteen hundred and thirty-three, by the sheriff of the county of Morris,
who has the said Antoine now in custody before me. He the said Antoine, upon his examination, now saith that his name is Antoine Le Blanc,
and that he will be examined here upon the charges aforesaid. And is
willing that Monsieur Amedee Boisaubin be interpreter on this occasion.
He says he was born at Chateau Salin, and has lived the last six years, of
his life at Bistroff, in Germany ;that his ordinary business, or occupation,
is that of a farmer, his object in coming to this country was to labour—he
landed at New-York about the twenty-fifth day of April last past. He
has boarded in three different houses, one German and two American—
he first boarded at an American house, near the water's-edge—he does
not recollect who kept it, staid there only a day and a half—and the next
house that he boarded at was near a large hotel that was burnt, and staid

---

* This Mr. Sayre is no connexion to the family of the deceased, although
of the same name.

two days—he next went to an American house near where a boat leaves the ferry every two or three minutes, and remained at this house about a day and a half—he changed his lodgings because his friends that were with him did so. He did not know the names of his friends, any farther than as some were called Francis and Joseph. That he had two hundred and twenty francs after paying his passage—he had about one hundred francs in gold, and the rest in five franc pieces—he changed the whole with Mr. Marrin, except two five franc pieces, into dollars, and half dollars—he had a marche de route when he left home—he did not follow it, because he met a Frenchman who came from the place where he was going to—who told him that he had been there two years, and could make no money, and was returning home : and another reason was, he could not find any one that could give him directions to go to Aratz, where many of his friends were. That Mr. Samuel Sayre called at the hotel where he last staid, and not finding him in, said he would call at 4 o'clock, and at four o'clock he saw him—he did not make any engagement with Mr. Sayre at that time—that there was some person that interpreted for him—does not know his name—the Interpreter took him to a gardener to find employment. When he came to work on trial with Mr. Sayre, at the end of ten or fifteen days they were to come to an agreement—he has worked for Mr. Sayre fifteen days and a half—he saw no person, while working for Mr. Sayre, that he was acquainted with before—and that he was not in the habit of conversing with any body in his own language—that once saw a German boy at one of the taverns, who was to have written a letter for him, but he did not see him afterwards—he was not acquainted with any one in Morristown, except he sometimes spoke to a baker that called there occasionally. He never went out in the evening but twice—once on Saturday evening, the first Saturday after he came, to get tobacco. And the Sunday following, he went to church, and the next time he came to get a letter written—the first Saturday he went to a large hotel where there was bushes before the door—he says now that he was mistaken about his going out the first Saturday after he came—it was on Sunday ; there were pillars before the tavern—that he returned home that night about 10 o'clock—he was absent that night from Mr. Sayre's about two hours. That on Saturday evening last he left Mr. Sayre's house about 8 o'clock—he went and asked leave to go of Mr. Sayre—he says Mr. Sayre understood some French words, and with signs gave him to understand that he wanted to go to get him a hat, and wanted to see the German, to get him to write a letter for him—he had no communication with the rest of the family, except by signs, and with Mrs. Sayre a little. When he left, to go to town, he, Mr. Sayre was in the kitchen washing his feet, when he asked permission to go to town—there was a small lamp burning at the time in the kitchen—he did not observe any other—he does not know whether Mr. Sayre shaved that evening or not—does not know whether there was any lamp in the entry or not—he believes that Mrs. Sayre was in the front room below stairs. Phebe was eating supper in the kitchen when he left to go to town—he thinks that Mrs. Sayre was hard of hearing, as when they spoke to her they spoke very loud—they burnt lamps and candles both—that on Saturday night last, when he went to town, he went from house to house, to look for the baker, who was the person who promised to write for him—he first stopped at a store, he did not want to purchase anything —he wanted to find the German baker—he staid perhaps an hour in the store—he bought four segars, and three glasses of cider ; he then went

round the town, and stopped at the tavern, where he bought a glass of
brandy—it was the same tavern where he had been before—he believed
they gave him a segar, but he did not ask for one—it might have been so
undersood—he passed again near the baker's house, but not finding him,
he went home—was not at the tavern over a quarter of an hour—he was
absent from Mr. Sayre's house perhaps two or three hours—in returning
home he walked sometimes on one side, and sometimes on the other side
of the road—he saw no person whom he knew on his way home—the
last person he saw on his way home was a person who went into a blacksmith shop, where there were three persons at work, it was where Mr.
Sayre's sulky was mending—the person whom he saw last went into the
door of the house next to the blacksmith shop, he thinks, he will not be
positive, there was no light in the street along where he went—it was
near eleven oclock—he stopped only two or three minutes on his way
home to hear the conversation of two or three persons that were talking,
was about twenty minutes on his way before he reached the house—he
found the oxen in the street and turned them in, and did not go to the
barn or stable before he went into the house—he says he did not go to the
barn or stable after his return home that night—(being shown a roundabout) he says he had it on, he put it on before going to supper after fin-
ishing his work—he put it down cellar where he had his clothing—(a cap
being shown him) he says he wore it that night, he left the cap under the
back piazza by the kitchen door, (being shown a pair of pantaloons) he
says he did not wear them that night, nor that day (being shown a hatchet)
he said he used it in the garden trimming that day, and after using it he
put it in the piazza or Mr. Sayre put it there, and his great coat under the
piazza that evening—(being shown a large club) he says he does not recollect of seeing it before, it was not used to fasten the barn doors at present—that two days before a carpenter had fixed the barn doors—the
back doors were fastened with a latch—(being shown a striped vest) he
says he did not wear it on Saturday—he wore a black silk waistcoat that
day—the last time that he wore the striped vest was on Friday, the day
before, and left it in the cellar—he slept in the first room of the cellar,
but before, when he slept with Mr. Sayre's other man, he slept in the
back room, and when he removed into the first room Mr. Sayre's man
that slept with him removed these pantaloons of velvet, into the front
room—he carried the pantaloons into the first room, thinks he put them
under the bed as a pillow—thinks he wore them on Saturday last, and
took them off about two or three o'clock in the afternoon, because they
were wet and dirty a digging holes for the posts for the garden gate on
Saturday last, the first work he did was to curry the horses and to cut
straw, then turn the cows to pasture, then feed the hogs, then breakfasted,
after breakfast put a large ladder behind the house, and then cut straw
almost till night, when he was called to set the posts, and then went after
the cows, they were lost, and he got wet all over—he then changed his
pantaloons, and did no other work but clean out the stables—at the time
he changed his pantaloons he rolled them up, but does not know whether
he put them under the bed or not, as he was called by Mr. Sayre to feed
the hogs and afterwards went to dam the water, he watered the horses,
and Mr. Sayre gave them their oats—(being again shown the velvet pantaloons) he says that Mr. Sayre sent him to get lime or plaster, he dont know
which, it was put into a peck measure or a half bushel measure, and he
took it to Mr. Sayre, who mixed up corn with it; he has not observed any
white on his pantaloons, he says that on Thursday and Friday Mr. Sayre

and the other man put the plaster on the corn, but on Saturday he, Antoine, mixed it—at noon and in the evening—and that which was mixed in the evening was put under the back Piazza—the barrel of plaster was put under the shed at the barn near the stable, about four or five o'clock that afternoon—he did not overturn the barrel—the other man had dressed and gone off, he, the other man, was in the habit of going off before night every Saturday—(being again shown the pantaloons) he says it cannot be blood that is on his pantaloons—(being again shown the striped vest) he says that the carpenter and the other man can account for the blood on his vest, he frequently bled at the nose, he has a handkerchief somewhere that is full of blood—it is a yellow pocket handkerchief—his nose bled while he was in the garden, he kept on working and did not let his nose bleed on the ground, but used his handkerchief—he has two handkerchiefs, a red one and a yellow one, the yellow one he used on Saturday, (being shown a blue coat) he says he wore it last Sunday a week ago, he left it in the cellar. He says he entered Mr. Sayre's house on his return from town last Saturday evening by the back door, he was only in the house three or four minutes, that is all that evening before he finally quit it. After his return from town he found a light burning in the kitchen, he does not know whether it was the same he left, he cannot tell whether it was a lamp or a candle—there was no lamp burning in the lower entry—there was a light in the front room below stairs—the only difference in the condition of the kitchen was a looking glass on the table—he did not go to bed because he was frightened—because he saw no one in the house—when he started to go into the cellar he was taken with affright—the entry was dark—in going into the kitchen he had a presentiment that he would be murdered, and without seeing any thing to lead to it—it is the first time that he ever had such a fear or dread—when he left the kitchen he started to go down into the cellar, he was affrighted, it was all done ie a flash, he turned and immediately went up stairs straight up into the garret, to see if there was any one there—he went into no room on his way to the garret—he saw no person but the girl, who was dead—hn took the candle with him that was in the kitchen—he called out as loud as he could for the girl and for his master—he ran to Phebe's bed and seeing that she was dead, he ran down and in his hurry tumbled down stairs, the candle went out, he cannot tell what covering was on Phebe—for to save his life he cannot tell what wounds she had, he saw the blood and then started, and being in the dark he ran and left the house immediately—said he picked up in haste what he could in the dark, and ran out and went on, it struck twelve o'clock at the first house in the village he first arrived at, it was a clock in a house—he would have looked for Mr. Sayre if he had not seen Phebe—he did not search for the other man —he knew that Phebe slept in the garret, he could see her at the window there from the garden—he says there is a window in that part of the garret, he had never been in the garret before, nor in the front room. When about to start, being in the dark, he picked up what he could find in a small room in which there is a bed on the same floor with the kitchen, near the cellar steps—there was a great many things in a drawer in that room which he took at one grasp—he says if he was to die for it he could not tell what things he took—the watch was the most valuable thing that he took—he took some shirts and a coat and he cannot tell what else—a vest and many other articles he cannot tell what they were, all in the same drawer—some things were in a bag, which he supposes were ear rings—he made no bundles in the house; he found two bags among the clothes into which he put the clothes, but did not make bundles of the goods until he got to Newark, or this side of Newark, he first put the clothing in a great coat—(being shown a strap marked K 3553) he says he had it in his pocket when he came to Morristown, on Saturday night last, he has had it in his pocket since a week before; he wanted to cut it for to make suspenders, he says he bought it in Germany to fix his travelling bag with —he put all the articles that he took into Mr. Sayre's great coat, and strapped it with a circingle, and carried them so until he got near Newark, when he took this strap marked as aforesaid from his pocket, and used it in carrying the bundle—he found the silver money in the same drawer wrapped up in a sheet of paper—he did not know that he had any money until he arrived at that house near Newark, except his own—he believes that he put the aforesaid marked strap into a bag at the aforesaid house, near Newark—(being shown a bead bag) he says he never saw it before—(being shown an opera glass with a bag covering it) say he dont know that he has ever seen it—he says that about five or six miles from this place, as he was sitting under a tree near the road side a horse passed him at full speed, does not know whether the horse had on a saddle or bridle—nor could he tell the colour of the horse. He says that an umbrella was open under the Piazza when he started, and he took it—that what he took made but a small bundle, and therefore he was able to carry the umbrella by carrying the bundle under his arm—(being shown the gold watch) he says he never knew what he had until he arrived at that house—(being shown a red pocket-book with a clasp) he says that he had one, and thinks that he saw it—he found the gold watch in a little bag among the articles he took—(being shown two visiting card cases) he says that he found them at the house where he stopped to make up his bundle—(being shone a gold hair ring, set with pearl) he thinks that he saw it among his things—(being shown a pair of gold ear rings, broken, and a golden belt hook for a watch, and a ring) says he has seen them before, and found them in a small bag where the watch was in—(being shown a small box with a gold chain in it) he says that he had several small articles and thinks that they were among them—(shown a number of trinkets from a small box in the bead bag) says that he never saw them— (being shown articles taken from the bead bag in a small box) says he believes that he has seen them—(being shown a large breast pin taken from the bead bag) says he has not seen it—(being shown some white stockings) he says he has stockings like them, but did not put them there—he says that he took the coat, the shirts, and all the other articles that he carried from that house except the vest, from one drawer—that he found the vest under the Piazza—when he thought that he heard a noise in the house he ran out of the back door—leaped the garden fence, ran across the garden, and made a half circle to get into the road, and stopped to listen —the reason why he stopped to listen was, that if he should hear his master he would return—he says that he passed from the kitchen through the board fence that was open across the potatoe ground into the rye, and from the rye field got into the road—returned towards the house where the roads forked, and went on—and when he got nearest the house he stopped to listen, and looked at the house—he imagined that he saw something in the house, but did not see any thing but a light burning in the house—he did not walk fast—(on being shown two razors) he said they were his, he shaved himself with them—(being shown a large knife with an instrument used in farering) said it was his—(shown a razor strop about six inches in length) says it is his—(shown a small brass padlock) says is not certain, he thinks his was a little larger—he thinks there was one in Mr. Sayre's vest that he took hanging under the piazza. He says that in the house where he breakfasted he changed his dress, took Mr. Sayre's coat from among the clothes that he took, and put it on under the piazza —he says it is the great coat that he took from under the piazza—says that he took the light bodied coat of Mr. Sayre and put it on before he went to the drawer, having first put his roundabout under the piazza— says that he took great coat and all and put it into a bag at the house where he stopped for breakfast—he supposes that they might have seen him—says that there was two small bags which he put into one bag, and carried them in that way, and when he was taken by the sheriff he had but one bag. He says he and Mr. Sayre had no dispute—he had no disputes with any of them—the money that he had in his pantaloons pocket was the money that he got out of the house, except the change of a five franc piece—he did not know the road to New York—he enquired as he went along—he stopped on the way, it was dark, he enquired of a person the way, they said go on.

Being asked if he did not murder Mr. Sayre and Mrs. Sayre, says he did not. (Here the examination of the said Antoine was closed for this day, and I committed him to the custody of the Sheriff of the county of Morris, until Monday next, the 20th day of May instant, for the further examination of the said Antoine.)

Monday the 20th day of May, A. D. eighteen hundred and thirty-three, the said Antoine, by my order, being again brought before me for further examination, on the charges aforesaid—he says, he had seven shirts belonging to himself, he thinks one or two were not marked with the initials of his name, and the rest ; were he cannot account for the blood on the shirt that he wore on Saturday, except that his nose frequently bled—while cutting straw on the Saturday in question, as he was whetting the knife the blood ran out of his nose a little, a few drops only ; he says, the shirt he had on that Saturday, he took off on the way and put on Mr. Sayre's: that it was among the articles found by the Sheriff; he had but these with him ; he did not change the shirt in any house, he changed it in the woods; he cannot tell where it was ; persons were passing at the time, and saw him, it was out of the road, over the hedge, it was after breakfast; being shown two white handled knives, he says they were in the pocket of Mr. Sayre's tight coat, cannot tell how they came there, he first discovered them when he changed his shirt, they were in the side pocket, opposite the left arm ; he had walked an hour, or an hour and a half after breakfast before he discovered them ; he stopped and took tea at the entrance of a long village, paid eight cents for it ; they gave him some bread and some fish, they were at breakfast ; he says it was scarcely light when he took his first breakfast, it was a piece of bread, and about nine o'clock he got his tea ; he did not pay for his breakfast ; it rained hard ; they gave him a piece of bread, and he went on, it was not a tavern : there was only a woman up at the house ; he went in to light his segar ; he recollects to have passed a bridge, where he paid for passage two cents ; it was not at the entrance of that place where he got his tea, but a good ways this side ; it was on the left in going that he stopped to light his segar, and got the piece of bread ; he cannot tell what kind of house this was, large or small ; being shown a circingle, he says he took that where the coat lay, under the Piazza—he says Mr. Sayre had three saddles, one was in the stable, and this cricingle they had put under the Piazza to brush and clean it, with two other saddles ; he now says that they were not there at this time, he did not know what had become of them, says he never rode with a saddle; being shown a tooth brush with sealing wax on the back of it, does not recollect of ever seeing it before ; being shown a hair brush, cannot say whether it was in his sack or not; he says all the articles which he took, except the great coat, the tight-bodied coat, the vest and the hat, were in the drawer, he found the hat hanging by the coat, near the kitchen; he said it was dark when he took these goods, as the candle was burning in the kitchen ; he put Mr. Sayre's hat on at the moment he made his escape while he was in the house ; he says he had but one cap ; when he left the house there was a light in the stove-room, the front room ; he says when he went up to Phebe's room, he went up to her, he said in German to her, are you asleep? she did not answer, he then touched the cover, saw the blood and ran, the blood was hissing and bubbling at the time ; he remembers that there was a long board in the stable, they used it to cover some feed that was there ; says that Mr. Sayre fed the horses himself, and he, Antoine, had no occasion to use a candle ; cannot tell how that plank was broken ; does not know that it was broken ; says that he had never used a light or a lantern in the stable, and never knew of one being used there ; has never seen about Mr. Sayre's premises a lantern made of glass, in the form of a globe ; the only lamp or light that he has seen or noticed, is a small tin lamp used in the kitchen; says he had on his own boots when he was taken ; he says he did not know that he had the circingle until he had got several miles from town ; the clothes were slipping about, and when he discovered the circingle he bound it around them, having first tied the bundle with the great coat sleeves, a short time before ; says that the woman of the house where he first eat in the morning gave him the rope that he had round the bundle, that he made a sign that he wanted a rope, and she went and got it.

Taken before me,    }
    R. K. Tuttle. }

The foregoing examination being offered to the said Antoine Le Blanc, he refused to sign it.

## Witnesses for the Prosecution.

**John P. Feusier,** resides in New York, keeps a boarding house at 75 Fulton street, is acquainted with prisoner ; came to witness' the 26th of April, remained nearly 3 days. Mr. Sayre called there, and asked witness if he knew of any person who would go into the country and work his farm, showed him prisoner, but could not recommend him, being a stranger ; did not see Mr. Sayre again. Mr. Sayre told prisoner to come up the next day, on trial. Prisoner's counsel here requested the court to have the testimony interpreted to prisoner. *By the court,* we know of no law for the court to appoint an interpreter for the prisoner, but as he does not understand our language, the court is willing to allow some one to give prisoner the substance of the testimony, or even word for word, if necessary. Mr. A. Boisaubin was, therefore, requested by the court to interpret for prisoner. Witness continued—about the last of April, prisoner left witness' house ; stage driver called for him ; prisoner's bill was $1 75, prisoner paid 75 cents ; $1 due witness ; prisoner could not pay, as he had no more money ; does not know that he remained at any other house whilst in the city ; came to witness' same day of his arrival from Havre ; does not know whether he applied to any other for employment; was to leave a pair of boots in pledge, for the payment of the $1; went off without so doing; cannot designate the stage driver.

*Cross examined*—Mr. Sayre communicated with witness in English; communicated the conversation of Mr. S. in French to prisoner; paid witness in American money; prisoner told witness, the day of his arrival, the boots were too small for him, and wished to sell them, never saw the boots; prisoner had a bag containing his effects; never demanded the boots of prisoner, but thought Mr. Sayre would pay it; several came over with him; prisoner did not go out much, the others did; six came with him to witness' house in company; knows a man by the name of Merlin, was a cabin passenger in the vessel with prisoner; Merlin has gone to Bogota; at the time the bill was pre sented, he promised to leave the boots; left there about 10 o'clock.

*Direct, resumed*—No one but witness talked with Mr. Sayre about prisoner; knows nothing of the business between Merlin and prisoner; prisoner told witness that he was a Frenchman, but spoke German.

*Paul W. Piper*, sworn. Is acquainted with prisoner, brought prisoner to Morristown in the stage from New York, from the house of last witness, in the latter part of April last; witness paid prisoner's passage in the boat from New York to Elizabeth Town Point; Mr. Sayre paid for his stage fare; does not know why prisoner did not pay his boat fare; witness did so by direc- tion of Mr. S.; left him at Mr. Sayre's.

*Cross examined*—Do not recollect that prisoner called for any thing to drink on the way; did not go within the house of Mr. Feusier; prisoner left the stage a short time at Springfield; does not recollect of any person in the stage that spoke French; pri- soner had his clothes in a knapsack, with straps to go over his shoulders; bundle not very large, weigh probably from 20 to 25 lbs; no communication with prisoner relative to his having mo ney.

*Samuel Stansborough*—Worked for Mr. Sayre at the time of his death, went there the last week in March, and continued till his death; prisoner first came there on a Saturday, in April. The Sayre family consisted of Mr. and Mrs. Sayre, daughter Mary, Phebe, the coloured servant, and witness, when the prisoner came. Mary left a few days afterwards, probably a week; she went to Newton, Sussex county; did not return un- til after her father's death; prisoner assisted in removing brush, the first labour he done; prisoner principally laboured in the garden; witness remained with deceased continually, until the murder, except Saturday night, when he went home, and remained until Monday morning ; lived at Basking Ridge, 7 miles ; at first prisoner and witness slept together about a week ; did not like to sleep with prisoner, as he did not think him decent, being uneasy in bed, and kept witness awake ; prisoner was removed to the 1st room to sleep, and witness kept his old room ; witness generally kept his door fastened, as he did not like the manners of prisoner ; was ugly at times, and would not be instructed ; prisoner arose once in the night, went out, returned, and got into bed with his clothes on, whilst they lodged together ; it was possible for prisoner to go through the house without knowledge of witness ; prisoner was filthy in his manners ; never saw him wash his feet on going to bed, although working barefoot ; was similarly treated with witness, and eat with him ; never saw him drink liquor ; appeared to work as if he was accustomed to it ; done but little but plant corn and work in the garden ; Mr. Sayre could make himself understood by prisoner, in broken French ; prisoner would talk and make signs to witness, but could not understand him : knew of no one visiting him ; prisoner spent his evenings in the kitchen, generally smoking ; does not recollect of prisoner's going out at night ; Phebe got the victuals for them ; she frequently went to bed previous to the others ; Mr. Sayre generally wished all in the house by 9 o'clock ; all retired before Mr. and Mrs. Sayre ; prisoner and witness generally retired soon after supper ; Mrs. S. generally fastened the kitchen door ; Mr. and Mrs. S. slept in a bed room adjoining the kitchen, at the end of the hall, about 2 steps from one door to the other. Mr. S. sometimes shaved in the kitchen ; has a small glass to sit on the table ; shaved in the evening ; sometimes wore slippers in the evening ; does not know of Mr. S. having but one pair of boots ; generally had a tin lamp in the kitchen ; there was a lamp fastened up in the hall ; was never lighted whilst witness was there ; did not notice it the morning after the murder ; had frequently seen it, did not know if it was smoked. Mr. Sayre's bed room has but one window, looking to the rear, towards the barn yard ; a carpenter was at work there, who kept his tools in the left side of the barn ; he had two chisels, one wide, the other narrow ; thinks they were in the barn the Saturday of the murder ; saw one of the chisels in the house after the murder ; witness generally took care of the horses ; sometimes prisoner did ; taken care of about sun set ; knows of no light being used in the stable, but once ; had a glass lantern for that purpose ; it was kept in the kitchen, on the cupboard, in plain sight. Stable door not locked at night ; fastened with a latch and hook ; had a club or stick to fasten the door open with, (the club of solid white oak, shown witness,) that is the stick ;

last saw it on the Saturday of the murder, near the stable door; deceased had two horses, the mare a light gray, the horse dark; kept in the stable, and fastened with ropes; the mare stood near the door; the mare was the most active, and best riding beast; Mr. Sayre generally used her. Was a large heap of manure in front of the stable; a load or two had been taken the week previous to the murder; the barn is a few rods from the house, towards the town; the stable beneath the barn, and the door at the corner, towards the house; a shed projects from the barn, towards the house, and opens towards the stable door; a barrel stood under the shed, with ground plaster in it, about half full; was placed there about ten days previous; was there the Saturday evening in question; on Sunday morning it was turned over, and rolled 8 or 9 feet from its former position; it had been rolled in an ascending position; the plaster was procured to put on the corn, &c.; was at deceased's house the whole of Saturday, excepting about an hour, he came to town to shell seed corn; prisoner was occupied principally that day at cutting straw in the barn; in the afternoon prisoner assisted in putting up a ladder against the house; towards evening, Mr. Sayre, prisoner, and witness, went to set a bar post; witness fed the horses before he went home, about 6 o'clock; prisoner was then around, not doing much; prisoner went after the cows after the fence was repaired, but did not get them; prisoner wore a pair of black velvet pantaloons that day, and his blue frock; the manure was thrown out of the stable a few days previous to the murder. At 1 o'clock court adjourned for 1 hour.

2 o'clock P. M. Court met; Stansborough's direct examination continued—A pair of pantaloons exhibited to the court. Witness, those are the pantaloons worn by prisoner; at half after 6 o'clock on the night of the murder, prisoner had them on; he believes the vest also in court; at that time prisoner was feeding the hogs; a saddle and bridle were in the stable when witness left there, hanging on the left hand of the door as they entered; a circingle was presented; does not recognize it, probably belongs to one of the two side saddles in the house. No plaster sown or used that week; that in the barrel was for the use of the corn; when witness left there, deceased and prisoner were at the hog pen; Phebe was returning home from town, when witness met her; Mrs. Sayre was in the kitchen; the hatchet presented in court belonged to deceased, and was usually kept on the back piazza; had seen it there on the Saturday of the murder; the knapsack presented in court was the one prisoner brought his clothes in; goat skin, dressed with the hair on. A person standing at the stable door, could not be seen from the

street, or any neighbouring house, as the shed obstructs the view ; it is a retired place, and woods below it.

*Cross-examined.* _ The hatchet presented is the only one used about the premises ; witness put in the helve ; planted the corn in May—the week of the murder ; rolled the corn in the plaster ; prisoner dropped some, and deceased also ; dark night of the murder ; rained some during the day ; never saw prisoner on horseback ; the horse the most gentle ; plaster in the yard where the cows run ; stood against the side of the stable under the shed ; witness complained to Mrs. S. of prisoner, and Mr. S. altered his lodging ; deceased gave no liquor to his hands—only cider ; witness drew cider when he wished it ; no misunderstanding of import between prisoner and witness, except the Saturday in question, when witness wanted the box to cut straw ; does not recollect of any except this one. A daughter of deceased left there previous to prisoner coming ; black man named Martin ran away from deceased a short time previous to the arrival of prisoner—probably a week ; knows of no difference between Martin and Mr. Sayre ; Martin was a servant in the family ; never have seen Martin since his elopement ; Martin ran away in the night ; he was about 19 years of age ; there are no marks on the chissel spoken of by which he could swear to it, but judge from general appearances ; does not recollect how long previous to the murder the carpenter worked there ; plaster had been sown on the oats ; prisoner had sown no plaster ; it was talked of that witness's wife was to come and stay there, and clean the house ; prisoner's bed was prepared for him previous to talking of witness's wife coming ; cannot swear positively he had the vest on in the afternoon, or any part of the day ; had his frock on when he went after the cows ; had no waistcoat on over his frock ; Phebe was Martin's sister.

*Examined Direct.* The front room was the usual sitting room ; lamp in the hall below would shine above ; never saw prisoner's nose bleed ; the strap presented has the appearance of one in prisoner's possession, with his other articles ; belt marked " K. 3553 ;" belts of the knapsack marked the same manner, were all white buckskin tanned.

*Nathan B. Luse.* Witness first saw prisoner either one or two weeks previous to the murder, on a Saturday night ; came for something to drink ; next time saw him at his house, on the night of the murder, from nine to half-past nine —prisoner took a glass of brandy and water and a segar ; remained in the bar-room about ten minutes ; Mr. J. Wilson, Mr. Ford, Joseph Brown, D. C. Martin, C. Robertson, and others, were in the room at the time ; was very mannerly when he left the house ; wore a blue-mixed round-about, and similar pantaloons; did not particularly notice his dress; he next saw him at the half-way house between Newark and New York, between twelve and one on Sunday, the day the murder was discovered; witness was talking with the landlord relative to the murder, and on turning to go to the door he discovered prisoner on a bench in a corner near the door; stepped up to prisoner and asked him where he was travelling; prisoner looked up—witness told landlord this man was the murderer, at which time the sheriff and Mr. Z. Drake arrived; prisoner attempted to go out of the back door, but was prevented; was taken to the front door, where his bundles were; in his bundles, the first article was a blue frock coat of Mr. Sayre's—next, a shirt with deceased's name marked on it; prisoner was tied and searched; in his pocket were one or two small pocket books or wallets, with the name of the family, as also visiting cards; the ladies' kid mitts shown, marked with the name of Mary Sayre, were taken from his vest pocket; tooth brush, watch chain, seal and key, buckles, thimble, hair brush, two case knives with ivory handles, ear and finger rings, pillow case marked S. S. S., several pair of woollen-stockings, &c. &c. were taken from the pillow case witness opened; there were two pillow cases filled and tied together; first stopped at Drake's hotel in Newark; arrived at Morristown a little before sun-down; was in Newark about two hours; witness went with Sheriff Ludlow to Newark; he took a sulkey and went towards New York, a few minutes in advance of the Sheriff and Z. Drake.

*Cross-examined.* Prisoner could see witness when he first went into the tavern where he was arrested; did not rise from his seat until witness tapped him on the shoulder; was in about one minute before he saw prisoner; the front door was open; the bundles were on the front piazza; prisoner appeared fatigued; the small articles were taken from his pockets; the watch was in the prisoner's vest pocket.

*William H. Wetmore.* Saw prisoner before; was at witness's store, and purchased cider and segars the evening the murder was committed; paid for the articles a five franc piece; had on a black cap, similar to the one presented.

*Joseph Brown.* Saw prisoner at Luse's hotel, on the evening of the murder, about half-past nine; he called for brandy; had on a dark round-a-bout coat, dark cap, dark pantaloons; witness left the tavern about 10 minutes after prisoner, and it was 10 minutes of 10 o'clock when he got home; distant about a quarter of a mile.

*Cross-examined.* Prisoner was in the tavern about 20 minutes; prisoner's pantaloons darker than the coat.

*Daniel C. Martin.* · Saw prisoner at Luse's hotel, on Saturday evening the 11th May ; had a dark hair cap on his head, a dark round-a-bout coat, and dark pantaloons, striped vest, similar to the one exhibited ; prisoner came into the tavern about nine o'clock ; as he was a stranger, witness took particular notice of him, and also as to his manners, &c.

*Cross-examined.* Do not know whether the pantaloons were wet or dry ; was very polite when he left the room—bowing to those in the room.

*David B. West.* Resides on the Reeves farm, adjoining the farm where S. Sayre resided, and beyond it ; was in town until nearly 10 o'clock on Saturday night, 11th May, and left for home with Edward N. Rogers ; overtook C. Robertson and J. Wilson, near J. Wood's house ; parted with Robertson and Rogers at their residence, between town and Mr. Sayre's ; at the time of parting with them a clock struck 10 ; continued on homewards ; parted with J. Wilson at his house, also this side of Sayre's ; Mr. Wilson's house is on the opposite side of the street from Mr. S.'s ; continued that side of the street until opposite Mr. S.'s, and crossed on a small bridge from the walk to the road ; Mr. Sayre was sitting by the window, and Mrs. S. about the centre of the room ; there are 2 front windows in the room ; the window up was nearest the town, at which Mr. S. was sitting, reading a newspaper ; did not perceive Mrs. S. doing anything ; was from five to 10 minutes going from Mr. Rodger's to Mr. Sayre's ; saw no window blinds ; the town clock struck 10 about the time witness parted with Mr. Wilson ; saw a white-faced ox rubbing against the barn in the yard ; was well acquainted with Mr. S. ; saw no light in any other part of the house ; believes a candle was on the chimney piece, and one on the table at which Mr. S. was reading.

*Cross-examined*—Mr. Sayre had on no coat, a dark vest, no hat ; a dark cloudy night ; could not well distinguish a person across the street ; was on the opposite side of the street, where he saw the ox.

*Edward N. Rodgers,* recollects returning to his house in company with D. B. West, on the evening of the 11th of May ; saw Mr. Martin, Mr. Wilson, and Mr. Robertson ; as witness opened his door, his clock struck 10 ; did not hear the town clock strike ; it is a little over a quarter of a mile from witness' house to Sayre's.

*Cross-examined*—It was a cloudy evening, might discover a person 4 rods.

*Moses Cherry,* has had the charge of the town clock for a number of years ; regulates it every Sabbath morning ; regulated it the morning of Mr. Sayre's death, was 4 minutes too slow ; regulated it by Luse's time, which is considered correct.

*George Johnson*, was fishing on the night Mr. Sayre was murdered, with Isaac Cole and Lewis Jaggers ; started to go about 7 o'clock ; passed Mr. S.'s house in going, saw nothing to attract notice about S.'s house ; went to Post's pond, about 3 miles from town ; left the pond after 12 o'clock ; went down in a one horse wagon ; left the wagon at Mr. Ogden's, a quarter of a mile from the pond, this side ; had 2 time-pieces in company ; walked to the wagon ; the horse was put to the wagon, and came directly home ; passed Mr. S.'s house on their return ; saw a man inside the house as they passed, through the window next the piazza ; came from the hall to the window, and looked out as they passed by ; the person had on a dark coat ; did not notice whether it was Mr. Sayre or not ; was a light in the front room and hall ; the wagon made some noise ; the window-blinds were partly up ; lives about 200 yards towards town, from Mr. S. in the same street ; sometime after he got home, looked at the time, which was half past 1 ; nearly half hour after he got home ; there was a dim light over the hall, up stairs ; very bright light in the hall ; could discover it as the door was open leading from the hall.

*Cross-examined*—Saw the light over the door below, a fan light ; the light in the room appeared to be in the centre of the room ; the man had no light in his hand ; first saw the light as they came to the garden, a short distance from the house, from the end window ; drove home pretty fast ; set on the opposite side of the wagon, from the house ; the person continued looking from the window for some time ; some remarks made as to the light in the house, at that hour ; dim light at the other window ; the blinds probably being down ; the person appeared to be middling sized ; dont recollect as to having on a hat ; heard no noise around the house ; came to the window as they passed, and looked directly out ; noticed no cattle about the house or barn; the rattling of the wagon could be heard in the house ; formed no opinion at the time as to whom it was.

*Isaac Cole*, was fishing in company with Johnson, on the night Sayre was murdered ; when they left the pond it was a quarter past 12 o'clock ; was 10 or 15 minutes going to the wagon, and getting the horse ready ; about 3 miles from where he lives to the pond ; as they approached the house they discovered a light in the house, and thought it a late hour for the people to be up ; as they got opposite the house, some person passed from the hall to the front room ; witness turned his head as the person came into the front room ; saw a dim light in the 2d story, over the hall ; saw no light only where he has mentioned ; thought the man had on a dark dress ; was a common sized man ; about the size of prisoner ; the hall was lighted up.

*Cross-examined*—Saw a bright light in the hall, when coming up ; saw no lamp or candle ; drove pretty fast ; did not look at his watch until he went to bed ; Mr. Sayre was about the size of prisoner ; when witness went to bed, it wanted 20 minutes of 2 o'clock.

*Lewis Jaggers*, was in company with the two last witnesses ; was not quite 7 o'clock when they passed Mr. Sayre's, saw no one there ; quarter past 12 o'clock when the horse was ready to start, by his watch ; first saw a dim light in the 2d story window, at the gable end ; saw a light in the front room and hall ; a man came from the hall into the front room, and looked out ; had on dark clothes ; cannot tell whether a long or short coat ; no hat ; bright light in the hall, as also one in the front room*; a short time after he got home, looked at his watch, and found it 25 minutes past 1 o'clock, not more than 2 minutes after passing Mr. Sayre's.

*Cross-examined*—Saw no candle any where, only the light. At 7 o'clock court adjourned until 8 to-morrow morning.

Aug. 17, 8 o'clock, court opened.

*James W. Wetmore*, sworn—Saw prisoner the evening of the murder, about half past 8 o'clock ; he was in the store about 15 minutes ; he drank 4 glasses of cider ; gave witness a 5 franc piece in payment ; dont know which course he took when he left the store.

*Cross-examined*—Four of the glasses would make 3 half pints ; pretty hard, strong cider ; saw him have no other money.

*Lewis K Halsey*, resided in the house owned by Jabez Rodgers, on the 11th of May, in South street, 100 rods from Mr. Sayre's, towards town ; on the morning of the 12th of May, passed Mr. S.'s house about half past 6 o'clock, after his cow and calf ; went down on the side of Mr. S.'s house ; running down ; went about 40 rods towards Mr. Ford's woods ; on his return, found a bundle of clothes on the old road, a little before its junction with South street ; a pretty good sized bundle, wet and heavy ; with a buckskin strap buckled around it ; the one presented was the one ; (same as recognized by Stansborough, as prisoner's) ; as witness returned, on the side of the house towards town, picked up a black cloth coat, and bombazine do., black cloth pantaloons, flageolet, a piece of black silk, a piece of calico, 3 handkerchiefs, yellow pocket handkerchief ; the pantaloons were in the strapped bundle, one of the legs hanging out ; in the strapped bundle were 4 coarse linen shirts, marked A. B., with red thread, in the breast ; no fine shirts in it ; flannel waistcoat, yellow vest ; the strap was loose, as if articles had fallen from it.

Picked up, also, a small white handkerchief, marked Harriet Sayre, and a flag silk do. ; brought the whole to Mr. Rodgers' shop, near witness' dwelling, and spread them out on the logs ; some of the neighbours examined them; whilst witness was breakfasting, the neighbours went to S.'s house, and as witness went down, met Mr. Robsetson, who told him that the family were murdered.

*Cross-examined*—There is a deep gully where the articles were found, sufficiently so for a person to get on a horse ; the scattered articles found nearly opposite the lane leading to the stable, first found them 10 or 12 feet from the bridge spoken of by West; they were lying in a circular form, as if they had been dropped by a person going round ; the flageolet was in the middle of the road, and the last article found ; the gully is a place where there is little or no travelling ; the clothes were all wet, both in the strap, and those scattered ; the gully spoken of, is a water course.

*Collin Robertson*—Lives in South street, quarter of a mile from Mr. Sayre, towards the green ; on Sunday morning 12th May, rose half past six, the young woman called witness and stated that something unusual was going on opposite at Mr. Rogers' ; went over, and asked Mr. Rogers what was the matter ; after some conversation, requested Mr. R. to go to deceased's house with witness, as probably the house was robbed ; they went, first thing they saw was the barn doors open, fronting the road ; cows and oxen in the yard, articles in the barn in confusion, the cattle having been in ; stated to Mr. R. this was unusual for Mr. Sayre ; they passed to the gate leading into the stable yard ; in that passage found a japanned lamp lying on the side on the ground ; a few steps further discovered a horse with a rope around its neck, in a lot adjoining the stable yard ; the large gate leading from the stable yard to the lot, was open ; went to the stable, found the door open and the other horse missing, also the saddle and bridle, supposed the horse stolen, and the house robbed, saw a glass lantern lying on the side in the stable, under a plank which reached from one side of the stable to the other ; no floor to the stable, grease on the plank as if a spermaceti candle had been stuck to it ; if a candle had been placed there, light would shine out the door under the shed ; on going to the house, they discovered the large gate open at the street, leading from the stable yard to the street ; observing some articles there, they went up the lane and found a part of a large paper of tobacco about midway to the street, a round hair brush with a glass in the back of it, the one presented to court was the one, or similar ; a blue cloth coat, the one prisoner now has on, hung the coat on the fence, two black silk handkerchiefs were also found ; near the

stable door, under the shed, witness found a hatchet lying on a
shaving horse, also the blue mixed round-a-bout coat presented;
the hatchet is the same recognized by Stansborough, saw some
plaster spilled under the shed, and barrel lying on its side ; they
went to the front door and knocked repeatedly pretty hard, and
called also, but no answer given. Mr. Rogers went after Jacob
Wilson to go into the house with them ; Mr. R. returned with
Mr. Wilson and a Mr. Camp. Whilst Mr. R. was absent, went to
the rear of the house, and there saw a German pipe on a bench
on the stoop ; lifted the kitchen door latch, and found it was not
fastened, retured to the front door until the others came; the front
door was locked ; Mr. W. came, they all went around the house
and in at the back door; Mr. W. took a dung fork in his hand by
way of precaution ; on the kitchen table was a dressing glass,
and a cravat nearly under the table, also a pair of coarse men's
shoes under the table, the quarters down ; a decanter of some
kind of liquor was on the table, they went into the hall, saw
nothing material until they came to the bed room door at the end
of the hall, about 4 feet from the kitchen door; in that room the
secretary was broken open, the papers, clothing, &c. scattered
around, one or two of the draws broken ; a carpenter's chissel
was lying on the secretary, the draws open and contents principally taken out ; the clothes of the bed were turned down from
the pillow as if a person had been preparing to go to bed; the bed
not tumbled ; from thence to the front room and saw nothing in much disorder ; went up stairs and there found a large
quantity of bedding, men and women's wearing apparel of every
description in great profusion, on the floor ; there are three
rooms up stairs leading this hall; bandboxes were emptied of their
contents on the floor in the hall, the doors up stairs were all
open, some trunks in the hall broken open and contents turned
out, a blue paper curtain hung at the front window in the upper
hall ; the back room over the kitchen they first went in, there
was a bureau with all the locks broken, the draws partly out, and
mostly of the articles apparently removed to the hall ; in the upper hall found a set of silver teaspoons lying together, but not
tied, found all in disorder in the other rooms ; from thence they
went to the garret; as witness got on the floor, discovered the
feet of Phebe projecting from beneath the bed clothes, saw a
large quantity of clothes on the bed, and a buffalo skin over all ;
took the articles off, and found her dead, the buffalo skin was
over her face, a large quantity of blood and froth was lying in the
bed as if it came from her mouth and nose, two gashes or holes
in the temple, similar to those made by a pitch fork ; told Mr. W.
the girl was dead; going down stairs suggested that the alarm

be given in town ; witness took the horse, rode through town and gave the alarm; was absent probably half an hour ; saw no marks of blood about the house except in the bed of the black girl. The stable is about 25 feet long, and from 10 to 12 wide, the top of the stable is not as high as the street; lights in the stable door could not be seen from the street ; from the street could see no one at the stable door ; the shed projects 20 feet or more from the stable door : it is what is called a *cellar stable.*

*Cross-Examined*—Thei e is a window at the gable end of the house below, saw Yankee blinds to it afterwards ; stable had but little litter or manure in it, the shaving horse was in its usual place, the dark gray horse was in the lot in the morning ; the spoons were discovered in the midst of the articles, in the upper hall ; after his return, saw a table set of silver, tea and coffee pot, sugar dish, milk cup, sugar tongs ; first saw them in a closet in the lower front room, noticed no other articles of silver in the house ; believes the blinds in the lower front room were raised; one of the windows in the upper front room was raised, the other was down, and the paper curtains all rolled up, is not certain ; the third window, at the gable end towards town, witness believes was up ; three windows in the lower front room, the two front with venetian blinds, the end, paper ; the rope around the neck of the horse was long enough for him to use as a bridle, and appeared to have been untied ; there were no tracks of cattle in the plaster on the ground ; a ladder was up to the west gable end of the house, very heavy, and about 30 feet long, could not be managed by one man, no; near enough for a person to enter the window, is not positive as to its position ; deceased was a small man, not quite so tall as the prisoner ; prisoner could go from his bed room to the cellar, and thence out of doors, or up stairs into the lower hall. Prisoner was dressed when at Luse's on the evening of the 11th, similar to what he had seen him wear previous ; pantaloons darker than his coat; prisoner had no appearance of intoxication ; the pipe presented witness believes is the same he found on the rear piaza.

*Examined Direct*—The round-a-bout exhibited is the one witness found on the shaving horse under the shed, and the same prisoner had on the evening previous at Luse's.

*Jabez Rodgers.* Resides in South Street, a quarter of a mile from deceased, opposite Mr. Robertson's ; went to the house of deceased on Sunday morning, with C. Robertson ; the reasons for going were [similar to those given by Mr. Robertson ; first observed a glass on the kitchen table, a razor partly open, lather box and brush, a decanter of liquor near the end of the table in rear of the glass ; merely looked in the front room to see if any

person was there ; a liquor case was in one of the rooms broken
open ; fully corroborates Mr. Rohertson as to the situation of
the interior of the house ; believes it would take 2 or 3 hours to
commit such a depredation ; it would take a persons 5 minutes
to walk from E. N. Rodgers to the bridge nearly in front of deceased's house ; it would take about 20 minutes to walk from
Luse's to the house of deceased—about 3 quarters of a mile ; the
impression of witness that he picked up the pipe in the stable-
yard, and put it on the rear piazza of the house—it was either
the pipe or the lamp ; the plaster was scattered in something of
a circular manner ; the track of a man's shoe was discovered in
the plaster under the shed ; thinks the lantern was laying on the
plank ; it was a dark and cloudy night ; rained before morning.
  *Cross-examined.*  Took particular care about avoiding to
tread in the plaster ; saw some remaining in the barrel ; it did
not strike them forcibly on discovering the plaster ; went under
the shed when they came out of the stable ; saw several prints of
person's feet on the edge of the plaster ; took no measurement of
the size ; discovered the tracks immediately on going under the
shed ; does not think it possible witness or Mr. Robertson could
have made the tracks ; corroborates Mr. Robertson as to the
windows ; will not be positive, but believes the plaster barrel was
standing up, either the first or second time he saw it.
  *Jacob Wilson.*  Was at Luse's hotel on the evening of the
11th May ; prisoner came in after 9 o'clock, and left there about
half past 9, about 5 or 10 minutes previous to witness ; it was 10
when witness arrived at his own door ; Mr. Sayre's house is
about 350 yards from the residence of witness ; went to the house
of deceased on Sunday morning ; fully corroborates the two last
witnesses ; saw one or two bandboxes in the upper hall, empty ;
the upper hall was the principal place of deposit, but articles
scattered in the other rooms ; it must have taken 2 or 3 hours to
have broken the locks, and examine the several articles, and
make selections ; the room in the rear of prisoner's was locked,
the only one he saw which was not broken open ; the large trunks
in the garret where the black woman was killed, were broken
open, and contents taken out ; no partition in the garret ; a quantity of lumber was near the house ; deceased was about building
a kitchen.
  *Cross-examined.*  Do not recollect the situation of the windows ; prisoner had on the coat presented at Luse's ; had seen
him wear it previous ; when prisoner came into the bar-room,
some one asked who it was, when witness replied he lived with
Mr. Sayre ; prisoner took water with his brandy.
  *William Jaggers.*  Was at Mr. Sayre's on Sunday morning,

12th May ; went down with Alexander Robertson and others ;
went about a quarter past 7, on acount of Mr. Robertson's in-
forming them that the black woman was killed ; went down the
lane leading to the stable yard ; on going to the stable door,
Alexander Robertson discovered calico under the straw, and said
he found some more clothes ; on pulling at it witness saw the leg
of Mrs. Sayre ; they also saw the foot of Mr. Sayre projecting
from the manure ; they went up to the gate until others came,
and then went back and dug the bodies out of the dung heap ;
Mrs. Sayre was lying across the front of the stable door, and a
horse could not easily be taken from the stable without walking
over her ; Mr. Sayre was lying 6 or 8 feet further out ; feet
towards the stable door ; Mrs. Sayre had an old hood on her head,
and one coarse shoe on one foot ; saw wounds on the head ; Mr.
Sayre had on a straw hat, and coarse boots on his feet ; his pantaloons had not been pulled down after putting on his boots ;
wounds on his head and temples ; his arms were drawn back
over his head at full length ; had a silk pocket handkerchief
around his neck ; had the appearance of being dragged from
towards the stable by his hands to the hole in the manure ; the
head of Mrs. Sayre was lying towards the head of Mr. Sayre ; if
Mrs. Sayre had been drawn to where she lay, she must have been
drawn from under the shed ; the plaster spoken of was about 10
feet from her feet ; the club was near the corner of the stable,
near the door ; the one presented witness believes is the same ;
the hatchet present was lying on the shaving horse ; the bodies
were drawn a little down hill to the manure ; Mr. Sayre was
buried the deepest ; the bodies were taken into the house soon
thereafter ; taken into the kitchen ; Mr. Sayre had on mixed
clothes ; Mrs, Sayre had on a calico gown.

*Cross-examined.* Knows not whether Mr. Sayre was in the
stable that night ; saw no marks of his having been dragged ;
supposed he was dragged into the hole from the circumstance of
having his arms over his head ; blood on his face when discovered ; appeared to have run from the temple ; the position of
his body was about level ; saw no blood about the plaster ; the
plaster was lying in a circle ; did not suspect Mrs. Sayre had been
dragged any—but, if so, must have been from the direction of
the shed ; blood around her head ; her arms were lying in front
of her ; the bodies were fully dressed.

*Examination direct.* Mr. Sayre's hat was drawn down almost
over his nose ; saw a candle on the plank ; believes the coat in
court was the one on the shaving horse.

*Alexander Robertson.* Was at the house of Samuel Sayre on
Sunday morning, 12th of May ; went there on account of the
alarm of murder ; went there about 7 o'clock ; went into the lane

leading to the stable yard, and saw a silk handkerchief, then a
coat, then some calico, as witness thought, and said there were
more clothes in the dung heap ; a small piece of calico appeared ;
took hold of it to take it up, and found it was Mrs. Sayre's frock ;
some one observed there was Mr. Sayre's boot, then went to the
lane, and informed the people the bodies were found ; was then
sent to Bottle Hill, to inform Archibald Sayre ; got home as they
were taking the bodies into the house ; the coat presented (the
one identified on prisoner at Luse's the previous evening) was on
the shaving horse under the shed.

   *Dr. John B. Johnes.*   Was at the house of deceased on Sunday morning, 12th May ; the alarm given of the murder induced
him to go ; Mr. and Mrs. Sayre were on the dung hill in the yard,
and the coloured girl in bed in the garret ; Mr. and Mrs. Sayre
were taken to the kitchen, and examined in company with Doctors
Canfield, Cutler, and Condict ; the wounds on Mr. Sayre's head
were in two places; one on the left side of the head, a bruise in
the flesh sufficient to draw a little blood, but not break a bone—
sufficient to knock a person down ; appeared to have been done
with a blunt instrument, but not heavy ; a blow on the forehead
sufficient to change the appearance of the face, crushing in the
bones at the junction of the nose and forehead ; no skin broken ;
the nose and forehead bones broken and depressed ; altogether
much shattered, so much so that the brains were forced from the
nostril ; some of the brains were taken from off the breast ; the
fracture on the forehead sufficient to produce death, and no doubt
produced the death of Mr. Sayre ; undoubtedly repeated blows
were made use of ; the club presented (heretofore identified) was
sufficient to produce death, and the indentation of the bones
would lead them to suppose it was produced by a bludgeon ; on
Mrs. Sayre's head were several wounds ; on the back was one
which bruised through to the skull ; a round opening, the size of
a shilling, as if done with a stick ; on the left side of the head
one similar to the first one on Mr. Sayre's, but bruised through
the skin ; on the forehead were two marks similar to one made
with the corner of the head of the hatchet ; on the right temple
Mrs. Sayre had a severe blow which fractured the bone from the
cheek to the eye.   The wounds on Phebe first presented themselves as if she had been stabbed in the left temple, being a hole
about the size of a goose quill ; on opening the scalp the left temple bones were all shattered, as if done with a blunt heavy instrument ; had also a wound on the left side of her head similar to
that of Mr. Sayre, and the skull fractured ; blood had issued from
her nostrils apparently rapidly, as on the bed near her face was a
large quantity of froth, say a quart ; in the rim of the left ear
was an incision ; appeared to have been made by a sharp instrument, but very little blood ; from the nature of the wounds she

must have been killed instantly, as apparently she had not moved even a muscle ; a great many arteries in the head evidently were instantly opened ; life necessarily is not taken when suddenly stunned ; it is not possible for a person to commit the deed, walk down stairs and immediately back, and find her gasping ; but if one went down and another up, and find her gasping, they must have met on the way ; the quantity of froth designates the rapidity of the flowing of the blood, and the suddenness of the death ; she lay in bed as if asleep, and a person would so consider her if no blood or wound was perceptible. When first saw Mr. Sayre, his arms were stretched above his head, and had the appearance of being much strained ; the blows on Mr. and Mrs. Sayre were very similar on the left side of the head.

*Cross-examined.* The wounds on Mr. S. appeared to have been inflicted with the same instrument ; on the head of Mrs. S. were 5 different wounds ; the one on her forehead was evidently done with an instrument having a square corner ; the others *may* have been done with the same instrument, if struck square ; but the one on the side and back of the head were similar to those on Mr. S.'s, but the skin was cut through ; much blood was in Mrs. S.'s bonnet ; it is *possible* the wounds on both were made with one instrument ; but the one on Mrs. S. was evidently done with a cornered instrument ; the blows on the head of Phebe resembled those on Mr. and Mrs. Sayre, on account of appearing to have been done with a blunt instrument : she had a long fracture, some 2 or 3 inches, extending from the temple to the ear ; the long wound could possibly have been done with the side of an axe if struck fair ; judged Mr. S. had been dragged, from the appearance of the position of the hands, and having discovered blood in the stable about 8 inches in diameter ; had a recent appearance of being placed there ; could not have been there long, or it would have been disturbed and scattered around more ; appeared to have remained as it run from the wound ; the blood must have came from the nostrils of Mr. S., if it came from him at all ; the stable door sill is raised its depth from the ground ; about a half pint of blood ran in the stable ; the blood on the door sill had the appearance of having been wiped off by drawing Mr. S. over it ; the hole was dug below the manure to cover the body of Mr. S. ; the spots on the vest presented, were spots of blood, and could have proceeded from the nose of Mr. S. when struck on the forehead ; the spots on the pantaloons have the appearance of blood ; the white on the bottom is apparently plaster : the grease on the vest and pantaloons has the appearance of coming from a spermacetti candle—similar spots could have proceeded from a rapid and sudden bleeding of the nose, or blowing of the nose whilst bleeding ; did not see the vest in two weeks after the murder ; the bodies appeared to have been dead some hours—equally rigid and stiff. Witness's opinion was, that the blows on them were first on the back of the head and fell, afterwards the others.

*Dr. Isaac W. Canfield.* Was at the house of S. Sayre the morning after the murder was discovered ; examined the wounds on the corpses ; concurs with the statement made by Dr. Johnes ; believes the club presented was a proper instrument for committing the murder ; the hatchet *could* have been made use of ; the witness's opinion was at the time, and now is, that they were first knocked down by the blow on the side of the head, and then dispatched by those on the forehead ; the principal one on her was on the right side of the head, near the eye and temple ; she had evidently received several glancing blows ; on Phebe's head was a severe wound on the left temple ; the bone fractured extending to the ear ; she was lying on the right side in a sleeping posture, and apparently had never stirred after the blow was given ; the system must have been immediately parallyzed ; the head of the hatchet in court appears to have been the instrument to have given the death blow, or blows followed up with a club ; it is not within the range of possibilities, that after the severe blow, a buffalo skin could have been spread over her, a person go down 2 pair of stairs to the street, come up again, and find her gasping.

*Cross-examined.* The blow on the side of the head did not probably produce death with Mr. Sayre, but stunned him : was sufficient to prevent an outcry from him ; they had been dead evidently several hours previous to the examination ; Mr. S. was more bloated than Mrs. S. ; it is *possible* that a person could have gone from the lower room to the garret, and found Phebe gasping ; she could not possibly have lived over 3 minutes.

*Examination, direct.* Saw the vest soon after the murder ; the spots were blood, and much plainer than now ; the bottom of the pantaloons was covered with plaster, or something similar to it, and much plainer than now ; the blood spots on them was also much plainer ; the plaster has been much shaken off since ; saw the clothes a very few days after the murder ; observed the incision in the left ear of Phebe.

*William A. Carmichael.* Was at the premises of Mr. S. on the morning of the murder ; saw blood on the straw and hay in the stable, 4 or 5 feet from the door ; saw the blood in but one spot—a place as large round as the crown of a hat ; took the straw in his hands to examine more distinctly ; the blood appeared to be fresh ; was there between 8 and 9 A. M.

*Bernard M'Cormick.* Was at the house of Mr. S. on the morning in question, about the time Mr. and Mrs. S. were discovered ; went into the room of prisoner and Stanberry ; the latter was not fastened ; it was some time after his arrival before he went down ; Stanberry was there some time previous ; did not observe the liquor case until the following day, when he saw that the lock of it was broken ; had charge of the house with others, 8 or 9 days ; saw no trace of blood in the house except in the garret ; was in prisoner's room ; bedstead, bed, and chest in it ; examined the chest and found a piece of crape similar to what was worn on Mr. S.'s hat ; behind the chest found an opera glass, and a note given by John Crissey to Sally Crissey, for $152, dated Feb. 3, 1815 ; (the name of the former Mrs. S. previous to her marriage) ; found the vest and pantalooons (now in court, and previously spoken of) spread under prisoner's bed, on bed-quilts, which rested on the bed cord ; found these articles on Monday following ; were spread on the quilts ; there were old strips of rags in the chest also, with a pair of old suspenders ; don't re-collect of any thing else ; gave the clothes in the charge of the sheriff ; Mr. S. apparently had been shaved the previous evening.

*Joseph Fairchild.* Was at the house about 7 on Sunday morning after the bodies were found ; saw a coat on the fence, from the pocket of which witness took a hair brush and a book ; the coat is the one the prisoner now has on—dark blue ; was one who took charge of the house ; remained 11 days ; was present when the vest and pantaloons were found ; saw the blood on the articles much plainer when found than now ; the white on the pantaloons was much higher up, and more on than now ; thought at the time it was plaster ; thinks it was Wednesday the opera glass was found behind the chest ; the note was *in* the chest, as also a pair of shoes said to belong to the prisoner ; the ladder was about one-third the distance from front to the rear of the house ; on Sunday evening endeavoured to light the lamp which was fastened to the ceiling of the stair way ; it would throw light into the upper hall ; the glass of the lamp was very black ; there was considerable oil on the floor under the lamp.

*Cross-examined*—The clothes were nicely spread under the bed on the quilt ; the book was a French Roman Catholic prayerbook ; got the oil from the kitchen to fill the lamp ; it was in a decanter.

*Examination, direct.* The circle of the plaster was about 10 feet ; the barrel was on end when witness saw it ; Stansborough's room was locked when witness first went there ; it was open afterwards ; witness is a blacksmith ; prisoner brought to his shop a pair of sulkey wheels to be repaired on Saturday ; on Saturday evening witness was at a singing society ; it broke up about half-past 9, and went directly home ; got home before 10 ; the shop is nearer the green than the house—the next door.

*Cross-examined.* No other door in the house had locks ex-cept the front door and upper front room, except Stansborough's.

*William Kirk.* On Saturday evening previous to the murder was at the singing society, at B. A. Sherwood's ; Mr. J. Fair-child was there ; broke up about half-past 9.

*George H. Ludlow, Sheriff.* Was at the house of Mr. Sayre on Sunday morning, 12th May ; the bodies of the deceased had just been discovered ; the plaster under the shed was similar to that described by the other witnesses ; did not observe that it was shuffled about ; most of it under the shed, and extended outward towards the stable door ; thinks the barrel was lying down ; saw the plank in the stable ; saw nothing on it of consequence ; remained on the premises but a short time ; suppose it would require a person at least three hours to derange the house in the manner it was ; the lamp was attached to the stair casing about 6 feet high ; would illumine the upper and lower hall ; saw no lock in the house but what was open ; every drawer or trunk in the house was forced open ; the drawers generally apparently were forced open with a chisel about one and a quarter inch in width ; some of the locks appeared to have been driven in ; the note spoken of by Mr. M'Cormick was given witness by M'Cormick ; on Monday after the murder was informed of the discovery of the pantaloons and vest ; the spots and other marks on them now not so bright ; the bottom of the pantaloons covered with plaster nearly to the knees, when first discovered ; have frequently been examined since ; Mr. S.'s private papers were in and about the secretary in his bed-room, all displaced and in confusion ; some on the floor ; subsequently found $180 in paper money, in three parcels, and $3 in specie.

Adjourned to 9 o'clock on Monday morning.

Monday, 9 A. M. court met. George H. Ludlow still under examination. The lamp in court is the one attached to the stair case in the lower hall of Mr. Sayre's house, it is one of unusual structure, and requires much skill to prepare it ; witness went in pursuit of prisoner on the 12th May ; started nearly 10 A. M., in company with N. B. Luse ; went to Newark —there changed horses and took Z. Drake ; went towards New York ; Luse passed them ; at the half-way house Luse came to the door as they drove up, and said he believed they had the murderer ; witness went in, and prisoner was sitting with a part of a glass of cider ; Mr. D. and Mr. L. took hold of each hand and led him to the door ; witness took from his vest pocket a small gold watch, and a pair of ladie's kid mitts marked Mary Sayre ; in his vest pockets were 3 small pocket books—articles of jewelry, trinkets, &c., finger and ear rings, gold watch, chain and seals, silver thimble, &c. &c. ; ladie's gold watch hook found next day in prisoner's pantaloons pocket ; the watch presented is the one in his vest pocket, with ribband around his neck ; steel for striking fire ; jack knife, and 2 razors ; 2 case knives in the breast coat pocket on prisoner—the coat belonging to deceased ; the hat of deceased on prisoner's head, with the name in it ; black cloth vest of deceased ; pair of black pantaloons in one of his bundles ; 2 pillow cases presented, marked S. S. S. No. 7, were filled with articles tied together with a rope, and a cane and umbrella passed through ; the latter was written on the border, " Samuel Sayre, Morristown, N. J. ;" other articles identified as sworn to by N. B. Luse ; 11 cravats, the name of S. Sayre on some of them ; bombazin shawl ; 1 linen sheet, marked C. L. S. ; (the initials of Mr. S.'s first wife) 4 pair of ladie's cotton, 1 pair silk, 1 pair worsted stockings, and 1 pair marked Mary E. Taylor ; 2 pair white pantaloons ; 1 white vest ; 1 pair of muslin drawers on prisoner ; 5 linen shirts—Samuel Sayre marked on some of them ; 7 muslin shirts ; prisoner was brought to Newark, and remained at Drake's hotel about 2 hours ; got some irons at the prison at that town, and returned to Morristown, the sun about half hour high ; on Monday morning went to his cell— stripped him, and took from him the articles belonging to deceased ; next to his skin was a leather belt buckled around his body, with $42 in specie—one 5 franc piece, two Spanish dollars, the remainder in American half dollars ; about $15 dollars in small change in his pantaloons pocket, no piece over a quarter ; his feet were clean, and had on a clean shirt when examined ; prisoner understands some English words.

*Cross-examined.* Witness believes he has seen the lamp lighted in the hall ; did not observe oil on the floor ; 2 windows in the hall below ; saw the barrel of plaster ; had evidently been intentionally rolled from one side of the shed to the other, and the plaster much scattered, some places about 4 feet wide, some places merely sprinkled, and others an inch thick ; there were 12 large silver table spoons, 12 desert spoons, 24 tea spoons, tea and coffee pot, milk cup and slop bowl, silver premium cup, and several plated candlesticks ; witness did not see the bank notes when first discovered ; $30 in bank bills were in a secret drawer of the secretary, which appeared not to have been discovered ; there was 230 or 235 dollars worth of silver, as was appraised ; was in the house when the paper money was found ; it was in the secretary rolled up in a piece of paper, and had evidently been overhauled ; the silver money was in the same desk ; the drawer in the secretary in which was the $30, was not locked ; saw no track of cattle or horses in the plaster ; it was observed by some that the plaster was evidently sprinkled to cover blood ; examined one or two places but saw none ; the candle on the plank must have thrown its rays directly on the line of the plaster ; the notes in the drawer were lying loose ; the plaster lay in a line from Mrs. S.'s feet to the rear of the shed, and the light would have shown from her feet to the rear of the shed ; when prisoner was arrested, was much confused, and talked much and fast, but could not understand a word he said.

*Catherine Killerine.* First saw prisoner at Mr. Drake's, on

Sunday, the 12th May, about noon ; asked prisoner what he had
been doing, in German language ; he told witness, he went out
from deceased's house to get a letter wrote home in German—
when he came back he wanted $5, and could not get it ; said he
came home about 11 in the evening, and found no one about the
house, and went up stairs and found the black girl in the bed
dying, which frightened him so much that he went down into the
cellar and got his clothes ; he took 6 shirts, 1 watch, Mr. Sayre's
hat and frock coat—he took the horse and then run away ; he
rode the horse so hard, that the horse fell down and threw him,
and could not catch the horse again ; (witness here repeated the
conversation in German to the prisoner)'; prisoner asked witness
if he must die right away—witness said no.

  *Cross-examined.*   Native place is Germany ; been in this country 3 years ; arrived at New York ; could not speak English before she came to this country ; lived 2 years in New York and 1
year in New Jersey ; several present during the conversation ;
Mr. Drake requested witness to converse with prisoner ; explained to the sheriff and others what he said.

  *Archibald Sayre*—Resides at Bottle Hill, about 200 rods from
the turnpike, on the Hanover road, is a connexion with deceased ;
deceased was frequently at the house of witness, and generally
rode or drove a gray mare, when he did not come with his family.
Knows James A. Campfield, he resides about 2 miles from witness, at Columbia, on the same road ; witness resides about 4
miles from Morristown.

  *Moses Force*—Resides at Bottle Hill, about 20 rods beyond
Archibald Sayre's, on the Hanover road ; heard some one pass
his house about 4 o'clock on Sunday morning pretty fast, it rained at the time, wife of witness was sick, and witness was sitting
up, it was a little before daybreak.

  *Cross-Examined*—Did not look out ; horse was on a gallop,
had not slept that night, heard no other person pass that night,
commenced raining about 12 o'clock, and continued until after
sun rise.

  *James A. Campfield*—Resides at Columbia, Chatham township, on the road leading from Bottle Hill to Hanover church ;
on Sunday morning, the day on which he heard of the murder,
saw a man pass his house, was called up earlier than usual, and
was in his barn yard ; the man came past him on a pretty fast
trot, with a large bundle on front of the rider, it was a gray horse.

  *Cross-Examined*—Saw but one bundle, saw no overcoat on
the rider, broad day light, before sun rise, it was not raining,
thought it was a pedlar broke down; about 500 feet from witness.

  *David Morehouse*—Lives in Livingston township, Essex
county, on the Newark turnpike, about 3 miles from Columbia ;

on the morning of the murder, saw a light gray beast coming from the direction of Newark, towards witness' house, with saddle and bridle, the reins of the latter were resting on the mane near the saddle ; could plainly discover where a man had sat on the saddle, as it was dry, the remaining part wet, the beast was walking, witness took her up with some difficulty, and tied her to the door yard fence until church time, when she was put in his stable ; at the intermission saw handbills describing the beast; previous to his arrival at home, some other person had taken her; it had rained during the night, the hair lay close, did not then think had been rode hard, did not raise the saddle.

*Cross-Examined*—Lives about one and a half miles from Campfield, about 9 miles from Morristown, via. Bottle Hill, took up the beast about 10 minutes after sun rise, no mud about the beast except what would collect by travelling.

*Samuel Wade*—Lives in Livingston township, about a quarter of a mile beyond Morehouse's, towards Newark ; on the morning of the murder saw the tracks of a horse going towards Newark, and another return ; afterwards went towards Newark about 4 or 500 yards, saw the track of a horse leave the road to the bank, and then take a circuit in the road and returned towards Morristown ; lives three quarters of a mile this side of Joseph Courter's, saw the tracks between 6 and 7 o'clock A. M.

*Cross-Examined*—Saw no place where a horse had stumbled and fallen.

*Joseph Courter*—Lives in Livingston township, about three quarters of a mile from Wade's, the last witness ; on Sunday morning, 12th of May, after sunrise, saw a man on foot coming with a large bundle on his back, about the size of a pedlar's pack, looked as if a dark great coat had been put around it to keep it from the rain, a strap like a circingle around it, a stick on each shoulder attached to the bundle, and his arms extended in front of him ; common sized man, with dark whiskers, took particular notice of him, from the singular manner in which he carried his bundle; could not swear the prisoner was the person, as he was a darker complexion.

*Cross-Examined*—No appearance of his being in the mud ; thought he had a blue coat on, hat on, did not speak to prisoner.

*Peter Cook*—Lives about a mile from last witness ; has seen prisoner before ; first saw him on Sunday morning, 12th May, not far from 6 o'clock ; prisoner was going toward Newark, and a few rods from witness, when first saw him ; had a large bundle, thought him a pedlar ; bundle covered with a dark coat ; had an umbrella on the right shoulder, and a stick on the left attached to the bundle by a circingle ; could not understand prisoner; prisoner came up to witness and made signs by putting up his

hands, &c., understood New York only ; walked pretty fast ;
umbrella of the description of the one in court, and heretofore
recognised as belonging to deceased.

*Cross-Examined*—No mud on him, as if he had fallen ; prisoner's countenance is familiar, but not so dark, and thinner in
flesh.

*Mary Harrison*—Thinks she saw prisoner before this ; lives
half a mile from Peter Cook's, towards Newark ; prisoner was
walking in the road ; witness was at the well opposite the house
when prisoner came along ; he had a large dark bundle on his
back ; prisoner kept looking at witness as he passed, and afterwards ; between 6 and 7 o'clock of the morning she heard of
the murders.

*Cross.Examined*—Prisoner had on a black hat ; no appearance of having fallen in the mud ; lives 4 miles from Orange.

*Lewis Freeman*—First saw prisoner the day he heard of the
murder ; saw him as he went through the toll gate ; his father
keeps the gate ; prisoner was on foot, and going towards Newark ; about 7 o'clock ; had a large bundle, described by the
other witnesses ; the bundle was carried on the ends of an umbrella and a stick, one on each shoulder.

*Cross-Examined*—Prisoner asked for *Newick.*

*Mary Freeman*—Lives at the gate spoken of by last witness ;
saw prisoner pass through the gate about 7 o'clock on the morning of the 12th May ; had on black coat and vest, and mixed
pantaloons ; had a large bundle apparently done up in a dark
great coat, as the sleeve hung down ; a circingle was around it ;
carried the bundle as described by the others.

*Cross-Examined*—Prisoner endeavoured to ask the way to either Newark or N. York ; had some trouble to understand him.

*Elizabeth Harrison*—Resides in the upper part of the town
of Orange, one quarter of a mile from the Episcopal church ;
prisoner arrived at witness' house between 7 and 8 o'clock on
Sunday morning, 12th May ; had on a black coat, dark mixed
pantaloons ; came on foot, with a large bundle, and very heavy ;
endeavoured to remove it from the door, and had to drag it ;
came in in great haste, and understood he wanted something to
eat ; took breakfast at witness' house ; could not understand
what he said, only *caffee*, the remainder by signs ; was about
half an hour at the house ; witness lives about one mile from the
gate ; paid a 10 cent piece for his breakfast ; looks like the man
at her house ; appeared to be in a great hurry for his breakfast,
by his motions ; was getting breakfast for the family ; does not
keep public house.

*Cross-Examined*—Witness' door stood open when prisoner
came in ; did not speak the word coffee very plain, but understood him ; prisoner laid the money on the table ; looked very

nice in his dress; at the time thought his countenance showed he was unhappy; looked sorrowful.

*Valeria Harrison*—Recollects to have seen prisoner on Sunday morning referred to, between 7 and 8 o'clock; came to their house on foot; remained about half an hour; saw the bundle, with a blue coat wrapped around it; could not speak the English language; the collar of his shirt was clean; was not in the room when prisoner left the house; let the bundle fall off his shoulders when he came in; much fatigued.

*Alfred Pierson*—Saw the bead work-bag now in court; found it in the road leading from Bottle-Hill to Columbia, about 150 rods beyond Archibald Sayre's; found it about 8 o'clock, A. M., 12th May; in the bag were 2 pair ladies' cotton stockings and 1 of silk; 1 pair was marked C. L. S.; 1 finger-ring, set with pearl; sewing silk wound around a card; 2 plated stock buckles; braided hair bracelets, with gold snaps; several small gold clasps; gold locket; do. breast-pin; 1 large do.; 2 gilt buckles; 1 gilt scarf ring; several other small articles in the work bag; found an old pillow-case, muddy and torn, about 2 rods from the work-bag; articles found about 4 1-2 miles from Morristown.

*Mary W. Sayre*—Is daughter to the deceased; the bead work-bag found by the last witness belongs to witness; was at Newton on the 12th May; had been there about 10 days; the bag was left in the next to the upper drawer in the bureau, in the back chamber; nothing in it; the room was witness' bed room; the large finger-ring was left in a dressing glass drawer in witness' bed room, on the bureau; there were two; both presented in court; the gold broaches were in the same drawer; gilt and paste buckles, same place; the sewing silk was in a paper box, in the bureau;1 pair silk stockings were in the under drawer of the bureau; 1 pair cotton do., in the same drawer; these articles were all in the bead work-bag. The opera glass belongs to witness, and was left in the next to the upper bureau drawer; the needle case belongs to witness' mother; was in the bureau drawer in her father's bed room; the gold chain belonged to witness father, and was in the same drawer with the needle case; the large seal was in witness' bureau drawer up stairs, and the small seal was in her mother's work basket; the chain and seals were not heretofore put together as they now are. The gold watch, &c. belonged to her mother, who frequently wore it, and when not worn, wes kept in the bed room; ear-rings and drops belonged to witness, and left in her bureau drawer; were not broken; the ivory handled case knife belongs to a set kept in a trunk in the upper front room, rolled in a paper, and near the bottom; the bone handled one belonged in the closet in the front room, down stairs; witness' father's best clothes were

kept in a trunk in a small bed room, at the end of the upper hall;
he usually wore a black coat, and frequently black vest ; the
woollen stockings were usually kept in the under bureau drawer
in father's bed room, down stairs; the shirts and cravats in the
same bureau ; the clothes identified are her father's ; the flageolet was witness', generally kept on the table in the front room,
down stairs; piece of calico belonged to witness' mother, and in
the bureau drawer, down stairs ; the lamp in court was fastened
to the stair way, in the hall below ; was sometimes lighted when
witness was at home, but seldom without ; it would always
smoke when the wick was two high ; it would give a light up
stairs sufficient to go about ; the articles in the house were re-
placed before witness went to the house ; all the locks broken
except two, and they were forced without breaking ; there were
some old trunks in the garret ; father generally retired about 10
o'clock ; black girl frequently went first ; sometimes would
shave in the kitchen ; almost always set up until his work hands
returned at night ; he preferred seeing the house fastened at
night ; the hood which her mother had on when found belonged
to the black girl ; the stockings marked Mary E. Taylor belonged to her cousin : witness' father seldom permitted a light to go
to the barn, but when they did, took a globe lantern ; the one in
court was the one ; he conversed with prisoner principally by
signs ; knew a few words in French ; took the New York Observer, and got it on Saturday evening ; he generally took off
his boots and put on slippers some time previous to going to
bed ; there were 2 side-saddles in the house, kept at the foot of
the stairs in the basement story ; the circingle belonged to one
of them ; there was a chest in prisoner's bed room ; sometimes
a lamp and sometimes a tallow candle burned in the kitchen ;
spermaceti candles occasionally burnt in the other part of the
house ; hair brush belonged to witness, left in the upper front
room, on the table ; father lost a relative after witness left home;
Phebe wore a pair of coarse shoes in wet weather ; the one presented belonged to her ; generally left them in the kitchen when
she went to bed.

   *Cross-Examined*—The closet below, in the front room where
the knife belonged, was the place where the plate was kept ;
5 pair plated candlesticks up stairs ; father did not usually read
by a sperm-candle; not generally used except when company
was there ; black man left witness' father a short time previous
to prisoner's arrival ; no serious difference between them ;
threatened to correct him about a month previous to his going
away ; went so far as to make him take off his coat ; was not
as obedient as formerly ; was not aware of any specie in the
house ; knew nothing of her mother's funds ; the black boy

which ran away from her father was a brother to the black girl which was killed.

*Jabez Rodgers, called again*—Saw the gray mare of Mr. Sayre's, at Mr. Morehouse's, on the Orange mountain ; took her to Newark and brought her home; believes Mr. Sayre wore crape on his hat.

*James Rodgers*—Is a carpenter ; worked for deceased, quit on Friday noon, previous to the murder, left his tools in the barn; on Saturday towards evening went down there and put the tools up on some corn stalks in the barn, and covered them up with straw; prisoner was the only person saw witness put them there ; prisoner was in the barn cutting straw, wished prisoner to know where he put them, that he would not move the stalks and let them fall down; Stansborough had gone home when witness put up the tools

*Cross-Examined*—Saw Stansborough go past witness' house on his way home ; Stansborough worked the farm ; witness was about putting up an addition to the house ; the chissels belonged to witness, and were those he put up among the cornstalks, saw the remainder of the tools in the place he left them ; saw a part of a barrel of plaster lying on the side under the shed. A week previous to the time witness left there, prisoner was sitting on the ground with his head down, asked Mr. Sayre what the matter was, who answered that he expected his nose was bleeding; prisoner's back was towards them, saw no blood ; did not get the chissels until Monday; heard no complaints of, or from the black fellow, appeared to work as well as any other person in his condition, prisoner usually wore a black velvet pantaloons, and blue frock, no vest on when it was represented his nose was bleeding, never saw him wear any other.

*Elizabeth Shannon*—Was at the house of the deceased on the day of the murder ; whilst putting away the articles saw two linnen sheets which had been opened and blood on them as if a person had wiped blood from their hands; the linen was in the upper part of the house, the bodies of Mr. and Mrs. Sayre were laid out below stairs in their bed room ; would not suppose a person laying out the body of any of the deceased, would take a clean sheet in a different part of the house to wipe their hands upon, when there were plenty of towels, &c. in the same room.

*Sheriff Ludlow* was called upon to show a letter which he found in a writing-desk in the lower front room, it was considerably bloody: discovered it in the course of the week, whilst arranging the papers ; the blood similar in appearance that it now has.

*Stephen Vail*, remembers Sunday morning the 12th May last ; held the inquest over the bodies of Mr. and Mrs. Sayre, and Phebe, the coloured woman ; witness forbid the rummaging of the articles about the house after the inquest was in session ; it would take from 2 to 3 hours for one person to do the mischief that was done ; the Jury were cautious about handling any of the articles, or suffering any other person ; the locks were broken on the liquor case and pantry door in the cellar ; the handboxes appeared to have been drawn from under the beds, and pillaged ; the plaster barrel was thrown down, and the contents thrown therefrom, as if it had been rolled; discovered some blood under the shed, and apparently was a considerable struggle there ; walked from Luse's house to Sayre's house in 14 minutes ; the blood on the sill of the stable door looked as if it had been wiped off ; discovered some clothes on a line near the head of Phebe, which were sprinkled with blood ; have since seen blood on the rafters over where her head lay, from 2 to 3 feet over her head.

*Henry King.* Phebe, the coloured woman of deceased, came to the post office for letters and papers for deceased, on the evening of the 12th May ; deceased took the New York Observer, which paper comes on Saturday ; she came towards dusk.

*John L. Ward* was present when prisoner was stripped and examined on Monday morning after the arrest ; his feet were clean ; was at the house of deceased on Sunday ; saw the chissels afterwards.

*Cross-examined.* Prisoner had boots on ; does not recollect as to stockings ; was searched in the prison ; it was sufficiently light to see every thing.

The preceding examination of the prisoner was here given in evidence ; Amadee Boisaubin, the Interpreter, was sworn, and says that he was present at taking of prisoner's examination, was at that time sworn to act as interpreter.

*Cross-examined*—The examination was voluntary on the part of the prisoner ; prisoner made no objections at being examined.

After the reading of the examination, Mr. Boisaubin rose and stated to the court that it was properly translated to the prisoner at the time, as he (Mr. B.) was sworn so to do ; but he must beg of the Court to be excused from serving longer, for whilst Mr. Ford was reading the examination, prisoner made use of many vile epithets, calling him, (Mr. B.) a liar and villain, and Mr. Ford a Jew, and that the examining Court had no authority to examine him. At the request of the Court, however, he concluded to remain and act during the remainder of the trial.

*Victor Fleury* is a baker, takes bread, &c. around the town ; has taken it to the residence of deceased ; frequently saw prisoner there.

*Cross-examined.* On one occasion Mr. Sayre asked witness if he could talk German, said he could, and attempted to converse with prisoner, by asking him where he came from, &c. ; had but a few minutes conversation with him ; this was about a week previous to the murder ; prisoner never asked witness to write a letter for him ; never saw him in the village ; was at home at 9 o'clock on the evening of the murder, and the remainder of the night. Court adjourned to 10 to-morrow morning. August 20th—10 o'clock—Court met.

*Wm. N. Wood.* Was at the house of deceased shortly after the discovery of the bodies ; went to the stable door, there saw blood on the straw in the stable, about 3 or 4 feet from where he stood ; about the size of his hat ; a light on the left side of the stable-door would reflect its rays directly under the shed ; could not be seen in the lane.

*Catherine Kellerine* recalled. Prisoner told witness that Phebe was gasping when he went to her bed.

*Dr. J. W. Canfield* recalled. From the nature of the wound on Phebe, life might not have been extinguished under 2 or 3 minutes, and physicians could have discovered life by the pulse, and a very feeble respiration, like a person fainting ; but believes that she could not have gasped 1 minute after the blows, and probably never did gasp ; a hard blow on the temple, breaking in of the brain, and a profuse flow of blood from the nose, would produce immediate death.

*Cross-examined.* Cannot distinguish human blood from the blood of animals, when put on articles whilst warm ; the substance on the letter presented has every appearance of blood ; saw the pantaloons directly after they were found, and had far more the appearance of blood than it has now.

*Dr. John B. Johnes* recalled. From the nature of the wound on the head of Phebe, the respiration must have been very weak and short ; she *might* have gasped one minute, and the respiration continued from 3 to 5 minutes ; the substance on the letter in court has the appearance of blood, but would not swear it was blood ; saw no brains in the case of Phebe, on the outside ; a rush from many blood vessels must have been made suddenly through the nostrils, and discharged itself some 3 or 4 inches from the face where the large bunch of froth was found; but little blood between the froth and nose ; she lay on her right side, with her right hand under her face, and back towards the stairs.

*Samuel Stansborough* recalled. Never saw prisoner with stockings or shoes on ; wore boots ; never saw a sperm candle burned in the kitchen; prisoner had two coats, the round-about, and the blue cloth coat prisoner now has on ; the chissels Mr. Rogers kept in the barn, sometimes on the mow ; saw no plaster on prisoner's pantaloons before they were found under the bed ; Mr. Sayre attended the funeral of a relative a short time previous to the murder, and wore crape on his hat.

*Cross-examined.* There was a chicken killed on the Friday, it may have been on Saturday ; left there about half-past six o'clock ; no one used the chissels but Mr. Rogers; knows of no use Mr. Sayre had for them ; witness killed the chicken in the

shaving-horse, with an axe; threw it down in the yard, and could
not have got to the stable-door ; knows of no other killed.

*Amadee Boisaubin* recalled.   Prisoner told witness that Mr. S.
gave prisoner a 5 frank piece on the evening of the murder; prisoner said he asked deceased for a shilling, when he gave the piece.

*Cross-examined.*   The knapsack in Court is such as is used
by the Swiss soldiers, as also by persons travelling on foot in
Germany, for carrying the clothes, &c. ; should say that the
mark on the belt denotes that it belongs to a military person.

*Zebulon W. Conklin.*   Was at the house of the deceased on
the 12th May ; was a little after 8 ; there was a Yankee blind at
the gable end window, towards the garden and foot of the stair-
way ; it was rolled up about one-third of the way ; would permit
the light to pass through that part which was not rolled up ; the
light from the lamp would, from its position, throw the light
through this window, into the upper hall, and also into the front
room when the door was open.

The Counsel for the prosecution here rested their case.   The
defence was opened by N. W. WEISE, Esq.

' *Joseph Fairchild* recalled.   Saw a dead chicken in the cellar ;
there was considerable oil on the floor.

*George H. Ludlow* recalled.   Found a shirt in the bundle of
prisoner, belonging to prisoner, but saw no blood on it.

The passport of prisoner was here read and interpreted by Mr.
Boisaubin, given by the General Police of France to Antoine Le
Blanc, to go into foreign countries.   Description : 31 years
old, 5 feet 5, brown hair, do. eyebrows, gray eyes ; sailed in the
Manchester, 16th March, 1833, from Havre.   The second
paper is a certificate of his birth, copied from the records, 21st
Jan. 10th year French Republic.   The 3d paper gave directions
to go to Canada.   The native place of prisoner is where some of
the greatest battles in the section of that country ; it had been conquered by Napoleon.   The certificate and passport are evidently
correct and genuine.   The language of the passport is similar to
that given by our government to persons travelling to France.

*Mr. Medina* is agent of the government of Colombia to this
government ; passports are frequently handed to witness to give
them new ones to pass to South America ; French government
very particular in giving passports ; a convict would not receive
one as his having been a criminal ; a certificate of birth is necessary before he obtains a passport.

The defence being here closed, Mr. Brown, at 12 o'clock, opened the case in behalf of the State until 1.   Court adjourned to 2.

Two o'clock, Court met.   Mr. Brown continued his argument
until half past 4, when Mr. Halsey rose and addressed the jury in
behalf of the prisoner until 8 o'clock in the evening.   Adjourned
until 9 to-morrow,

Aug. 21. Court opened at 9 o'clock. Mr. M'Culloch addressed the jury in behalf of the prisoner, which continued until half past 12, when the Court adjourned until 2. Two o'clock, Court met.

Mr Miller concluded the argument in behalf of the State, and closed at half past 4.

Judge Ford then charged the jury as follows:—

GENTLEMEN:—You have before you the evidence of three most direful murders, marked with such atrocity as surpasses all others in the annals of the county. You see a private dwelling deliberately ransacked through every one of its apartments; its secretaries, bureaus, drawers, trunks, chests and bandboxes, after every individual of the dwelling had been first cut off, in the night, save one, and he the person accused of perpetrating these bloody deeds. He is now on trial for the murder of one of the three persons, Samuel Sayre, the owner of the dwelling house, the husband, the father, and head of the family. You are enquiring upon this indictment for only his blood, and whether the prisoner at the bar is the man who shed it.

Here I beg leave to make two observations that should be remembered at each step of the investigation, and be present at each moment of your deliberations. The first is, that you must discard every report and rumour concerning this offence, which you could not but have heard before you came to the book, and form your opinions entirely on the evidence here in court. You are bound by the terms of your oath, to render a verdict according to evidence; and these opinions, reports, and rumours are so far from being evidence, that any admission of them by the court would pollute it all.

Remember in the next place that no direct evidence has been given that the prisoner committed the murder in question; no eye witnessed the perpetration of the deed; the proofs are drawn from facts that are circumstantial and presumptive merely. Now circumstantial evidence is to be examined with the most studious care; and my second observation is, that if the circumstances shall leave on your minds any reasonable doubt of the prisoner's guilt, it will be your duty to acquit him of this murder. I do not mean if you can excite yourselves into a doubtful mood, by surmising possibilities that have no probable support in a spark of evidence, for such are not to be called rational doubts—they are the creations and vapours of fancy, lighter than air, and nothing more than nervous affections. But if the evidence of the witnesses shall leave on your minds one single, serious and rational doubt of the prisoner's guilt, it will be your duty to acquit him. Let the evidence be of what nature it may, whether circumstantial or direct, if it fail in establishing his guilt to your entire satisfaction you ought to acquit the prisoner of the indictment.

The law concerning murder as it stands in the statute of our state, is expressed in these unequivocal words—' Every person who shall commit murder, on being convicted thereof shall suffer death.'—It was said at the bar, by the prisoner's counsel, that the justice and policy of this law have been arraigned and denied by many respectable and worthy men, who hold it to be the relic of an abolished dispensation; that human life is the gift of God, and man has no right to take it away. How strange it is that this sophism should be cherished by one who acknowledges a God and believes in revelation. That *Being* who is infinitely just and righteous, once condescended, *Himself*, to enact laws for the government of a great nation, and one was, that whosoever sheddeth man's blood, by man shall his blood be shed. That people has long since ceased to exist as a nation; but the civilized world has felt confident that it could not err in copying from *Him* who is the very perfection of justice and righteousness. Those casuists who would excite you to forsake *His* counsels should take heed not to advance Satanic policy in giving to murder a free scope. But what have you or we to do with the justice or policy of the laws of the state? Is it any part of our business to make laws for this republic? Where is our commission?—On the contrary, we are sworn to the faithful execution of them, and what is resistance better than rebellion?

Another branch of our law is alleged by the prisoner's counsel to be complained of extensively in society—that of convicting for a capital offence on circumstantial evidence. But do these carpers know their own meaning? Do they wish a free license to murder, on condition that it be done without an eye-witness; or, if there happen to be one such, do they wish it safe also to murder him, before the trial comes on, secretly, and obtain impunity for one murder by committing another? Then he who assassinates one in a large family shall be hung; but if he shall murder them, all, he shall go clear! Believe me, Gentlemen, there is no such law; he who asserts that there is, slanders the institutions of the state. Circumstantial evidence is allowed to prevail to the conviction of an offender, because it is capable of producing the *highest degree of moral certainty*. What is called direct, positive testimony, may not be more certain. The person called an eye-witness may be instigated to swear falsely by malice, by revenge, by conspiracy, by political or religious rivalry and hatred, or may be himself the murderer. The truth is, that innocence has suffered in more instances by what is called direct and positive testimony, than it ever has done by circumstantial evidence. And I lay it down as a settled law, that convictions may be founded on circumstantial evidence, for the high crimes of murder, arson, rape, burglary and robbery, no less than for the inferior offences of larceny and other misdemeanours. If the circumstances beget an entire conviction in your minds, of the prisoner's guilt, unimpaired by any countervailing rational doubt, you are bound to find the verdict according to such conviction. You cannot say you find him not guilty with a safe conscience if your full belief is the other way. If you entertain a real doubt you ought to acquit; but neither sympathy nor mistaken humanity, should interfere with a stern, virtuous and conscientious discharge of duty.

It is not my intention to review the minor circumstances of this case, but to recall some of the leading ones to your consideration.

1. Were Samuel Sayre and family all alive that night, when the prisoner came home from the tavern to their house? David B. West had to pass Mr. Sayre's house in going home that night; he walked with three other persons residing in the same street till they successively turned into their respective houses, one of whose clocks struck ten as he was passing. Five minutes after it the town clock struck ten. He was then left by the last man of his company, and a walk of only five minutes more, brought him in front of Mr. Sayre's house. It was five minutes after ten o'clock, corroborated by those persons who were walking with him. The sash and blind were both up in Mr. Sayre's front room; there were two candles burning; and he saw Mr. Sayre at the table reading a newspaper by one of the lights, and Mrs. Sayre, his wife, sitting quietly in the same room. The family were all well at five minutes after ten. Now the prisoner left Luce's tavern *to go home*, as he says, at half after nine o'clock that night. The time of his leaving the tavern is proved by numbers who tarried longer, but having a less distance to walk had got home as the clock struck ten. The prisoner says moreover, in his examination, that he did not stop on his way home, after leaving the green, and that as he passed the house of Joseph Fairchild, the blacksmith (whom he well knew) he saw Mr. Fairchild enter his house and shut the door. Mr. Fairchild had spent that evening at a singing school; and when he got home and was closing the door after him, he well remembered that his clock struck ten. It is about five minutes faster every Saturday night than the town clock; but the latter is regulated and brought even with his every Sunday morning at the ringing of the first bell; and it being only ten

minutes of ordinary walking from Mr. Fairchild's to Mr. Sayre's house, the prisoner arrived at the latter house in at least five minutes after Mr. West had passed it. Were, then, all this family murdered, and two of the dead bodies buried in the barn yard, while the prisoner was in the house and he knew nothing of it? Mr. Sayre, and after him his wife, were the first two victims, and the black woman, Phebe, in the garret was the last. The prisoner says when he saw Phebe, she was making her last gasp, and before that Mr. and Mrs. Sayre were both missing; he took the kitchen lamp and looked, but saw them not, he called for them and received no answer. If, then, he was present from the commencement to the termination of these barbarous and protracted murders, you must draw from his presence your own conclusions. The influence appeared so irresistibly fearful to the prisoner's own mind that he was led to say that the family were all murdered before he got home. But how does this consist with the direct and positive testimony before you?

2. What length of time would it take to murder Mr. Sayre, dig his grave and bury up his corpse; next to murder Mrs. Sayre, dig her grave and bury her corpse; next after these double interments, to pass away from the barn yard into the house, and ascend to the garret on tiptoe, for fear of waking up this sleeping victim, accomplish her murder last, and there wait till death was evident by no flinch on slitting her ear? Could an active butcher accomplish these deeds in less than one hour, and could the prisoner have run in a panic, as he says, about the house during that hour and have had not a glimpse of these occurences? You must answer this question honestly to yourselves.

3. The innocent citizens who discovered the mangled corpse of Phebe first in the morning, saddled a horse and spread the alarm of murder over the town instantly. But when the prisoner alone by himself saw her shattered skull and gushing brain, her foaming blood and gasping mouth, he hid it all with the skin of a buffaloe, and buried up these facts in the deepest silence and secrecy of his heart.

4. These murders were not perpetrated in this hideous form for nothing; the guilty wretch must have had some definite object.—Now does the evidence, I repeat it, does the evidence before you disclose to you any purpose beside that single one of plunder? Then who was this plunderer? It was the prisoner, and no body with him to share in the booty. Every article taken from the house was found upon his person, or picked up early in the morning in the exact line in which he fled during the night.

5. Death is a spectacle that strikes those who view it with instinctive awe; but how did the presence of three dead and mangled bodies affect the prisoner at the bar? Did he employ himself in plundering all the apartments, and in forcing the locks of all the drawers? Did he coolly dress himself in the clothes of the dead, even to the primary articles of a shirt and cravat? Judge ye gentlemen of the ruthlessness of such a monster. I leave all minor circumstances, and lighter corroborations to your own recollection and judgment.

The jury, at 10 minutes past 5, after an absence of 20 minutes, returned a verdict of GUILTY. The verdict was then rendered in the French language to the prisoner, and also was informed that at 10 o'clock to-morrow morning, he would be sentenced, which would give him time to answer such questions as would be put to him why he should not receive such sentence as the law directs. Prisoner stated to the interpreter that he was innocent; that they only wanted to take his life, and he was willing they should have it.

Thursday morning, 10 o'clock, Court opened,

Mr. Ford, the public prosecutor, prayed that the judgment of the Court be pronounced on the prisoner. Judge Ford asked prisoner, through the interpreter, what he had to say why the sentence of death should not be pronounced upon him. Prisoner stated that he was not guilty of the murder, only of the robbery. Judge Ford then pronounced the following sentence :—

Antoine Le Blanc : You stand convicted of the murder of Samuel Sayre : wherefore it is considered and ordered by the Court, that you be detained in the jail of the county of Morris, in safe and secure custody, until Friday, the 6th day of September next, and that you be taken from the said jail on that day to a place of execution, and then and there, between the hours of 11 o'clock in the forenoon and 3 o'clock in the afternoon of the same day, that you be hung up by the neck till you are dead. And it is further considered by the Court, that after execution is done, your body be delivered to Dr. Isaac Canfield, a surgeon, for dissection. And may the Almighty God have mercy on your soul.

## CONFESSION.

I was born at Chateau Salin, (Meurthe,) in the N. E. department of France, on the 20th March, 1802, of reputable parents, who are still living. My means of education were not as limited as many others of similar circumstances, but I never was fond of study, nor could my parents prevail on me to employ the advantages which were offered me. My delight and sole aim was mischief, and the principal part of my time was occupied in playing truant and teazing our neighbours. My father frequently corrected me for my faults, but they were as soon forgotten, and I returned to my follies again. In his admonitions, my father has frequently and vividly pourtrayed to me my end, and many a time have his admonitory lessons recurred to my mind since I have arrived to the years of maturity.

Nothing of serious consequence occurred to me in my youth, although I was continually engaged in broils, as I was very passionate, and would on every convenient occasion give an insult, but never take one. In the autumn of 1826, I found that my situation was disagreeable to myself and friends, I was determined to leave my native place. I accordingly started for Germany, and after rambling about several weeks, I came to the house of Mrs. —— Smicht, a widow woman, residing at Bistroff, (Moselle,) on the borders of Germany. I engaged to work for her, and for several months we agreed very well. She was kind and affectionate to me, as well as her three daughters, Christine, Marette, and Marie. After I had lived with the family upwards of a year, I paid particular attention to the youngest daughter, Marie. She received my addresses kindly, and after much solicitation she consented to be mine. The consent of her mother could not be obtained, for she said that she was afraid

we never could live happily together, as I was passionate and
ill-tempered, and Marie was quite the contrary. I endeavoured
for a long time to gain her mother's consent by the most implicit
obedience to her commands, and the most humiliating conduct
towards the family. A certificate of my good conduct from my
old friends in France was demanded, but this, through several
excuses on may part, was never obtained, for I well knew I
could not get it. I was determined to make Marie my wife, and
as her pure soul was wrapped in me, and she the favourite of
the family, I changed my course of life, and became a different
person—I commanded instead of obeying, and my passion carried me so far as to chastise and greatly abuse the whole family,
from the mother to Marie herself? My passion and rage became unbounded—having been pent up for such an unusual
length of time, and burst forth with ten-fold vigour. I had a
friend by the name of Bouse, living a neighbour, who probably instigated me to commit these rash acts, and I now believe that his
object was to supplant me in the affections of Marie. This
course of life continued until about the first of March, of the present year, when, after lingering about the neighbourhood for a
long time, I found that I could not obtain my wishes without
blood shed, (for Marie would never disobey her mother, and I
had forfeited the confidence of the remainder of the family,) I
was determined to go America. I stole an interview with Marie, and told her my determination, which was, to go to New
York, and thence to some place near there to get into business.
That when I was properly settled I would write to her, and she
pledged herself to follow me. The last interview we had was
at Morhange, where we were pledged to each other. I there
said to her, that something within told me we should never meet
again in this world, but she endeavoured to quiet my fears, and
we faithfully promised before God never to marry another so
long as either was living. I left them, to the great joy of this
worthy family and the whole neighbourhood, with the exception
of Marie, and started for my native place, where I remained but
sufficient time to obtain the certificate of my birth, and from
thence to Paris, where I remained three days. I then went to
Havre, where I found a vessel which was to sail the next day for
New York. Having but little more money than to pay my passage and purchase sea-stores, I felt very unpleasant at leaving
my native country, and in company with entire strangers. The
good counsel of my aged and worthy parents would frequently
recur to my mind during the voyage; and as often would I re-
gret the pranks I had played upon the youth of my own age dur-
in the services in the church, or going or returning from there.
But for ten years had I neglected to bow the knee to my Maker,
which I sullenly was obliged to do whilst under my parents roof.

I contemned all his pious instructions, and laughed at his bigotry, as I termed it, as soon as he was out of sight. But as I was bound for the new world, these thoughts were soon forgotten.

I arrived at New-York on the 26th of April, and there found some persons who directed me to the house of Mr. Feusier, who keeps a French boarding-house in Fulton street. I now found myself far from my home, among strangers, and not one dollar in my pocket. I felt miserable. I thought of my native home, and how happy I could have been there. I thought of Mrs. Smith's— of Marie, how I had abused this excellent family, and compared my present situation with what it would have been had I behaved myself properly. These thoughts continually employed my mind, and prevented my going out much from the house. The third day after I had been there, Mr. Sayre came into Mr. Feusier's house, and inquired for some one to go into the country and work on a farm, as I learnt from Mr. Feusier. I told him that I would go ; and it was agreed that I should go on trial for two weeks, when we were to make a bargain for a year. This agreement was made through Mr. Feusier. I told Mr. Feusier that I could not pay him the whole of his bill, but paid him six shillings, and then intended to let him have a pair of boots as security. The next morning I left his house without leaving the boots, as I wanted them, and intended to send him the money as soon as I could earn it.

I had not lived with Mr. Sayre more than a week before I saw that I was considered more as a menial servant than a common hired man. As soon as my work was done for the day, I had something to do about the house, such as feed the hogs, take care of the horses, cut wood and bring it in, carry water, and the like, and was under the servitude of the servants around the house. I was further convinced of this when my lodging was exchanged for one of very inferior quality. I plainly saw that as I was a stranger and a foreigner, unacquainted with the customs and manners of the country, I should be made a miserable beast of burthen if I suffered it, to whom no pay would be returned but my food. From these considerations engendered the first idea of murder and plunder. I had longed to be in possession of sufficient money to either send for my betrothed Marie, or go to her. I saw that Mr. Sayre paid out and received considerable, and believing from my treatment I should never be able to earn enough by my labour, these murderous thoughts often came into my mind. I then began to pray to God to prevent me from committing so great a sin. Every time I thought of it I began to pray, but I found that God had left me : I had not confessed for ten years.

These ideas were continually recurring to me whilst I was at my daily labour, and my treatment determined me. I had formed my plans, but I waited several days for their daughter Mary to return, that I might murder her also, as she had a gold watch which I wanted. Finding that she did not return, and that daily I became the more degraded in my own eyes; after their hired man had gone away, on Saturday afternoon, I asked Mr. Sayre for five dollars, as I wanted a hat and some other articles. He gave me a five franc piece. This I considered an insult, for I had worked hard for him, and was willing to do the same justice to him a year to come. I had made my preparations by cleaning the stable properly, and feeding the gray mare more than I did the horse. I then went to town and got some cider and segars at a grocery store, and then went to a tavern, at which I had been once before, and took a glass of brandy and a segar; this was done to pass away the time until the people had gone to bed. I went home a little after ten o'clock, and remained around the barn some time, and then went into the kitchen, where I found Mr. Sayre shaving. I pretended to be frightened, and told him by words and signs that something was wrong at the stable. I ran out and stood inside the stable door for some time with a spade in my hands, waiting for him to come. At length I saw him coming with a candle in his hand, and as he came in the stable I struck him down with the back of the spade, on the left side of the head, which killed him without a struggle. I gave him another blow on the forehead to make sure work of it, and then dug a hole in the heap of manure, dragged him into it, and covered him up. As soon as he fell I threw the candle on the plank near by, to prevent any light shining out and exposing me. —I then went into the kitchen and decoyed Mrs. Sayre out in the same way : she came out in a hurry, but without any light; and as soon as she got past the shed I struck her with the same weapon with which I had killed her husband. It being dark, the blow glanced—she screamed ; I gave her another, but with like effect ; she screamed again and again, clinging hold of me, and begging for her life ; and it was not until I gave her several blows, that I brought her to the ground. I got tired of striking her with the spade, and then I kicked her on the head with my heavy shod boots. She died a terrible death, and I see her every time I close my eyes to sleep. When I found she was dead, I covered her up in the same heap of manure, and rolled the plaster over the blood which had run from her head whilst I was murdering her. I then went into the kitchen with a club in my hand, took a light, went softly up stairs to the garret, where Phebe, the colored woman, was sleeping, and with a single blow she passed into an eternal sleep. The blood spouted into my face and on my vest and hands : she did not stir after I first struck her. I then took the chissels which I had seen the carpenter put into the corn stalks, and opened all the drawers and trunks in the house. My object was only money. The silver money found in the belt around me belonged to Mr. S., as also the change the sheriff took from my pocket, except a few shillings left from the 5 franc piece which Mr. S. gave me. I would not take the paper money, as I did not know the value of it, and I was afraid it would lead to my detection ; nor would I take the silver spoons, &c. for the same reason.

Whilst I was plundering the house, I thought of my Marie.—I found a large quantity of jewelry, &c., which I thought would become her person, as also several articles belonging to females ; I therefore put them into my bundles for her. I well recollect the wagon passing with the men in it who had been fishing, for it frightened me much, and I went to the window to see if they would stop ; but as they did not, I continued my search after money, and such other articles as I could easily carry. Hearing a noise in the garret, I went up and cut a slit in Phebe's ear ; but I found that she was dead, and that a cat had disturbed me. After I had put up my two bundles in the upper entry, I took off my own clothes and put on a suit of Mr. S.'s, which fitted me very well. After putting my clothes under my bed, I went to the kitchen—took the glass lantern—went to the stable, and set it within the door. I put the saddle and bridle on the gray mare which Mr. Sayre generally rode ; took one bundle before me, and the other fastened over my shoulder, and rode out of the lane. The beast there did not go very well, and turned around with me once or twice, so that it loosened the bundle which was over my shoulder—spilled several things out, and finally I lost the whole of it after I was fairly started : this was about the breaking of day. I made the beast go pretty fast, and take her own course, as I believed, she knew the way to New York. When I went through a part of the first village I came to, she wanted to stop at a large white house, and troubled me here also ; and here I lost some valuable things which I intended for Marie. After it had got towards sunrise, I turned her out of the road and got off with the largest bundle. I here did not know what to do with her, and whilst I was resting myself by the side of the road, I made up my mind to cut the poor animal's throat. Before I arose, however, she turned away from me, crossed to the other side, and went back the direction from whence she came. It was my intention to go immediately to New York, and there take passage the first opportunity for my native country, with my booty, and fulfil my vows to Marie ; for I did not believe the murders would be found out until Monday, when I should be secure ; but I was unexpectedly overtaken when I thought no one but myself knew of my crimes. This is a full and frank confession of my many sins, for which I pray forgiveness, and for the truth of which I call upon that God to witness, from whom I hope to see salvation. The sentence is just, and I am ready to die.

*Morris County Gaol, August* 29, 1833.

# ARSENIC SANDWICH

THE FIRST EDITION of the *Life, Trial, Execution and Dying Confession of John Erpenstein* . . ., all two thousand copies, sold out within a few hours of leaving the press in 1852. Thus, explained the publisher, a second edition had been rushed into print, which is reprinted here.

John Erpenstein had in death turned a neat profit for the *Daily Advertiser*, Newark's leading newspaper and publisher of the Erpenstein manuscript. He may well also have brought some financial reward to the Reverend William Winnes, owner of the copyright, for it was into the minister's hands that the murderer had d.livered his manuscript as he mounted the gallows.

The chief beneficiaries of the several thousand copies, if the publisher could be believed, would be Erpenstein's three children. The pamphlet was expressly "published for the benefit of his children." Their benefit would of course be spiritual.

Winnes already had experienced spiritual rewards, for the publication clearly showed that Erpenstein had won grace through his association with the minister. The tract also was mildly anti-Catholic, for Erpenstein had been converted to Protestantism while in jail.

Erpenstein had been a happy, devout Catholic in Germany, where in 1832 he had met and married an eighteen-year-old Protestant girl named Fritzigen. Despite the dire forebodings of his family about such an "unblessed" marriage, the pair had nearly eighteen years of happiness that included three children.

But Erpenstein decided that America would fulfill the family's dreams. He left Hamburg on July 2, 1850, leaving behind his wife and children. They would join him later. The industrious Erpenstein earned seven dollars for tailoring jobs aboard the vessel. He also met the Müllers, mother and daughter.

Erpenstein said in his confession that "I attached myself to Mr. Müller's family." Erpenstein and the Müllers went to Newark, where he slaved and saved $45, which he sent to Germany as a step toward bringing his family to Newark. The money never reached Mrs. Erpenstein.

Successfully plying his trade at 25 Grand Street in Newark, he hired Dora Müller as a seamstress in March 1851. Related John: "She flattered me and caressed me until I would rather have died than say aught to her. . . . What followed I will pass over."

Dora's mother also was lonely, and, wrote Erpenstein, "The mother's passion was often kindled also—God knows it all." The daughter wistfully hoped, "Oh, that once we could be married."

Alas, John told Dora, if his dear wife and children came from Germany there never could be a marriage, but if they did not, he would surely marry Dora.

Mrs. Erpenstein suddenly arrived from Germany, as a surprise, on November 20. She soon learned of the cozy life that John had been leading with the Müllers. She decided to return to Germany with the children.

John tried suicide, first rejecting his straight razor, then trying arsenic, which he promptly threw up. He decided on murder-suicide by means of an arsenic-laced sandwich, which he made on January 8, 1852. Mrs. Erpenstein ate her half, but to John's horror (he later recalled) his half fell into a stream. Mrs. Erpenstein died. John lived.

Erpenstein went on trial within a few days, fast even for those days of swift justice. He was found guilty on January 24 and sentenced to death by hanging on March 30. In a show of sentimentality, Erpenstein asked that he be executed on a Tuesday, the same day as he had been married. The wish was granted, although Friday was traditionally "hanging day."

According to Winnes's translation of Erpenstein's confession, originally written in German, the murderer was treated poorly by Catholic priests. He turned to the Protestant faith and embraced it before he strode to the gallows to pay his penalty. Looking on were two hundred law-abiding spectators, augmented by prisoners who were "allowed to witness the scene from an upper corridor."

Dramatically, as he stood on the gallows, Erpenstein made a short speech before handing his rolled-up confession to Mr. Winnes. Minutes later he was dead. He was buried in the Potter's Field, next to his murdered wife.

SECOND EDITION.

# LIFE, TRIAL, EXECUTION

AND

# DYING CONFESSION

OF

## JOHN ERPENSTEIN.

## CONVICTED OF POISONING HIS WIFE,

AND

EXECUTED IN NEWARK, N. J., MARCH 30, 1852.

*Written by himself, and translated from the German.*

[ PUBLISHED FOR THE BENEFIT OF HIS CHILDREN. ]

NEWARK:

PRINTED AT THE DAILY ADVERTISER OFFICE.

1852.

# TRANSLATOR'S PREFACE.

THE TRANSLATOR of the following "Life and Confession" has had not a little difficulty in putting the ill-constructed sentences and disjointed composition of its author, into a readable shape for the American public. In attempting this, he has aimed at being as faithful to the original as the idioms of the language would permit. In no case has the sense been altered; and wherever any important passage has occurred, a literal rendering has been given, though perhaps at the sacrifice of perspicuity. The document was drawn up with great rapidity, and consequently does not express all which would have been otherwise communicated in it, and which was stated verbally to the Rev. W. W. Many individuals may be disappointed that Erpenstein has given no more indications of true penitence. Those who have conversed with him, will see that he has not done justice to himself in this respect. The time for writing was short and much broken up by visitors, and the concluding statements were hurried through fragmentarily. But whatever may be the truth as to his final spiritual state, his history, as here sketched, adds but another confirmation to the truth of those warnings which Solomon has given us against yielding to the seduction of an illicit passion. "His own iniquities shall take the wicked himself, and he shall be *holden with the cords of his sins*. He shall die without instruction, and in the *greatness of his folly he shall go astray*." Even so was poor Erpenstein enmeshed in the snare of his own evil acts; and his last crime was evidently a final desperate measure resorted to for the sake of disentangling himself from the perplexities of his situation. "As a bird he hasted to the snare, and knew not that it was for his life."

# TRIAL AND EXECUTION OF ERPENSTEIN.

THE first edition of the following " Life and Confession" of John Erpenstein, of *Two Thousand copies*, having been exhausted by the public demand, within a few hours of leaving the press, and a large demand still made, the present edition is published with the following brief notice of the trial and execution :

John Erpenstein was tried at the January term of the Essex County N. J. Court of Oyer and Terminer, for the murder of his wife, Frederika, by poison, in the December previous. Justice E. B. D. Ogden, of the Supreme Court, presided, with the Judges of the Court of Common Pleas of the County. B. Williamson, Esq., the Prosecutor of the Pleas, appeared as counsel for the State, and Ex-Gov. Wm. Pennington, Esq., and J. F. Burrage, Esq., for the prisoner. A jury was selected without difficulty, and the testimony adduced showed clearly to their minds that the affections of Erpenstein, having become estranged from his wife, whom he left in Germany, had fastened upon one Dora Müller, who appeared to return the passion. The unexpected arrival of his wife and three children, from Germany, apparently annoyed Erpenstein, who subsequently administered poison, in some cake, as was inferred from the evidence ; but from the confession it seems that it was given her with some bread and butter a day or two previous.

After able arguments on both sides, and an impartial review of the case from the Judge, the jury retired on the evening of January 23d. On the following morning they returned into Court with their verdict. Breathless silence pervaded the crowded room when the fatal word " GUILTY" fell from the lips of the foreman with a thrilling effect. The condemned prisoner sunk into his chair appalled ; then wept, and became violently agitated, but shortly after conversed with Constable Bachmeyer, to whom he gave directions as to the disposition of his property, his dress, &c., for the execution, which he desired might take place on TUESDAY, being the same day of the week upon which his poisoned victim died.

The SENTENCE was pronounced by Judge Ogden, Jan. 29th, the Court room being thronged with people. The usual question, "Whether he had anything to say why sentence of death should not be pronounced," &c., being interpreted to him, he answered in German that he was innocent of the crime of which he had been convicted; that proofs of his innocence had come to light since his trial; that the evidence to convict him had not been sufficient; and that he was the victim of a conspiracy, and he concluded by a passionate appeal for clemency.

His counsel, Gov. Pennington, then moved for a rule to show cause why a new trial should not be granted. He said that he had had several conversations with Erpenstein since the conviction, with a view to ascertain the truth in the matter, and although it would be improper to relate those conversations, he had determined to make this application, on the ground that Erpenstein had been convicted upon circumstantial evidence alone, and that all those circumstances might be true and yet he be innocent. He asked that this application be considered as made before sentence.

The Court refused the motion, as no reasons had been given to impugn the veracity of the witnesses, &c., and there was no reason why the Court should interpose between the culprit and the due administration of justice. Proclamation was then made and the Judge delivered an appropriate and affecting address, recounting the leading incidents of the prisoner's life, the lessons taught by the discovery of the crime, and closed by sentencing him to be hung on the 30th of March.

The prisoner stood composed and firm till the words which fixed his dreadful doom were pronounced, when his muscles instantly relaxed; he fell, as by an electric shock, into his seat, covered his face with his hands, and sobbed like a child. The scene was heart-rending to every one present.

The prisoner continued to protest his innocence of the crime till applications for reprieve or commutation were refused, and all hope had fled, when he confessed the crime, and sought relief in the consolations of religion and preparations for his eternal welfare.

The Rev. Mr. Balleis, of the Roman Catholic Church, attended him; but he subsequently renounced that faith, and embraced the Protestant. He was attended to the last moment by the Rev. Mr. Winnis. The Life and Confession which follows, was written by himself, in

German, and was delivered to the Rev. Mr. Winnis, from the scaffold, a few moments before the execution.

The execution took place in a large hall of the Jail, on Tuesday, March 30th, which was a departure from the custom of appointing Friday, so commonly known as hangman's day. The prisoner was engaged during the night previous to the execution in devotional exercises, and his three children also then paid him a farewell visit. The nterview between them is said to have been touching. The gallows were erected at the end of the hall, and some two hundred persons were present, including the clergy, physicians, members of the bar, county officers, &c. The prisoners were also allowed to witness the sad scene from an upper corridor.

A large crowd of persons were collected upon the outside of the jail, which was surrounded by the Columbian Rifle Company, Capt. Brintzinghoffer, in full uniform and well armed, to prevent any disturbance; nothing of the kind however occurred.

At eleven o'clock the passage was cleared from the door to the gallows, and the mournful procession entered, composed of the Sheriff and assistants, escorting the prisoner, who walked between his spiritual advisers, the Rev. Messrs. Winnis and Lehlbach, with a firm, solemn step. He held in his hands a copy of a German Bible, and his confession, written also in German, tied in a roll by a string. He was dressed in a white gown reaching to the knees, gathered around the waist by a black scarf, and with a broad collar, also gathered by a black ribband at the neck. The cord by which he was to be suspended from the gallows, was also already adjusted. A pair of light colored striped pantaloons, light figured mittens, black cap upon his head, with a black cape to fall over his face, and slippers upon his feet, completed his last earthly costume.

On arriving at the gallows the prisoner knelt with the Rev. Mr Winnis, who implored the Divine Mercy in an earnest prayer in the German language, into which the prisoner entered with a heartfelt and sincere devotion. The prayer being finished, Erpenstein rose and with a firm and clear voice delivered a brief address in German, expressing a hope that his sins and his enemies would be forgiven; his thanks for the humane treatment received during his confinement, and the justice of the laws. As a proof of his full repentance he delivered his full confession into the hands of the Rev. Mr. Winnis. Then holding the Bible, he spoke of the consolation it afforded him, and prayed that no contention might arise after his death on account of his conversion

from the Catholic faith. Kissing the Bible, he handed it to Mr. Winnis, and broke out with impassioned warmth into a fervent prayer :

"O, Father! I commend to thee my soul : take my spirit unto thee,
Father, for my career on earth is now ended. I have wandered on a
strange path, in a strange land, and I now return to thy fatherly
house. O, God! have mercy upon me : Jesus, thou art my Saviour,
and in thee, O, Jesus, I live and die! I am thine, alive or dead!"

Turning, he waived his hand, saying, "I am ready to die now; I
have commended myself to God." The record of the trial, &c., was
then read by the Clerk, and the Sheriff, Dr. W. Pierson, proceeded to
execute the sentence. Having attached the cord from the prisoner's
neck to the gallows, he stepped into the inclosure through which the
weights were dropped, and severed with a chisel the string that held
them. In the twinkling of an eye the body of the condemned
swung into the air a lifeless trunk, and his earthly existence was over.
He probably felt not a pang, and no motion was apparent, except a
few of the usual muscular contractions, when all became still, and
breathless silence pervaded the assembly. The scene was deeply impressive ; and sad, melancholy emotions were depicted on the coun-
tenances of all present.

The body, after hanging about half an hour, was pronounced dead
by the physicians, and was lowered into a black coffin, in which it was
subsequently carried to the Potter's Field, and there interred beside
the grave of his murdered wife.

The following pages contain the Life and Confession written by
himself, and delivered to his spiritual adviser from the gallows.

## A POOR SINNER'S LIFE, AND HIS GUIDANCE, UNDER GOD, TO THE LORD JESUS CHRIST.

MY DEAR BRETHREN: Ye who are walking in this Vale of Tears, accept these lines as a memento to remind you of me after my death.

I was born of Catholic parents, the 24th of December, 1812, in Suetz, Prussia. My father was an officer in the 21st Regiment of Infantry. My mother was a toll-gatherer's daughter. I was educated in the common school learning, according to city customs, and in the Catholic religion. When 14 years of age, my father died. A life of poverty ensued, for a family of seven children, the eldest of whom was 18 years old, and the youngest only fourteen days. My poor mother often went hungry to bed. In order to relieve her cares, in July, 1826, I took my departure into the broad world, furnished with only a single suit of clothes, and endowed with a mother's tears and prayers.

The first night I slept in a stable. On the morrow, after prayers, my breakfast was my tears. There I stood as a lost sheep—no business, no money, no father or mother, and but a helpless child myself. Weeping, I traveled on five miles, until my strength was exhausted. Then with my last pittance I bought a bit of bread. The third day I reached a tavern. There, in order to pay for my supper, I did some hard chores. Yet I was glad that my mother was relieved of the burden of caring for me. Eleven weeks I tarried at this place, performing severe work. I did my own washing besides. While here, I met with a young fellow, who invited me to travel with him to Leipsic. I gladly consented, and took leave of my benefactor with child-like thanks.

On the road, I carried my friend's bundle, of 50 pounds weight. We journeyed each day from 30 to 36 miles. I often fell to the ground, from weariness and exhaustion. In Sclafe, a great city, I lost my friend ; he deserted me. Oh, God! here I was, worn with hunger— without money—lost as a bird! I went outside the walls. In the suburbs I saw a musical concert going on. There sat many gentlemen and ladies. I was prompted to beg of them alms. My heart smote me—I was but a child. But God was gracious to me. Poor, innocent, in my hunger I approached the first ladies, who gave me some cakes. I kissed their hands. One of them bade me apply to the gentlemen. I plucked up courage, and did so. They collected for me a little over a dollar. Oh, how happy was I. One dollar! I thought of sending it to my mother. But alas! my shirt, coat, boots, all were going to pieces. I knew not where to lodge. I purchased two shirts, and got my boots mended. It was all I could do.

Continuing on, I came to a village called Bosehikowa, and stopped at a Catholic priest's. A countryman of mine, who happened to be in the place, related to him my circumstances. Here I remained 45 weeks, and was compelled to much severe extra labor. I had also the opportunity of observing with what blindness the poor people were smitten. Every Sunday I was obliged to traverse a large circle of six villages, to gather offerings of eggs, fish, chickens, butter, sausages, geese, ducks, &c. These were extorted from the people. These gifts were not always the best, and then the priest would strike them with his fist, and put them under the ban of the church, or expose them at public service. During fast days, the priest would himself indulge in meat; while the poor people, as if only his servants, were forced to eat (instead of flesh) bread dipped in linseed oil. I cannot describe all. Though but a youth, I wept often over what I saw. Oh, God! how it went with the poor people. How often were offenders obliged to creep around the church on their knees to do penance! I soon left the spot. The wages I received were some bread, fish, and five groschen, (about a shilling.) With these I came to Berlin and stopped at a victualing-house. The young people there I saw to be happy, while I, on the other hand, was wretched enough. In the evening there came a master workman to look for apprentices, whom he wanted to hire. The host pointed to me. I was then questioned about my native place, and replied that I was from Danzig. The man then gave me a glass of beer. That night I lay on the table, with my arm for a pillow and my coat for a coverlid. Fear and anxiety prevented me from sleeping. In the morning the host ordered me about my business. Oh, God! what could I do? Some one advised me to go to one Freitag, tailor to his Majesty. Thither I went; but such was my dread, that I dared not go in. For two hours I lingered round the spot, praying. Finally I took courage and rang the bell. The door opened, and I was led up to the second story. My heart chilled on looking into the room. There were 200 workmen before me. But it could not be helped; go on I must. In approaching the foreman I explained my errand, and was at once set to work. How things go! Shortly the workmen left for dinner, and I remained alone, to stay my hunger with my tears.

Two days passed on. In the meantime I finished a pair of pantaloons, and thought no painter could have made them look more beautifully. But my labor was to no purpose. The foreman bade me get back the money I had paid for learning my trade. My heart sank within me. I then told him my history; that I was an orphan, and left my mother for the purpose of relieving her from her burdens, and what was my present distress. My master was a Christian—a believer in Jesus. He encouraged me, and asked me if I desired to learn the trade. I answered " yes, most gladly." With all zeal and industry, not only by my work, but also by obliging conduct in the family, I soon acquired a favorable position. Frequently I helped the ladies at the social parties given in the house. I became thereby a general favorite, and was often invited by other wealthy families to assist at festivals. Through this means I was enabled to lay up about 33 thalers by the end of one year. At the same time I was promoted to the position of "journeyman," for which I paid twenty dollars, and with the rest of my funds obtained a suit of clothes.

My Sundays I spent in reading various books, and soon learned how the Catholic Church had persecuted other Christian communities. I perused the story of John Huss. I found how true Christians, scattered here and there, have been tortured to death, or put under a cruel ban ; and how even the body of the Emperor Henry Vth was prohibited from burial until four years after his death. Often I wept from sympathy ; and yet, me-thought, it was only what they deserved, as they would not become Catholics. I grew indignant against the books which the Popes had interdicted. I felt I had sinned in reading them, and invoked pardon from Saint Anthony for what I had done. One Sunday I was requested to read to my master's children out of the Bible. How I trembled at doing it ! I dreaded lest the Catholics would find it out. I knew not what to do. At the confessional I was silent.

In 1828 I left Berlin for Danzig. There I fell in with my uncle—a rich man. His wife was a Protestant. I often said to him, " What have you done ? My aunt is accursed. Why have you married her, a heretic ?" He would laugh and reply nothing. Often I thought of her lost condition. From this place I traveled on over the mountains into Poland to Warsaw. Here everything appeared right. There were in the city 130 cloisters. Frequently, during the whole week religious processions would train through the street with drums and music. How delightful it all seemed. But I often observed that the people would get drunk, and spue in the streets like swine while in the procession. Even the priests, from very intoxication, would stagger with the pix in their hands. While here I got the position of foreman in a shop. There were under me 52 journeymen, 8 boys, and 10 girls. My master put confidence in me. He was a true Christian. Often I was set to instruct the children in reading, and always out of the Bible. I read with reluctance. Often I came across passages in the New Testament which were a stumbling block to me. But when I was in the Old Testament the dress and pomp of the priesthood and such like things pleased me. I was glad that in this the Catholic priests had the superiority, and were evidently appointed of God, and were worthy of giving salvation to the souls of men. Once I had occasion to enter a cloister. How beautiful it was there. I was delighted to see it so adorned with gold and silver. Ah! thought I, the saints make us happy ! The Prior received me cordially. I began to ask him questions about this and that. In the course of talk, he remarked, " The Pope was sent of God to be God upon earth." This started fears. How will it go with me I thought; I am reading the Bible. With all respect I inquired of him whether Lutherans could be saved ? " No," he said, " they will be damned; Martin Luther is now bound in the chains of Lucifer." I asked, " Why are Protestant books allowed to·be published ?" He replied, " it was the devils who had transformed themselves into books ; where there is a Catholic child reading a book there you see a devil." " How," said I, " can a man detect the devil ?" He answered, " the moment we priests look at a man who is in the habit of reading such books, we know him at once that he has a devil." " Good," said I, " then it is not well for a man to dwell too far from the church." He told me, furthermore, that the priests are empowered to summon devils out of hell. Here I paused. I wanted to tell him something, but was troubled. Soon left. In a short time after, I received certain books, in which the barbarous treatment and anathematizing of scattered Christians were narrated, and it seemed as if I heard a voice declaring, that this was innocent blood. My heart was chilled. The Bible lay in my room. I feared to read it. But one night, in the year 1829, I had a vision, in which I was bid to read all I saw. In the course of conversation I told the priest I had learned that a foul murder had been committed in a cloister at Elbing, where I was acqainted. There were, it was said, many maidens snatched off in the place from time to time by a griffin. A journeyman, whom I knew very well, on his arrival at home, heard that his sister while in the cloister had been carried away by the monster. He went into the chapel for devotion and sat down in a corner. While there he fell asleep. In the night he was awakened by a door opening, and on looking up saw his sister and several priests coming in. They led her to the altar, shrived her, and then, one opening the covering of a pit, the others pushed her backwards, and she fell in. He remained quiet until morning. When the doors were unlocked he ran out, hastened to the Court and made known what he had seen. The cloister was thereupon surrounded by the soldiery. The priests within hid themselves in the tombs. On searching the pit many bodies were found there, among these were several little children. This story I told to the provost as something which I had received by letter. He answered that these persons so found were all damned. 'What,' says I, 'the little ones, too?' He said 'yes.' I would have kept silent, but involuntarily these words flew out of my mouth, " The children belong to heaven." He looked at me and said, " What, do you also read the devils?" He begged I would visit him often ; but I went there no more. However, I bethought myself, if these poor fellows are damned, I will not read these books again. Returning home I went to bed, and dreamed that I married a Lutheran girl, and would have a poor beginning in life; furthermore, that in 1839, I got into a trial at court with a Catholic priest respecting a child, and that it resulted, as it always does with Protestants, in like circumstances. I stood firm, and appeared to be the deliverer of many. On waking I laughed, and it all became fulfilled, as follows:

1832, I travelled in Russia, visited Rugen, Petersburg, Moscow ; also Odessa, on the Black Sea. I desired to go to Constantinople. There was a war between the Egyptians and the Sultan. It was not possible to cross the mountain ; was ordered back. After this lived some years in Prussia, and was subject to the Poll tax. In Petersburgh I was enrolled as soldier, but in 1833 deserted and came to Germany. Here, also, I was regarded as a deserter, because I had escaped the usual time of service in the army here. Before I was discovered I entered of my own accord the 1st Regiment of Hussars, and continued as an under-officer until Jan. 25th, 1835, and then was discharged. I put on a civilian's dress, took what money was due me, and returned to visit my mother and brothers, whom I had not seen for ten years. My native city lay in ashes; 100 houses were consumed, and 8 only left standing. The beautiful church, and a fine tower of 80 stories in height, were also destroyed. I was struck down with despair. Where could I now go ? While standing there crying over the prospect, my aunt approached and did not at first recognize me any more than I did her. Finally, discerning who I was, she exclaimed, "John, is that you, or your ghost?" In tears, I responded, "Yes, aunt, it is I;" and then inquired for my mother and brothers and sisters. She replied, "Your oldest brother lives in this house"—pointing to one near by—"and see, there goes your mother towards the church, and your other brothers and sisters are out to service in the village." I forbade her saying anything, and passed on by my brother's window. She then rapped on the glass, and sung out "Joseph, come here; who is this?' He answered "that is the Landrath's secretary." I did not stop to look round, but hurried on to overtake my mother, and came up with her close by the church. I greeted her, and she returned my greeting as if I were the actuary. I passed on rapidly and returned again in a quarter of an hour. Many persons had gathered about the church. Went directly up to my mother and stood still before her, and said, "How do you do?" "Not well," she replied, "all my property is burned up." My blood boiled; first, at the sorrowful message, and, secondly, that she did not know me. I kissed her hands and said, "Mother, mother;" she fell into my arms and wept copiously. Recovering herself, she exclaimed, "My son, would that your father could come out of his grave and see you. But where shall we go, you see our dwelling is consumed, and I must now lay my old bones on some bench at your brother's." I went with her to my brother's, but he also did not know me. We could not speak, and fell into each other's arms, and did nothing but weep. My sister came also, but did not know me; I seemed like a stranger. There was among us great joy and great sorrow. I went after my trunk and money, which had come on by stage. Here a mother's love showed itself in outbursts of affection. I made her presents according to my ability. My sister-in-law, however, evinced displeasure. She feared I would take her husband's custom away. Seeing this I left the place in six hours and came to Mersohfriedland, and found there a kind friend, with whom I lodged. On the first Saturday evening I walked out and met with my wife, who was then employed at service. At first glance my heart began to beat with fearful apprehensions. Sunday, P. M., went to a dancing party, being a practiced dancer. Fritzigen was there too. I invited her to dance. At the close I accompanied her home, and inquired by the way where she was from. She replied about 8 miles (German) from here, and that she was a poor child. Her father also, had been at service for 18 years, and since his death the family had lived in poverty. Her aged mother, too, was now leading a sorrowful life, "The same thing has happened with me," said I. "Be comforted, I will take you as my bride," She was astonished, and began to weep. The following week I rode with her to visit her good old mother, and solicited her daughter's hand; she gladly consented, but said she was poor and had nothing to give her daughter. "Mother," replied I, "I did not ask for money, God has given me ten fingers and joyful courage."

Thereafter I went to Schloppe and became a citizen and master workman. Our courtship lasted eleven weeks. In the mean time I visited my brother, and there learned that she was a protestant.

My brother and I were both troubled. On returning home I told the whole story to my uncle, who was a priest. My friends were all disturbed, and my mother threatened to disown me as her son if I married so. I kept still, as my conscience told me that I had gone, like a child, into the broad world, without father or mother; yet God nourished me. Also, I remembered my dream, and accordingly I was married on the 7th of Oct., 1835, by the Superintendent, Stipke, in Domberg, Pomerania. Two orphans stood before the altar with none beside them ; but God was with us. On the days following we wandered forth seeking nourishment, like bears through the fields, and traveled on till we came to Schönlanka Matters continued as they begun. By the end of the year I managed so as to lay up $50. This I put to interest for 6 months. In that time I laid up $50 more, and in 3 years my hoardings amounted to $320. This sum I loaned to a merchant. He failed and fled, and was finally apprehended in Hamburgh. For 5 years he lay in prison, and I lost all but $43. I worked at my trade with 7 assistants and gradually laid up more. In 1839 my dream again occurred to me. My daughter, Bertha A., was born there. My wife came near dying with fever. I did as was customary on such occasions, and sent for the Catholic priest, Kranz, on Saturday evening, that he should baptize the child on Sunday. But as he was intending to be absent on Sunday, he wished me to have it done on Saturday evening. To this I did not consent, as I desired to have a God-father stand with the child at baptism. The priest left. I sent to the Superintendent, Hartman, (Protestant,) and invited him to perform the service. He was ready at once. I inquired "What was to pay?" He replied it was an act of brotherly love, and bade me pay the priest the sum. I sent what was due by the nurse, and requested to have the name inscribed in the church records. The priest was offended, and complained of me to the Consistory at Posen. I soon received an order from the magistrate to go myself to the priest. Though an officer myself, yet was I subject to law, and accordingly obeyed.

I went in person to the priest, and told him that I was sent to inform him respecting my child. He struck me with his fist and bit me on the middle finger of my right hand. There was no witness and I went out quietly, and got some to go in. Again the priest did the same. I entered my complaint. The case hung along 4 years. I was put under ban in the church, excluded from the Lord's Supper, and had my life threatened. In my mind I was calm, and I went to the Evangelical church with my wife, arm in arm. In 1842 I purchased some real estate. During the progress of the above mentioned trial the priests sought to prejudice me in every way. I traveled to D. Crone, where my sister lived. During the journey my money failed. In the village of Ruge dwelt a neighbor's daughter. I went to her and begged the loan of 3 dollars. Her father was a sexton. Three days after I learned that an inquiry had been instituted about the money. It was laughable. I remitted the 3 dollars thro' my deceased wife, and asked for a receipt. The man threw the bills into the fire. Priest Kranz, Canonicus, Dosokinsky, the sexton and teachers, all swore that I had taken the money from the woman as a claim in another man's name. I was prosecuted, fined $62, and imprisoned 4 months. It was evident I could not hope to receive justice in the other suit pending. My Captain of horse, Baron Von Planse, intervened in my behalf. I was set right, and got my case.

In the year 1846, sold out my real estate, and bought another piece in Fisher-street, near a large garden. My married life in this city was a happy one. Once in a while a dark cloud floated over, but seldom did the sun set before it was clear again. In 1848 I was forced into the wars, and was twice wounded. In 1849 there was no quiet, and my wife said, " How many are leaving for America—why dont you go to ?" I was ready at once, and soon procured my passport. But my affection for my wife and children was so great that my heart was almost broken with grief at the thought of leaving.

The whole night long we sorrowed waking. I could not stand it, and gave up going. For a fortnight I was ill at ease. Finally taking with me $55, I bade farewell to my family, and traveled to Berlin. Told some there that I was going to America. On the morrow my father-love returned, and I went back. Everybody laughed at me— even my wife ; yet I was delighted to be again at home.

On the 25th of June, 1850, I engaged passage for America. My fare amounted to $32 ; and having provided myself with necessaries, and engaged lodgings for 5 days at port, I remitted the surplus to my beloved children and sorrowing wife. On the 2d of July, about 5 o'clock in the morning, I finally embarked, having with me but 4 shillings, Hamburgh money. There was a merry company on board, in all about 280 in number ; but my heart seemed ready to dissolve in tears. I stood on deck and watched the retreating hills of my Fatherland, where dwelt my loved and deserted ones. The will of God was my support. I soon found the society around me agreable. My meals I took at the Captain's table. At intervals I worked at my trade, and earned thereby about $7.

August 1st we reached N. York. I attached myself to Mr. Müller's family, who were my fellow voyagers. They had resided about 80 miles from me, and were country people. The first night in N. York one dollar was stolen from me. The next morning we left for Newark, a company of 11 persons. I carried a note of introduction to a German Doctor ; spent much time in hunting for him from place to place, and at last gave up from weariness. At last coming into William st. and stopping accidentally at Stiefbolds, I fell in with Doctor E. For want of lodging place he kindly accommodated us in his apartments, when the whole 11 of us slept on the floor. Next morning all took some refreshments, save myself. I could not think of eating until I had obtained some chance of earning something for my poor family at home. Accordingly Dr. E. went out with me to 129 Market st , where I found work at the rate of 5 1 2 shillings for one coat. Before nightfall I finished one of these and sank down exhausted.

On Friday we moved into Green street, No. 25. Here I lodged two months on the floor, made my dinners generally on three potatoes, and managed to lay up in the first three months the sum of $45. What was then my joy on this occasion ! I communicated the fact to Doctor E., and was aided by him in remitting it to my family at home, thro' Schultz & Bleitnug, merchants, in N. York. The letter conveying it I sent on Dec. 1st, and it is now in the hands of the court. On the 10th of March a reply came to hand, and my joy was indescribable. On breaking it open, however, I discovered two sad messages— first my dear wife had received no money, and second, she declared her inability to come to me. The journey, she said, was too hard for her. Accordingly, she suggested my remaining here a few years, and then returning to Germany, where, perhaps, a residence would be better for me. I went immediately to Dr. E. and told him the circumstances. On the 12th went to N. Y. and wrote in return to my wife, that I had sent her some money, and that she would receive it through a firm in Frankfort on the Maine, begging, at the same time, that instead of writing in reply, she would come on in person herself, as it was impossible for me to go back to Germany. To this I received no answer.

On the 20th of March I took Dora Müller into business with me as seamstress. She was industrious, and sought to please me by her kindness and fidelity. I got to confide in her, purchased at one time a dress for her, costing $10; also a bonnet for $3, an arvine for $4.50, a parasol for $2, and other articles of clothing, including a ring worth $5, amounting altogether to nearly $30. She flattered and caressed me until I would rather have died than say aught to her. Her mother's friends delighted in the intimacy. What followed I will pass over. Our affection was great. The mother's passion was often kindled also—God knows it all.

In the month of April last, I know not exactly what day, whether the 6th or before that, one evening while parading on Market street, Dora said to me, " O that we could but once be married." It went so far that she swore to me that she would be mine with all her heart forever. I replied, " if my wife does not come, I will marry no one else but you ; but if she arrives in course of time, she must be my first." This was said on Market st., not far from Keller's, under the broad heaven. We were full of joy and love. Passion burned warmly. We were always together, and could not be separated. Our happiness continued until Monday of Pentecost, when we went to a ball—I, Dora, her mother, and two sisters. This evening we got provoked with each other, because I saw something wrong in Dora. I left and went home. On the morrow I demanded back my presents. Tears flowed freely, and she said, " Dear Erpenstein, if your wife does not come I will indeed be yours " I could not but weep. God knows how many tears fell. She said, " Dear Erpenstein, if your wife should come, I will destroy myself."

On the 30th of August, I received a letter from home. My joy was great. Three days before this, I had loaned Mr. Stiefbold $35, and Dora was also then with me. At the interview I expressed my astonishment at not hearing from my wife. Mrs. S. replied, " she will come and take you by surprise one of these days." On the receipt of my letter I ran with it to Mr. S. and Doctor E. Dined that day with Mr. Unger, and after this went home late. Dora's mother said on my coming in, " We are now a-bed—how is it with Dora ?" " How is it with Dora?" said I. "Do you think I will desert my children ?" Should I do it the very ravens would croak at me. I have always said when my wife comes she would be mine, and live with me.

On the 1st of Sept. I obtained through Doctor E. full power of attorney, to be transmitted to my wife. This I took to the County Clerk and had it signed and sealed. Afterwards I went with it in company with Dora to the Consul in New York, and got his seal affixed, and then sent it off. I soon parted with Dora. Eight days after I left her house and took up my residence with Mr. Bomberg, a tailor. Again, the week following, I returned. Here were the dear hearts. I'll say nothing of what followed. My joy returned. The mother herself seemed sometimes happy, and sometimes miserable. But let it pass.

Dora's sister was soon to be married. I traduced her character in order to persuade her lover to take Dora instead. Dora was vexed at this. I asked her why she was troubled. " You see," says I, " it is very possible my wife may be here." She rejoined, in presence of her mother, " Let come what will, I will have Erpenstein ;—and this is what a fortune-teller has predicted." I then went to Mr. Sachson's, not far from the market, and besought them to take Dora as a servant, telling him that if my wife did not arrive I would take Dora as bride.

On the 17th of Nov. I gave Dora $4, so that in case she could not obtain a place at service, she might pay her board at home. On the 18th went to New York in company with Dora, her mother, two little ones, and a friend. O, friends, dearest friends, I must not speak of what ensued. Sh. be silent; and you M. and you A. be silent about it. On the 18th, since I received nothing from my wife, mailed another letter to her. On the 20th, at 7 o'clock P. M., my baker came and said to me, " Go to Stief bold's." Says I, "What's happened ?" He replied, " I dont know." I then dressed myself and hastened to William-street. Methought, as I went, 'O God it may be my wife and children have arrived.' I reached the house. A man told me here, " Go quickly to New York, your wife is there." · I replied, " It cannot be." Thereupon St. brought out my son, who had hid behind the bar with the intention of surprising me. I screamed as I saw him and clasped him in my arms. My wife and the rest of the family next appeared, and we had a joyful meeting, not without tears. I ordered supper, and hastened back to the house, having left $60 there in my trunk unlocked. I was gone about 5 minutes, and returned with a ring which I had bought as a present for my wife. After supper we had a bowl of punch and made merry together. In the course of the evening we took a walk out, called on Mr. Braun and Dr. E., and then purchased three bonnets for $7. I was satisfied. I said to myself, " Now I have my wife, and have nothing more to do." It seemed all right. In the meantime my wife told me she was unfit to entertain company, not having washed since leaving the ship, and, besides, it was not convenient for me to remain at Stief bold's. So I returned to my lodgings. Found no one there. Left again and went back, but on the way met Dora and her mother. They had been listening at the windows and watching our interview. Contrived to find accommodations at Stief bold's, and was delighted to lodge with my family there, though on the floor. We could not sleep the whole night, so full of talk was every one. On the morrow met Dora agian. She was weeping. I gave her again $3, and bade her content herself, as my wife was a good dear woman, and I was determined to abide with her. I moved my furniture to Longworth-street, No. 10, and got every thing in order. On Saturday, I was asked to help kill a pig at Mr. Müller's. Then Dora kissed me in the stable, and said, " What is there now left for me ?—I will take my life." My old affection returned, and I wept with her. " Dora," says I, " dont cry, it was not God's will that I should have you ; I will make you a present of a velvet bonnet—or, as we have several beds, you may have one of these, an upper bed." She kissed me and wept. I went away. My heart was troubled. Ah, thought I, what can I do, I have a wife. I came to S's. Mrs. S. then informed me that a saddler's wife had told Mrs. Erpenstein all the circumstances respecting Dora.

I returned home and said to my wife—"Fritzigen what have you done? What did you say at Stiefbold's about Dora?" She replied that a man at Stiefbold's had said that Dora was pregnant. Thereat I laughed heartily, but the whole thing was unpleasant to me. S. was in fact the original author of the story. He told it to F., who passed it on to D., who in turn communicated it to my wife. The trouble was increased by Dora's calling on me the first Sunday after our new settlement. She sat in our room with tears standing in her eyes. I felt as if between two fires, and matters only grew worse daily. On the next Sunday my wife and I took a walk. We went into Mr. Unger's, where she being thirsty I got her a glass of sugar and water. Dora continued to blow the flame. My wife cried; I went home and cried also, from sheer distraction and rage. One more drop and my cup of trouble would have run over. God knows it all. Finally I resolved to run away from my wife and children; but my heart was bound to the little ones. I could get no rest. My wife went to Dora's mother, and by her, in an angry tone, was informed of all that had transpired. Let alone what followed. All was now ready. I knew not further what to do. I got my razor sharpened, and thought to find peace by means of that; went with it into the yard; a voice sounded in my ear—"You fool." I reflected on what course I should pursue. Something suggested, "Get arsenic." I went up Broad street to the corner of Market and turned into a German drug store. I asked for arsenic. The man laughed and said, "Be careful," and marked on the packet 3 crosses, x x x. I took it and went down towards the Depot into a side place alone, and there I took one small dose. The stuff had no taste. The poison was no sooner down than I threw it up. It had no other effect. So terrible was my state that it is difficult for me to proceed with my narrative. I will only state the facts as they occurred. Sadness oppressed me. I could hardly speak to any one, as the family of Deurich, the neighbors and St. will know. My wife lost her regard for me. I purchased furniture for my house at an expense of $39. There were besides $56 in my trunk. This was on Wednesday 24th. On the 25th was the beginning of the end. My wife informed me that a letter from me had reached my mother in Germany on the 23d of Sept. last. O God! how the information stung me. Instead of pleasure it started tears, and I call God to witness what I here say. Mrs. Müller had told my wife that she and Dora, and two little ones, and John, her friend, in company with me, went to New York on the 18th of Nov'r, and then that I sent a letter to my mother. The crisis was hastening. God, thou knowest. St. had said that Dora during summer was pregnant, and as to what was said concerning Dora's mother I will be silent. My wife cried day and night. Her heart was thoroughly alienated. Through all this trouble I was at a perfect loss. It seemed best to make an end of the whole matter—that we both should perish together. Again a voice within said,—" You fool, let your wife go back to her home." One day I observed that I would not like to be buried in Germany. The night here is better than the day there. My wife cried and said to the children " I would prefer to eat potatoes and salt in Germany than to feast on bread and flesh here;

and if any one would only give me means I would return." Further, she exclaimed, weeping, " Would to God my brother would send me some money." In the mean time more news kept coming in little by little. I was resolved to take the lives of both of us. But what in that case would become of the little ones !

The thought occurred, ' you write a letter and put it in the Post Office, inviting her to return to Germany with the children.' This was a relief. I wrote the letter at Mr. Such's, in Broad street [or Broadway New Yoik.] The letter arrived ; but the fire raged worse and worse. She was ready to go. I was content. But I would not surrender the children. I acted on the supposition that she had received money from Germany in this letter. She held the letter firmly, and would rather have died than to show it me. Even during the night she kept it close. So it happened one day that while walking, in attempting to snatch it, I hit her in the face ; and she bled a little. One of the children was with us. I wanted to end the affair, and run away ; but my wife said, ' Come Bertha, we will go, too, and live where he lives.' At this the child cried. We returned home. D. and H. came into the room where we were. I said, with feeling, "Fritzigen, ain't you ashamed." Thereupon I left her, with the words, " You shall see me no more." I had hardly gone a hundred paces, when my heart misgave me. Oh, God ! here once more the flames burst forth. Again I tried poison ; but, as before, it didn't go. At last quiet was restored. I went again to my work, and was on pleasant terms with my wife and children. There was a prospect of peace ; but alas ! it did not last long. On the 5th, news came again from Dora ; and on Sunday it was known at St——'s. I gave no ear to it. On Saturday evening I went with my son to Mr. Müller's, and saw Dora. From there I went to Steifbold's with my son, and staid till 9 o'clock ; then returned home. My wife was crying. She was not well. She said she had received from Mrs. D. some warm pastry. I was troubled, in appearance ; but then there was Dora. My wife exclaimed, " Oh, God ! how it goes with me here, and what is before me !" and wept. " What is the matter ?" asked I. "Ah," said she, "hear me. John ; I cannot tell you what the people are all saying. Here I sat by the window, and there passed by two women, whom I overheard saying, ' how ill it goes with that poor wife !' —as to Dora, I will remain silent." " Dear Fritzigin," said I, "this is not true, now don't trouble me about it." She replied "hear me husband, it is true. D. told me that if I would go to St. on Sunday, I would hear how the Müllers had smutted you," This was not true. What followed I need not detail ; the children know it all. Sunday Dora came. The tears were hardly spent when my blood kindled again. Hardly had Dora left, when the thought shot like an arrow across me, 'you shall now finish the matter.' In the evening a despatch reached me confirming the pregnancy of Dora. On the 8th inst. I went with my wife to N. York all in tears. I left all my money at home. Before starting, my wife asked me to prepare some bread to eat by the way. I took a slice, sprinkled it with arsenic taken up at one dip with the point of my knife, and covered it with butter ; then doubled the piece together and put it in my pocket. About half way my dear wife cheered up and asked me for the bread. I replied "I am not ready to eat—I have no appetite." She put her hand in my pocket and took out the bread. I said to her, "let us di-

vide it." So we did. I wanted to eat the crust. My part fell into
the water. Horror took possession of me. I sought to remove from
her. Gladly would I have escaped through the waves. It was in
vain. I hoped she would vomit—then that she would not die alone.
We reached New York. I could not drink punch with her. I bought
two cakes and two apples for her. Immediately she began to be sick.
It seemed hardly possible, she had taken so little of the poison. We
hurried to the Railroad Depot. She puked violently. Now I was
relieved. My feelings were distracted. My blood boiled. I supported her in my hands. My heart warmed towards her in every thing;
that God knows. On reaching home I stood by my troubled and oppressed wife in her extremity, full of tears. I fell on my knees by the
bed and prayed God to stand by her in her last moments, and performed
all Christian duties for her. I also said to my children, "tell the whole
truth." My last kiss to my wife——in death—she is calling me,
come my child.

On 9th instant, between the hours of 11 and 12, I received a severe beating from H. and D., at my house in Longworth-st., and afterwards was led away to the jail like a lamb to the sacrifice. In three
days I was visited by Mr. St., for the purpose of ascertaining what
should be done with my things. They were on the point of being put
into the street. I gave Mr. St. full power to preserve three beds—the
best of the house furniture—the new table—my things and my wife's
things, and to bring me my money; also a shirt. I went, however, 7
weeks in the one I had on, until God gave me favor with strangers,
who brought me one. O, God! thou knowest it. Forgive them, they
have done right. I deserved it all. Shortly I sent by Mr. Butner for
Mr. Balleis, the Catholic Priest, to visit me. He came. I told him
many things. He envied my good luck, and said " I was better off
than he was." I could enter Heaven cleansed of my original sin by
extreme unction. He promised to send me a Priest from New York.
One came on the 27th of January; heard me confess, and afterwards
imposed on me 9 ave marias, to be repeated three times a day. The following week he came again, and shrived me once more. I told him
everything. One day I received holy bread. Let no one be offended at what I write. I wish only to honor God's grace and truth.
Every one knows the reason.

Feb. 1, Friday.—I partook of the holy sacrament. Was absolved,
yet found no peace. Could not feel satisfied before God. My heart
was hard. In the mean time I looked out and obtained some interesting tracts, but the priest Müller took them away with him to New
York. Occasionally I received a call from Mr. Winnis in a friendly
way, who prayed with me. I also heard preaching and a prayer from
the chaplain at the jail, in behalf of me, a poor sinner. Though I
could not speak, yet I often wept at the thought that American gentlemen were not ashamed of such a wretch as I was. I perceived
that their interest in me was not hypocritical, but proceeded from
pure brotherly love. But my heart remained hard and impenitent.—
I wrote a letter to the Catholics here, and prayed them to intercede
for a poor sinner before the altar. I asked them also to get up a
petition in my behalf, for the thought of death was bitter. In the
early part of March priest Balleis visited me. I bewailed my misery.
He was taking leave, and I entreated him that he would pray once

with me—perhaps his prayer might prove effectual. He replied : "How can you make such a request? I see now you are no Catholic." Accordingly, these gentlemen paid me no attention. I was in deep trouble. My prayer was, that I might conduct myself properly; and I offered industriously penetential vows. My petition was, "O Lord, have mercy on me, a miserable sinner. Be gracious unto me. I ask no more than the salvation of my soul." I repeated the Lord's prayer and Hail Mary, and two litanies, 300 times in one day.— It awakened in me no repentance. There were two or three days in one week that I took no water in my mouth. I passed many sad hours, but was sometimes joyful.

March 12th.—Mr. Winnis called. I had a dream the night before. Therein I read Gal. 1 : 1-8; John 3: 16 ; Ex. 33 : 11th verse: We had a long conversation together about this. Before he left, he read a chapter, and prayed with me. During the prayer Mr. Balleis, the priest, came and stood by the door. He knew nothing of this—but I joined in the prayer with some anxiety. Immediately after this, he took his hat, came and bade me good bye. Mr. Balleis then entered with great rage, and said that he would no more visit me, nor attend on me at the execution. Neither would priest Müller call on me again : for he had ordered me to keep aloof from every body. I begged he would not be so hard on me. Said I, "I am a man. I have feelings, and for these 15 weeks you have been here to see me but four times. And besides, I have entreated you through my children, and through Mr. W. and others, to call, but to no purpose." This I can prove.— The same day Mr. Ballies told me that, God had already shown the Americans that I was no Catholic: therefore they pressed me hard, [for my confession.] "Yes," I replied, "if Mr. Winnis had not visited me, I would not now have been alive. Sir Provost have pity on me, I am still a man." Then falling on my knees, I clasped his feet, and said: "Dear Provost, have I then committed so great a sin. I only was on my knees, and all the prayer that Mr. W. made passed away unheeded." I was weak. Had eaten nothing for 24 hours. Said I, "Sir Provost, if I have committed so great a sin by this joining in prayer, I will fast on till Saturday :" (for I was resolved on weakening my body, as all my prayers had been of no avail.) The priest rose to leave, and insisted that I should, in presence of a justice, declare whether I meant to die a Catholic or not. It was not enough for me to signify this before Mr. Beach. I replied, "O! God, would that I were dead, that I might avoid the eyes of people." Said Mr. Balleis, "The Roman Church does not pray, but she must be herself suppli- cated." " O God," I replied, " I did not know this. You did not come to see me. Sympathizing Christians were not allowed to visit me. I could hardly keep from derangement. I am not without feel- ings." But without giving me any confort, he was on the point of leaving. I then tore up the German tracts I had, and scattered them over the floor. The Bible, also, I flung at his feet. A book which once belonged to my wife was lying on the table. "Is this also a Protestant book ?" said he. This also, I threw away. Do this like- wise, he said, before that Protestant priest." I kissed his hand, and he gave me a book of consolation, by Oldenburgh, and then left with- out ceremony.

I read this book and prayed until 3 o'clock in the morning, On the 13th I wrote him a letter as follows: "Honored Sir: Your visit yesterday troubled me much. Yet have I received much joy from the book you lent me. Had I had it twenty years ago I would have died a good Catholic. I believe I shall still. I kiss your hand, I, a poor sinner, John Erpenstein." But though I thus lay like a puppy at his feet he did not come near me. I waited for him all through Sunday, Monday, Tuesday, Wednesday and Thursday. Day and night I cried to God. He is my witness. The stones in my cell on which I knelt will complain to God against him. My fast welling tears exhaled to the clouds. Incessantly I begged for peace, and did not obtain it. I tried every conceivable method, and still my heart remained like a stone. I uttered every request that suggested itself, until at last, in the violence of my pleading, I became utterly lost to myself. I knew not where I was, or what I did. My situation was indescribable.

On the 18th Mr. W. called again. I reached him my hand coldly. He inquired how I was. " Well, I answered, I am reading always in my prayer book." Mr. W. said, " how is it with you? Have you a joyful spirit ?" I struck my book and said, " here have I my book, and through the intercessions of the saints can I obtain salvation ; and if it were not for the people around, I would turn you out doors." W. rose up to go, and said quietly, that he did not come with the design of troubling me "No, no, dear Erpenstein," he continued, "I doubt whether one of your priests has the love for you which I cherish." He then took his leave, and I was glad. I thought I had this day served the throne of grace. My mind was joyful. I went then again to prayer, and b-lieved that Mr. Balleis would come that day. Often did I pray earnestly that he might call, and thus I robbed my soul of petitions which it needed in its own behalf. At last, with all my earnest praying, my anxiety grew so intense that I knew not what to do. My shirt was soaked with perspiration. No Balleis came.—I was wrapped in despair. I wished to give myself up in God's hands, and that the tears I had dropped might honor him from the earth.

On the 19th, Friday, up came Mr. Beach, and said, "that I must step down to his room." I dressed myself and went. There I found a fine lady, and gentleman, and Mr. Winnis. I was startled. The visitors, however, did not behave like lords, but approached kindly and shook hands with me, a poor sinner—my heart was hard. They began to converse. I found that the woman was a real lady and the second gentleman was the Rev. Mr. S. After many kind words I was persuaded to give my child over to Mrs. D., with the request that she might be brought up as a good christian woman, and thanked her heartily for the pleasure she had imparted to a father's heart. To my great astonishment she brought out a Bible, entirely new, and furnished with a silk mark, and handing it me, requested that I should make therein some family records for my children. Having expressed my profound gratitude to her for the present, I returned to my cell, and as I went, showed to my fellow prisoners what a beautiful Bible I had received. On reaching my place I opened the book, and my eyes fell on Matt. 7: 13th and 14th—"Strive to enter in at the straight gate," &c. Immediately my whole state and circumstances came up before my mind, and I resolved never to cease praising God for the kindness he had shown me as a Father in Heaven, in sending so rich a lady to visit me, and kindly take me by the hand and minister consolation to me. The mother of my child, and was she not a mother to myself also? I had sadly fallen, and yet she had presented me a Bible. O, God! an arrow shot through my heart. Tears flowed upon tears. I could not refrain from weeping. My heart became at once entirely devoid of joy and comfort. There rang in my ears these words : " Ifwe confess our sins, he is faithful and just to forgive us our sins and cleanse us from all unrighteousness." All that night I cried fervently to God for forgiveness, as a poor lost sinner.— The perspiration rolled from me in my agony. About 4 o'clock I dropped on my knees and renewed my petitions for pardon. In that posture I swooned away and did not recover myself until daylight.— I felt calmed. I thought of Christ's words, " Go thy way, thy sins are forgiven thee." They spoke peace to my soul. An aversion to earthly things then sprung up within me. My joy was indescribable. I read Luke 15 : 4—11 ; also 21.—25, and Rom. 8 : 33—36 ; Jeremiah 33 : 1—8, and Rev. 7 : 1—5. So it continued from Saturday till Sunday. In the course of the day I experienced a change for the worse. Took my book and read till Monday morning 3 o'clock. I then lay down ; could get no sleep. An indescribable horror seized me. It seemed as if a hundred devils were surrounding me. My body and limbs became cramped. I felt as if my last hour had come. " Get thee behind me satan, I exclaimed, my Jesus' blood has blotted out the handwriting against me. This is the blood of that Lamb of God which taketh away my sins." This lasted about three quarters of an hour. I remained the victor. The perspiration was then dripping from the ends of my hair. God helped me with his grace thro' Jesus Christ our Lord. Amen.

On the 5th came Priest Müller and another gentleman from New York. They asked permission to see me. I begged to be excused, for I was too exhausted for an interview. They may here see how God has revealed Himself to me, a poor sinner, as my Heavenly Father. Read the following :

> Jesus nimmt die Sünder au,
> Wehe dem der diesen glauben,
> Diese erste Zuversicht
> Sich-von-Satan lässet rauhen,
> Dass er in der Sünden Angst ;
> Immer fröhlich sagen kau,
> Jesus nimmt die Sünder an.

I believe, my brethren, that you are walking in darkness, and you may come into the light. Would that you all may be crowned with glory, and be united with our Lord Jesus Christ. This is written by a poor sinner of this world, yet cleansed by the blood of Jesus Christ.                    JOHN ERPENSTEIN.

# NOTE.

I need add but a few remarks to the above. A few days previous to his death E. experienced many struggles and deep anxiety for his soul, in view of his rapidly approaching death. As I was endeavoring to console his spirit, he remarked, "Death is bitter; and I am a sinful man. Yet indeed the Saviour went through severe struggles, though he was a God; but I am a poor man." He often prayed with great earnestness, and slept but little. His ear hung upon God's word, because it had become precious to him. Much prayer was offered for him and with him. A day before his death, God removed his anxiety. It was astonishing to hear him talk of his death. His mouth overflowed with joy at the thought of becoming a redeemed sinner in Heaven. If he saw any troubled concerning him, he would bid them be calm, as he hoped soon to be with his redeeming God. During the last day and night he sang several religious hymns. Especially did he derive great consolation from the last supper administered to him the day before his death, in company with a few friends. It seemed as if this was his last desire upon earth; and in the evening he repeatedly observed that he had greatly enjoyed the day. The last night was spent in prayer, singing, and reading the Bible. In this calm frame of mind he remained until the last.

WILLIAM WINNIS.

A view of the Egyptian-style Essex County courthouse in 1855, from
*Ballou's Pictorial Drawing-Room Companion.*

A view of the Middlesex County sheriff's residence and jail, from Everts & Stewart, *Companion Atlas Map of Middlesex County, New Jersey* . . . (Philadelphia: n.p., 1876).

# "The Doctor Liked Me"

F EW PERSONS, if any, had ever suggested to servant-girl Bridget Dergan that she was desirable, so her young Irish heart pounded when she heard (or thought she heard) Dr. William Coriell, of New Market, say in 1867 that he wished his wife "was dead or out of the way."

According to Bridget, "I made myself think from this remark that the doctor liked me, and I did really think that he wanted to get her out of the way, and this so preyed on my mind that I thought I must kill her."

Shortly after midnight on February 25, 1867, New Market echoed with cries in the street of "murder" and "fire." The Coriell house was in flames. Mrs. Coriell was found in the building, stabbed more than sixty times.

The next morning, a local jury summoned by the justice of the peace charged that Bridget Dergan, the servant-girl, had killed the doctor's wife. She was sent to the county jail to await trial. Requests for seats to the trial promptly poured in from newspapers across the nation.

Strangely, the writer of the pamphlet failed to mention a single word uttered by any witness, taking refuge in a bland statistical reference that eighty-seven witnesses had been sworn after the trial began on May 11. The total of witnesses, not what they related, appealed to that reporter, despite his declaration that the trial probably "was altogether one of the most remarkable in the criminal annals of the country."

After twenty days of witnesses the jury took less than an hour to find Bridget Dergan guilty. She was sentenced to be hanged on August 30.

Significantly, for more than four months after she was arrested, Bridget refused to admit guilt of any kind. Then in late July, she allegedly made two confessions, one to her attorney and the other her jailer. Both had to be written by others, for Bridget could neither read nor write.

The anonymous writer of the pamphlet admitted, "her confessions were not obtained from her all at once, but only in answer to questions put to her at different times and often in an indirect manner."

The two confessions differed in many details, but basically, they boiled down to Bridget's belief that Dr. Coriell might have chosen his Irish maid if only his wife were "out of the way."

While the convicted murderess was doubly "confessing," she also was getting ready for the hanging. The hangers-to-be were equally busy, chiefly in selecting the guest list of those who wanted to be inside the prison wall to watch the execution.

"The sheriff was terribly annoyed," the pamphlet said, "by the demand for tickets of admission." He gave away about five hundred, "and we judge a greater portion of them were used."

On the morning of August 30, Bridget Dergan left her cell. A black cap covered her head. The crowd, termed "boisterous" to that point, quieted and parted to let her through. Then it rushed madly forward to get good vantage points.

Bridget kissed the jailer, shook hands with the sheriff, and the rope was put around her neck. She shouted, "Don't let a Protestant touch me!"

The weight dropped, the former servant-girl was jerked three feet into the air. Her pulse continued to beat for thirteen minutes (ready volunteers taking the count). She had been strangled with horrible slowness, not killed suddenly. No one seemed to mind.

Outside the jail, two thousand persons waited for the sounds inside the jail to tell them that justice had been done. Most had hoped, in vain, for a possible extra ticket, much like gate crashers might at a sporting event. But, as the pamphlet related: "Before twelve o'clock the usual quiet of the neighborhood was restored, we hope never to be disturbed again by such a spectacle."

The writer meant the murder, of course, not the crowd that had gathered to witness the end of Bridget Dergan.

# THE LIFE AND CONFESSION

OF

# BRIDGET DERGAN,

## WHO MURDERED

## MRS. ELLEN CORIELL,

THE LOVELY WIFE OF DR. CORIELL, OF NEW MARKET N J

TO WHICH IS ADDED

## HER FULL CONFESSION

AND AN

## ACCOUNT OF HER EXECUTION AT NEW BRUNSWICK

PHILADELPHIA:
PUBLISHED BY BARCLAY & CO.,
602 ARCH STREET.

# LIFE, TRIAL AND EXECUTION

OF

# BRIDGET DERGAN.

A LITTLE after midnight on the morning of Monday, February 25, 1867, the citizens of the village of New-Market, a place about seven miles from New Brunswick, N. J. were startled from their slumbers by the cry of "robbers," "murder," and "fire." Such an unusual outcry in their ordinarily quiet streets of course aroused nearly every individual in the village, and caused them to rush forth in quest of the cause of the alarm. It was not long before it was ascertained that one of the most horrible tragedies that ever darkened the annals of crime was discovered, that of the murder of one of the most lovely of females, the beloved wife of a respectable citizen, and mother of a helpless infant, and her dwelling on fire. The dwelling proved to be that of Dr. WILLIAM CORIELL, and the murdered woman his wife. The flames were soon extinguished, and the mangled body of his wife dragged from the building scarcely recognizable by her neighbors from the frightful wounds that covered it. Bruises innumerable, and stabs to the number of over sixty, were found on the body, giving evidence of a long and terrible struggle for life on the part of the murdered woman and the fiend who had destroyed her. From evidence in the case it appeared that the doctor had been called away early in the evening to attend upon a patient some two miles distant, the nature of the case requiring his absence nearly the entire night—leaving at his home his wife and infant daughter and Irish servant girl, Bridget Dergan. During his absence the dreadful tragedy took place, he not returning until sent for after the horrible affair had become known to the villagers. The next morning, NATHAN VARS, a Justice of the

Peace, summoned a jury and commenced an examination into the facts of the case, which examination resulted in a verdict that the murder and arson had been committed by Bridget Dergan, the servant-girl. Bridget was thereupon committed to the County Jail to await the action of the Grand Jury at the April Term of the Middlesex Courts. The Grand Jury found a bill of indictment against Bridget Dergan, and on Monday, April 29th, she was brought into Court to answer to the charge. Not having any counsel, the Court directed HON. GARNET B. ADRAIN and ABRAHAM V. SCHENCK to appear in her behalf. MR. SCHENCK declining to act as one of her counsel, WILLIAM H. LEUPP, Esq., was appointed in his place. The plea rendered was "Not Guilty," whereupon her counsel asked for a postponement of the trial, in order to give them time to make a proper defense of their client. After argument of counsel, the Court granted the privilege of a postponement, and the trial was set down for Monday, May 11, at 10 o'clock, A. M.

At the appointed time the prisoner was brought into Court and placed at the bar. The panel of jurors was called, and after eighteen challenges had been made a jury of twelve was finally selected. The trial then proceeded, with the following gentlemen as counsel. On the part of the State, CHARLES M. HERBERT, Prosecutor of the Pleas for Middlesex County, and GEORGE M. ROBESON, Attorney-General of New Jersey; for the prisoner, GARNET B. ADRAIN and WILLIAM H. LEUPP. The examination of witnesses commenced, and occupied the attention of the Court until Monday noon, May 27—eighty-seven witnesses in all being sworn. The counsel commenced summing up the evidence and occupied the attention of the Court and Jury until Friday noon, May 31st, after which Judge VREDENBERGH delivered his Charge to the Jury, and gave the case into their hands at four o'clock P. M. The Jury then retired, and in less than an hour returned into Court with a verdict of GUILTY OF MURDER IN THE FIRST DEGREE. Bridget was remanded back to Jail until Tuesday, June 17th, when she was brought into Court and received her sentence, which was that she be hung on Friday, August 30, 1867, "until she be dead." The trial was very ably conducted, both on the part of the State and in behalf of the prisoner, and was altogether one of the most remarkable in the criminal annals of the country, attracting probably more attention from the entire public press of the nation than any murder trial that has occurred for many years.

An application was made by her counsel to the Court of Pardons, (which consists of the Governor, Chancellor, and the six Judges of the Court of Errors and Appeals,) to have her sentence commuted to imprisonment in the State Prison for life, but after a hearing of the case the application was refused on the 9th of July, and the sentence of the Court allowed to take its course. The fact was then conveyed to Bridget that there was no further hope of her escaping the judgment of the law, whereupon Bridget sent for the Catholic Priest, Rev. Father Rogers, for the purpose of seeking the religious consolation her case demanded. It is understood that her religious adviser informed her that she could not expect pardon for her sins until she had made an open and full confession of her crime, which she for some time seemed unwilling to make. But at the request of Mr. ADRAIN, one of her counsel, she made a confession to him, and also one to her jailer, Mr. RANDOLPH, and to Recorder JEFFERIES, both of which confessions we lay before our readers. These confessions differ in detail, but substantially agree in the acknowledgment that she committed the horrible crime for which she has suffered the penalty of the law.

About a week after the sentence of death was pronounced by the Court upon Bridget, she expressed a desire to have a letter written to her brother in Ireland. Mr. Randolph, the jailer, immediately informed our reporter of the fact, and on the morning of the 27th of June, he entered her cell and wrote the following letter, which she dictated to him. Several letters were written and sent previous to this, but were returned again, having been misdirected. By referring to the map of her country he fortunately hit upon the right direction and the letter reached its destination. He placed her thoughts and suggestions in readable shape, and now gives the letter to our readers the same precisely as it was sent to her brother. We would have published it before, but we were bound by a promise not to do so until after her execution. The letter reads as follows:

MIDDLESEX COUNTY JAIL, }
NEW BRUNSWICK, June 27, 1867. }

MY DEAR BROTHER :—

I am now in jail charged with the murder of Mrs. Mary Ellen Coriell, in February last, at New Market, N. J., with whom I had been living as a servant. I have had my trial, it took place in the month of May. I have been sentenced to be hanged on the 30th of August next. I want to see you very much. If you start immediately you can see me in time. I have no friends to see me, and I wish you could come over. I have nothing to say to you now, but when you come I have much to say.

There are two more—one man and one woman—to be tried i·
September, at the next Courts, for the same murder.   I am in goo
health and try to keep in good spirits.   Please take good care c
little Patrick for me.   I hope you are all well and little Patrick als(

If you cannot come over to see me right away please write me a׳
answering letter and send it by the next steamer so that I can get ׳·
in time.   Give my love to mother and brother Patrick.   I heard ε
the time of my trial that father had died sometime in April.   Pleas
send me the particulars of his death as I wish to know all about i׳
Give my love to my sister Mary living in England, and to her hus
band Martin Kiverton, and to the little ones, and to sister Catharine
Remember me to Patrick Kiverton and to his mother and fathe׳
and to William Shaw, and to Mr. Thomas Ross and family, to my
cousin Peter McDonnell, his wife and family, and to all my friend׳
and neighbors   Don't fail to come or write.

BRIDGET DERGAN.

Please direct your letter Bridget Dergan, in care of Sheriff Clark
son, Middlesex Co., New Brunswick, New Jersey.

To Mr. JOHN DERGAN, Parish of the Dun Cliff, Sligo County
Ireland.

This letter carried the first intelligence of her condition to her
friends.   Her brother's reply Bridget received about the first of
August, and it had such an effect upon her that she broke forth in
long continued wails of anguish.   All night she continued to wail
most piteously, and kept all in the jail awake by her lamentations.
No doubt the sight of a letter from home awakened in her mind and
heart thoughts of happy days spent in her childhood, and the mem·
ory of kind friends and kindred in her native land.   Her brother
stated in his reply that he would come over if she thought he could
do any thing to save her from her doom.   Other letters were subsequently sent, but we understand that no other reply was received
by her.

Since her conviction she remained most of the time in an appa -
rently careless condition, not appearing to realize her situation, or
having much dread or concern for her fate.   She was peculiarly
reticent in her answers to all persons of an inquiring disposition,
and except to her counsel, the jailer, and one or two persons, refused
to converse at all in reference to her crime.   Her confessions were
not obtained from her all at once, but only in answer to questions
put to her at different times, and often in an indirect manner.   She
could seldom be induced to converse with strangers, and often would
hide her face when they called to see her.   She remained most of

MRS. ELLEN CORIELL.
From a Portrait by Frankenstein, painted only two weeks previous to her death

**BRIDGET DERGAN.**
From a Photograph furnished by her Counsel. All Portraits representing her horribly ugly are incorrect.

the time at her cell door, sometimes conversing with the other prisoners, but generally in a moody condition, playing with her hands
and beads in a sort of stupid manner that caused many to believe
that she was not a responsible being.

Her appearance was most truthfully described by Mrs. E. OAKES
SMITH, the poetess, who seemed to have more control over her than
any other one of the hundreds of persons who have visited her,
during her confinement in the jail.    Latterly she has paid considerable attention to religious matters, and listened respectfully and attentively to the teachings of her priest and other religious friends
of the Roman Catholic faith.    Not being able to read, her Bible
and Prayer Book has been daily read to her by persons connected
with the Sheriff's family.    She has generally rested well at nights.
except when disturbed by noises from the other prisoners, and had
a good appetite and enjoyed her meals, having been supplied from
the Sheriff's table with all the necessities and even luxuries of the
season.    Her treatment was kind and considerate, as she freely
testified to all who approached her on the subject.

Ever since her sentence large numbers of persons, from far and
near, often from fifty to a hundred in a day, called at the jail and
desired to see her.    The Sheriff and jailer were annoyed exceedingly by this morbid demand upon their patience, and it required
much nerve and discrimination to select the ones that could be admitted, for it was of course impossible and imprudent to permit all
who desired to see her.    Large numbers, however, were admitted,
but, as we have said above, few could succeed in getting into conversation with her.    The Sheriff was also terribly annoyed by the
demand for tickets of admission to the execution—often receiving
fifty letters in a day asking that privilege, saying nothing about the
" boring" he had to submit to personally whenever he made his appearance in public.    He issued about five hundred tickets in all, and
we judge a greater portion of them were used.

On Thursday very few were permitted to come in and converse
with her.    Fathers Rogers and Duggan called in the morning and
performed the ceremonies of the Catholic faith.    Miss Sullivan, of
the Catholic School and Mrs. Clarkson, the wife of the Sheriff, have
assisted in giving her spiritual consolation.    At an interview about
six o'clock in the evening she was very buoyant and cheerful, ready
and willing to engage in conversation.    She professed to have been
pardoned and seemed to be resigned to her fate.

When asked if she thought she could be as happy as Williams,
she remarked, " I do not believe he was very good and happy," and
" I would not be sure he was all right."

Her buoyancy of spirit continued until she retired. At various times since her sentence she has appeared sullen and often refusing to engage in conversation with any one, but now she seemed anxious to laugh and talk with all who were privileged to see her. In speaking of Ireland and the hundreds arriving at Castle Garden from her country, she said: "They had better stay away from Jersey."

Charles M. Herbert, the prosecutor for the State, called about seven o'clock in the evening to bid her "good-by," and hoped she had no ill feeling against him. She replied that "he had done what was right—she had nothing against him." Mr. Herbert remarked: "I was endeavoring only to do justice in the case."

"I hope," said Bridget, "you will do justice to Mary Gilroy, and let her go."

"I will think over the case between now and September, and if I believe your statements to be true, I will lend my influence to do justice to Mary," responded Mr. Herbert. He then asked: "Didn't Mary Gilroy know about it before?"

Bridget responded:—"Mary Gilroy didn't know any sooner than the people of New-Market."

Mr. Herbert.—"Did she not know it was to occur?"

Bridget.—"Mary didn't know any sooner than the people of New-Market."

Mr. Herbert.—"If Mary didn't know any thing about it, how was it that Mary Gilroy told Delia Coyn, her roommate, that Bridget was murdering Mrs. Coriell?"

Bridget.—"It must be because of her (Mary's) bad and ugly temper, which made her say she knew about it."

Mr. Herbert was about to depart and bade her "good-by," when she called him back, and said: "Mr. Dennett, the New York ex-policeman, who testified against Bridget in the trial, to having seen her and Mary Gilroy at the Washington Market, New York, and recognized them as pickpockets, had never seen her with Mary Gilroy in New York; she never knew Mary until she came to New Market."

Mr. Herbert.—"Do you know a person in New York by the name of Mary Gilroy or Kilroy, or something like that? Have you ever known a large and fleshy person like yourself, named Dergan or Dugan?"

She answered: "No, sir."

Mr. Herbert and the reporters bade her "good-by," to which she replied good-naturedly: "good-by, sirs."

## THE LAST NIGHT AND MORNING.

Bridget retired at about one o'clock this (Friday) morning. Father Duggan (the new priest of the Catholic church in this city,) remained with her until a late hour, when he left the jail. A couple of ladies remained with her all night. After going to bed she was for a time annoyed by the ravings of Simeon Hopkins, a crazy man in another part of the jail, but after a while fell asleep, and slept soundly and well for about three hours—in fact, better than she had for several nights past—arising at about half-past five o'clock in the morning.

Breakfast was brought into the cell at an early hour, but she appeared to have less appetite than usual, and ate but little. At her request, Mary Gilroy, the other girl in the jail charged with the same crime, was then brought into her cell, where they remained alone for a few minutes, and held a conversation which no one else heard—both appearing to be on the best of terms with each other. After remaining a few minutes together, they kissed good-by, and separated forever on this earth.

Fathers Rogers, Duggan and Misdziol, visited her at an early hour and held Mass in her cell, Bridget apparently entering into the spirit of the exercises with all the comprehension and feeling that could be expected of one in so low a mental condition. Prayers were afterward read by her spiritual advisers, and she otherwise assisted in her devotions by Miss Sullivan and the wife of the jailer, Mrs. Randolph. She appeared resigned to her fate, and declared herself ready to submit to the penalty of the law, having full faith in the prayers and consolations of her spiritual advisers. She remained in this calm condition until the appearance of the officers of the law, when she submitted herself quietly into their hands.

While the rope was being placed about her neck, she remained quiet, her face blanched a little at the sight of the instrument of death, and her eyes steadfastly fixed on a crucifix held in the hands of one of the priests, which she kissed once or twice. The black cap was placed on her head, and her arms pinioned behind her at the elbows, so that she could not raise them to her neck or face. She had on a brown paramatta dress, gathered at the waist with a black belt, and white cotton gloves on her hands, and an ordinary silk watch guard about her neck.

She was led out of her cell, when she walked across the hall of the jail and kissed a couple of young men prisoners, and bade them good-by, and also shook hands with William Roantree, the man who was engaged in the recent murderous assault upon his father-in-law and family, at New Market. The warrant for her execution was then placed in the hands of the Sheriff by the Clerk of the Court, Charles T. Couenhoven, when a procession was formed in the hall to proceed to the gallows.

## THE EXECUTION.

The Sheriff led the procession, Bridget being supported on either side by Fathers Duggan and Misdziol, one of whom held a crucifix immediately before her face, she looking at it constantly, neither casting her eyes to the right or left—Father Rogers, several Sheriffs and ex-Sheriffs from this and other counties, officers and reporters of the press, falling in the rear. A passage-way through the crowd in the jail-yard was opened by the police, and the solemn procession marched some thirty or forty feet from the back door of the jail to the gallows placed in the north-west corner of the yard. The gallows was the same one used in the execution of the negro Williams, and hoists the criminal by the dropping of a heavy weight on the cutting of a rope by an axe as it passes over a beam.

After she was placed under the rope, the one about her neck and the one dropping from the beam above, were fastened together by a hook. She was supported by Fathers Duggan and Misdziol, while Father Rogers read a brief prayer, Father Duggan whispering words of consolation and hope in her ear. She then bade good-by to the jailer by kissing him, and shook hands with the Sheriff. As the black cap was drawn down over her face, she said, appealingly: " Don't let a Protestant touch me !" In the next breath she exclaimed : " God help us, and have pity on my poor soul !" The rope, which held up the weight, was then immediately cut by the Sheriff, and her body suddenly jerked up into the air about three feet, probably before she expected it. When under the gallows she trembled with agitation, and the color came and went from her face until it was hidden from view. Otherwise she behaved heroically, and with less agitation than was generally expected.

About a minute after her body was suspended she struggled violently, drawing her limbs up with a strong shrug, her breast heaved, a slight gurgling sound was heard from her mouth, and the body dropped heavily back again, never to undergo another such struggle. For some time her hands remained tightly clenched, the blood rushing and darkly coloring her wrists, while her pulse beat violently for two or three minutes. At three minutes after the suspension, the pulse beat one hundred, and five minutes after, from seventy to eighty—all pulsation ceasing at thirteen minutes, when the physicians around pronounced her dead. It was the opinion of the physicians that her neck was not broken, but that she died from strangulation. Her weight being about one hundred and seventy, it was supposed that the sudden jerk she received would have certainly broken her neck, but this did not appear to be the case.

Bridget left the jail at ten minutes, and was suspended at fifteen minutes after ten. After hanging thirty minutes precisely the body was lowered and placed into a neat looking black walnut coffin. The cap was drawn from her face and her features were viewed by the physicians. In death she looked quite natural,—the eyelids were a little swollen, but were free from blood, the .mouth was partly open, the teeth set and a little blood upon the lower lip, on the right side of the mouth, her tongue having been slightly cut. The face was discolored, and turned quite purple when placed in the coffin.

The crowd within the jail yard were hurried out, the hearse was driven in and the coffin placed within it, and driven immediately to the old Catholic burying ground, where it was interred. Fathers Rogers and Duggan followed.

The excitement among the large crowd congregated outside the prison wall, when the hearse and coffin were brought out, grew more intense. The boys started after the body by scores, the women and children dispersed and returned to their homes, and in a few minutes the streets were almost entirely deserted, save a few standing in groups conversing upon the execution.

All of the arrangements connected with the execution were well planned and conducted in good order by the Sheriff. There was a little boisterousness by the crowd in the yard before the prisoner was led forth, in their strife to obtain good positions, but this ceased on her appearance. There were present over thirty reporters connected with the Press of New York, Philadelphia, and other cities, and the Sheriff very properly allowed only three or four to enter the jail, as more than that would necessarily have created confusion, probably disconcerted Bridget, and caused much trouble in the final preparations for the gallows.

Two companies of the New Jersey Rifle corps, companies I and K, of the Third Regiment, under command of Colonel URIAH DEHART and Captains BLUE and WANSER, paraded around the jail and court yard for the purpose of preserving order. Some two thousand people gathered in the streets in the vicinity, but they

"I then turned upon Mrs. Coriell and pushed her back on the bed, and with this white handled knife stabbed her repeatedly." Bridget's Confession.

"After waiting until all was quiet outside the house, I took up the little child's chair and struck her with it on the head several times."

could not gain admittance to see either the execution or the dead body of the miserable woman, as some of them hoped to do. Good order generally prevailed among the outside crowd. The spectators in the jail and the outside crowd soon dispersed, and before twelve o'clock the usual quiet of the neighborhood was restored, we hope never to be disturbed again by such a spectacle.

### HER CONFESSION TO MR. ADRAIN.

I am nearly twenty-three years of age; my real name is Bridget Deignan; my father's name is Patrick, and that of mother Hannah : my father is dead, but my mother is living ; she lives in the Parish of Dun Cliffe, County of Sligo, Ireland ; I was born there; I have two brothers living at that place, Patrick and John ; I have also two sisters living—the one who is younger than myself lives with my mother, and the other who is older is married and lives in England. I came to this country two years ago last Christmas ; I first lived with a Mr. Dolan, in Brooklyn, N. Y.; then with a Mr. Knapp, at Bull's Ferry, N. J.; then with a Mr. Dayton, at Piscataway, N. J.; then with Mr. Wylie, at Plainfield, N. J. ; then with Mr. Blackford, at Piscataway, N. J.; then with Mr. William M. Coriell, at Plainfield, and finally with Dr. William W. Coriell, at New-Market. I lived with Dr. Coriell about four months; all the time I lived there Mrs. Coriell was .very kind and pleasant to me; she was a very pretty woman; I never had any quarrel with her ; at about 10½ o'clock, (I will not be positive as to the exact time,) on the night of the twenty-fifth of February last, Mrs. Coriell was lying upon the lounge in the sitting-room; before lying down she complained of not feeling very well, and said she would not go to bed, but would throw herself upon the lounge and wished me to sit up so that I might watch little Mamy if she stirred, who was sleeping in the cradle in the small bed-room. As Mrs. Coriell was lying on the lounge, apparently asleep, I came out of the kitchen with the bread-knife in my hand that was exhibited on the trial, and picked up the kerosene lamp that was on the table in the sitting-room, and not lighted, and approaching her, struck her with the lamp on the neck; she started up in a bewildered manner and immediately went into the small bed-room, adjoining the sitting-room, and I followed after her; she stood up against the side of the bed, and as I came near her she grasped the knife out of my hand ; I then turned around and picked up another knife with a white handle that lay upon the table in the bed-room concealed by a table-cloth which I had thrown over it— this knife I had previously placed there, having found it in one of the drawers of the bureau in the bed-room; I then turned upon Mrs. Coriell and pushed her back on the bed, and with this white-handled knife struck her repeatedly; the knife she had grasped out of my hand had fallen upon the floor so she could not use it, and I did not use it that night, and do not know how it became bent; she made all the resistance she could, defending herself with the pillows. After striking her very often as she lay upon the bed, and supposing she was dead, I then picked up little Mamy out of the cradle and went with her into the sitting-room, and sat upon the lounge for a few minutes; I then arose and went into the kitchen, having Mamy in my arms, and washed my hands in the iron pot of water sitting on the stove; I then came back into the sitting-room and went into the bed-room, and found that Mrs. Coriell had left the bed and gone out of the house; I immediately went in search, and found her going down to the gate in the front of the house; I told her to go back again; she said nothing but went back, and as she was passing through the sitting-room she stooped down and kissed little Mamy, who was standing by the lounge where I had placed her when I went after Mrs. Coriell; Mrs. Coriell then sat down on the floor, between the sitting-room and the bed-room, and while she was sitting there I took the small child's chair, which was exhibited on the trial, and struck her with it two or three times about the neck; I never bit her on the neck as was supposed on the trial; I then drew her into the bed-room and laid her down upon the floor; I then came back into the sitting-room and sat upon the lounge for a few minutes; I then took Mamy's dress and some paper, and put them into the stove and lit them, and then threw them burning upon the bed; Mrs. Coriell was not then upon the bed, but on the floor; I did not change Mamy's dress that night, but carried her out of the house with me with the same clothes she had on when put into the cradle; I then went out of the sitting-room door down to the gate in front of the house and stood there, and while standing there I thought I heard a man walking up from Israel Coriell's store, and went back into the house again; I sat down upon the lounge for five or six minutes; I then rose, went out of the house and down to Israel Coriell's store to rouse them up, representing, as was detailed on the trial, that robbers had been there. I had on that night, when I killed Mrs. Coriell, a white skirt, and that skirt was not produced on the trial, although the Prosecutor of the Pleas, Mr. Herbert, had it in his possession; I had on no frock, having taken it off about ten o'clock before the murder; I went to Israel Coriell's store that night, and over to the Rev. Mr. Little's house, with the same skirt

on that I wore when the murder was committed. I never changed
my clothes that night after the murder, nor arranged my hair, nor
fixed myself in any way before leaving the house, except to wash
my hands. The blood on my clothes, which were exhibited on the
trial, was occasioned by my monthly courses, and not by the blood
of Mrs. Coriell. I never heard Mrs. Coriell say that night "Oh my
poor baby!" I did not hear her make any noise after she got out
of the house and was going down to the gate; I never used the
words that night, " Take Ellen back!" I was not up stairs that
night in the room, where the bureau is said to have been upset;
Mrs. Coriell was not up there that night, nor was any person to my
knowledge. Dr. Coriell was up there in the evening before he left
home, having left about five o'clock. He wanted his watch-chain
from that room and asked Mrs. Coriell to go up there and get it for
him, but she declining, he then asked me, and I said "wait a minute!" but he became impatient and said he was in a hurry, and went
up stairs himself for it; if the bureau was upset I did not do it and
don't know who did, and I have no recollection of saying to any one
after the murder, "I don't know whether the bureau was upset or
not." Mary Gilroy was not there that night; she knew nothing of
the murder and had no hand in connection with it whatever; she is
entirely innocent; I never knew her until she came to New Market
to live; the statement on the trial that I was seen with her and a
girl by the name of Connor, in Washington Market, New York, is
wholly untrue. I did not put the bread-knife, exhibited on the trial,
in the garden-house at Dr. Coriell's, nor do I know who did; the
other knife with a white handle which I used, I threw into the stove
that night; that night before Dr. Coriell left home, he prepared some
medicine for his wife to take—it was prepared in a tumbler, and she
took some of it during the course of the evening, and she complained that it made her sick and sleepy, and that was the reason she
lay upon the lounge, preferring to do so to going to bed. There was
no truth in the story that I told about two men coming to the house
of Dr. Coriell on the night of the twenty-fifth of February last; the
men, Patrick Doyle and Michael Hunt, and the girl Annie Linen,
whom I unjustly charged with the murder, had nothing to do with
it—they are innocent. *I alone am guilty.* There was no design or
attempt to rob the house that night; the murder was for another
purpose. I killed Mrs. Coriell thinking that I might take her place;
this alone led me to commit the horrid crime. The idea of murdering Mrs. Coriell that night did not come upon me suddenly; I had
thought of it a long while before the deed was executed. I have

told a true story. I am very sorry for having committed so great a crime, and hope God will forgive me.

### HER CONFESSION TO MESSRS. RANDOLPH AND JEFFERIES.

My name is Bridget Deignan and not Dergan, as I am called; I never have changed my name, and have received the name of Dergan from people calling me by that instead of by my right name. I was born in Ireland, county of Sligo, and town of Clough; my father kept a grocery store, and was in very good circumstances, at least it was said by some that he was well off; I have two brothers and two sisters—I was the youngest but one; I always lived at home at my father's house previous to my coming to America. My mother kept a dairy, and we were accustomed to take our butter to the town of Grange, (about three miles from my native place,) to market; my sisters generally went; I attended this market but once myself for my folks. One of my brothers kept a dry goods store, next door to my father's store. I heard that my father was dead, one day in Court, while my trial was in progress. I have not heard from home recently; I have received two or three letters from home since I left; I do not know of any member of our family being in this country but myself, excepting an uncle, who was here and died about ten years ago. I did not think of coming to this country but one day before I started, and it came about in this way: My brother kept company with a girl by the name of Bell Ross, who was a Protestant; my father was opposed to his going with her, and she made up her mind to come to America. I was keeping company with a young man by the name of Dennis Curran, who was employed to take whisky around the country from the store. My parents becoming acquainted with the fact discharged him, and he then went over to England, since which time I have not heard from him. Bell Ross hearing of this, coaxed me several times to come to America, and I promised her I would. I went to my father's chest and took from it twenty pounds in English money and left home. It only took nine pounds to pay my passage, so I gave the remaining thirteen pounds to a man whom I knew, by the name of Patrick O'Brien, to take back to my father. I left my native land and came to this country about three years ago next December, arriving in New York about two weeks before Christmas. I have heard that my father never received the thirteen pounds I sent back to him, and he wrote me, just after I arrived, to come home again and he would forgive me all I had done to him. I was brought up in the true Catholic faith, and was always

taught to respect my religious teachings, but like many others I
went to keeping bad company and followed the advice of others too
much.  When I first arrived I went to Brooklyn, New York, to
live with a family by the name of Doran; I lived with them but
two weeks, and then went over to New York and visited Michael
Blaueg and Pat. Nicholas and their families.  I then went to live
at Bull's Ferry, New Jersey, with Mr. Burrough Knapp—here I
remained three months, and not liking the place came back to New
York and stopped at Castle Garden.  Mr. Dayton, from Piscataway,
New Jersey, came there in search of help and took me out home
with him; I remained a servant in his family twelve or thirteen
months.  While in Mr. Dayton's family I became acquainted with
a girl by the name of Annie Hunt, from Plainfield.  She urged me
to leave Mr. Dayton's and go to Plainfield.  I was liked in the
family where I had worked; as I was leaving I stopped at one of
our neighbors, by the name of Robinson, and Mr. Dayton followed
me there and told Mrs. Robinson that he did not want me to leave
his house.  I next lived with the family of Mr. Wiley, at Plainfield.
Three or four days over a month after coming there I was taken
with sore eyes and had to leave.  I then went to New Brooklyn,
New Jersey, near Plainfield, and stopped with Pat. Winstead while
my eyes continued sore.  While I remained here I was visited
nearly every day by Dr. Coriell, who was my physician; he was
treating me for my eyes, and for the complaint called by him
Epilepsy.  I remained at New Brooklyn about four weeks under
his treatment, and when I got well I told Winstead I would like to
pay the doctor; Winstead told the doctor what I said, and the
doctor replied that it was time enough for pay—it would be more
pleasing to him to have me secure a nice place to work.  My eyes
having become quite well I did not like to remain longer in the
family, so I came over to Stelle Blackford's in Piscataway, to live
with him, and stopped about two months, and from there I went to
live with William Coriell, a cousin of Dr. Coriell.  Here I remained five weeks.  One Sunday evening I went down to New
Market and called at Dr. Coriell's to pay him what I owed; there
was no one home when I called except Asa, the doctor's hired
man.

    While I was talking to Asa, Mrs. Coriell came in from church,
and she asked if I wished to see the doctor; I told her I did; she
said he would be home about half past six or seven o'clock; I
waited until he came, and after that remained and took my tea with
them; before the doctor came home I told Mrs. Coriell I wanted to

pay him some money, and she told me she thought I had paid him while I lived with Stelle Blackford; I told her I did not; Mrs. Coriell asked me if I knew where she could get a girl to work for her; I told her I did not know; doctor then asked me where I was at work and I told him; he replied that he had told me when I was at Stelle Blackford's, that I must call at his house in nine or ten days, and he would employ me; I did not call on him then, as I had engaged to work for William Coriell; I had offered him the pay, but he refused to take it. After talking a short time the doctor told me it was too late for me to go home, and that I must remain at his house all night. The next morning while I was helping get breakfast ready, Mrs. Coriell asked the doctor where she could get a girl to wash for her; the doctor told her I would do it, and I did; I got through about eleven o'clock, and then got dinner ready and took a part of the clothes and ironed them.

After tea the doctor asked me if I would rather work for him than for William Coriell; I replied that I would rather work at William Coriell's, as I liked the place. He then said he thought their work entirely too hard for me; that there was too much heavy work. He asked me how many there were in the family; I told him four boarders, besides four in the family; he said it was too much for me, and if I got sick again, he would not visit me there; I told him I did not care if he did not; nothing more was said at that time. I waited until Tuesday morning and finished the ironing; the doctor went to New York this Tuesday morning and told me I must stay at his house until he came back. He returned in the evening; I was still there; Mrs. William Coriell came over in the afternoon and told me to come home; I promised her I would the next morning, but did not go until evening, when I went after my clothes.

The doctor asked me in the morning if I was going back; I told him I was; he replied that he thought that "one good turn deserved another." I asked him his meaning; he replied that I knew, and said that he had not charged me much for his treatment; that no doctor would have done it for so small a price; I told him it made no difference, as I had never seen or questioned his bill. He then promised to give me as much wages as I was getting at William Coriell's, and possibly more. I finally concluded to return to William Coriell's and get my clothing and come to live with the doctor. William Coriell and his wife wanted me to remain with them and get their house cleaned, but I would not; I then got my clothes and returned to Dr. Coriell's house, where I remained until the night of the tragedy.

There has been so many attempts to get from me a statement of the facts in this case that I have told a great many contradictory stories to try and make the crime appear as light as it was possible upon me. There were several statements that I wished to make before Court, but could not. I have attempted to throw the guilt from my own shoulders and make it to appear that others were con cerned with me in this horrible murder. But now I see no chance of averting my doom and I make this confession. I now in this my last week on earth realize my situation, and though encouraged by my counsel to hope, I ask not, nor do I feel that my life will be prolonged, and therefore, in full view of my approaching doom, I make this my confession to Recorder David T. Jefferies and Samuel Randolph, and as I hope for forgiveness before God it is the truth. I confess to have left the impression that innocent persons have been connected with me in the murder of Mrs. Coriell, but this impression I want to change. *I am alone the guilty party*, and it came about in this way:

While living with Dr. Coriell I was taken sick and did not feel able to do the work; I thought I would leave; Mrs. Coriell was pleased to think I was going to leave, but the doctor became exceedingly interested in my case; the weather being quite cold, he thought my bed-room too cold for me, and told me to make my bed and lie in the sitting-room; I was not satisfied lying there, so he wanted me to take the front room up-stairs, which Mrs. Coriell objected to. I was then induced by him to make my bed in the kitchen by the fire, which I did, when as he said he would stop by me. One night he placed the lounge out of the sitting-room and laid down upon it to watch me; Mrs. Coriell remonstrated with him about it, saying that he could let the lounge remain in its place in the sitting-room and watch me, as well as to pull it out in the kitchen where I was; the doctor got mad and remarked to me that he wished Mrs. Coriell was dead or out of the way. I made myself think from this remark that the doctor liked me, and I did really think that he wanted to get her out of the way, and this so preyed upon my mind that I thought I must kill her. So I thought I must say something to some one about it—as I thought if I put her out of the way I would be all right with the doctor and would be kept in his employ to take care of his house and his baby.

I took Mary Gilroy into my confidence so far as to tell her that something would happen over to Dr. Coriell's house, but the crime

I did not mention to her. This occurred several days before the murder, since I contemplated leaving the doctor's, but he induced me to stay until I got better. I heard him say that he was going away that day and might not return again until next morning or very late at night, and I went over to Mr. Vail's and told the girls there that he would not be home that night, sometime between eight and nine o'clock in the evening. Mrs. Coriell went to her bed-room, undressed and slipped on her old dark wrapper, and came out in the sitting-room and laid down on the lounge. After waiting until all was quiet outside the house, and for her to get to sleep, I thought it a fitting opportunity, and took up the little child's chair and struck her with it on the head once or twice. My mind had been previously made up to put her out of the way sometime when the doctor was absent. Mrs. Coriell was only a little stunned with the blows of the chair and jumped up, and when she found it was me, she exclaimed, "Don't kill me, Bridget," and grasped me by the throat to struggle with me for her life. I then bit her on the cheek to make her release her hold, and she picked up the large chair and struck at but missed me.

She then ran out of the door on the porch and I ran after and brought her back. As she came in, the baby stood in the middle of the sitting-room floor, and as she passed it she stooped down and kissed it.

I seized the bread-knife, which I had previously obtained and placed on the table in the sitting-room, and hit her two or three times; she grasped the knife, and in my endeavor to wrench it from her grasp, it cut her hands very badly. After releasing her hold from the knife, I took hold of her and pushed her in the bed-room, and as I was doing this she resisted and placed her bloody hands against the door; but I succeeded in forcing her into the bed-room, and threw her on the bed, and stabbed her repeatedly with the knife. As I was forcing her in the bed-room, the lamp, which was burning there, was upset, and after I got done stabbing Mrs. Coriell with the knife, I let her lay on the bed, supposing she was dead. I then picked up the lamp and poured the contents on the bed and over the person of Mrs. Coriell, and went out and shut the door. I then sat the child on the lounge and went up stairs with the light and commenced to ransack the bureau, to make an impression that robbers had been there, and in my haste to overhaul the things, the bureau was capsized. I had placed the lamp on the window, and after the bureau capsized, I ran down stairs and forgot the lamp.

I then changed the baby's clothes and took the little frock it had on, which was bloody, and rolled it up in a paper and put the end of it in the stove to light it. I then opened the bed-room door and threw it on the bed. I then shut the door and fastened it and sat down on the lounge and took up the baby. I then heard a noise at the bed-room window, and ran out on the porch, and saw Mrs. Coriell standing at the window with both hands clasping the window-sill. I pushed her and she fell dead upon the floor. I then returned to the sitting-room and took up the baby and left the house. When I reached the road gate I saw that I had left the light burning in the sitting room, and returned to the house and put it out, and left again and went over to William Coriell's house and knocked at the door to give the alarm, and when I found that they would not admit me, I went over to Mr. Little's, and he admitted me and took me into the room where his wife was in bed. Mrs. Little took the baby in with her to bed, and as I was sitting down, Mr. Little spoke of the blood on my skirt, when I put it under me so that it would not be more particularly noticed.

## BIOGRAPHICAL SKETCH.

BRIDGET DERGAN, who has just ended her career on the scaffold, was the daughter of Patrick Dergan, and was born in the parish of Duncliffe, in the county of Sligo, Ireland.

Her parents belonged to the respectable class of Irish people; her father kept a shop in the town where she was born.

From her earliest infancy Bridget exhibited a singular tenacity of disposition, and considerable ambition. She, when only two or three years old, would attempt plots at which most children of her age would shudder, and had the name of the most fearless child in the vicinity. Then, as now, in Ireland, the hedge schools prevailed. These seminaries of learning are to be found in no other part of the world. Each scholar pays a few pence for his tuition, and brings a sod as his contribution to the fire. Difficulties did not seem to appal Bridget, if there were a sufficient motive to overcome them. While her schoolfellows either pouted over their tasks, or silently rejected them, Bridget alone would ponder over the difficulty, and generally finish by accomplishing what the others had considered as impracticable.

One instance of her bravery must be recorded. This was related to us by an old neighbor. Bridget, and another little girl who was two or three years her junior, had been out walking, when the youngest was attacked by a good-sized dog. Both were alarmed, but Bridget soon recovered her presence of mind, and seizing the animal by the throat there held him till some one came to their assistance and both were relieved from their perilous position. The dog, which was afterwards snot, was mad at the time, and nothing but Bridget's ready tact and coolness saved her life and that of her companion.

Mrs. Dergan, who had superintended a dairy on a large scale, purchased a tract of land, and with the assistance of her daughters made butter and cheese, which was sent to market. Bridget, who was now growing into womanhood, assisted her mother, and no matter how unruly a beast came under her notice, it was sure to acknowledge her as mistress. Although ambitious at school, still other matters divided her attention ; and after she quitted the grocery and went to the dairy, she did not pay much attention to books, but was rather more devoted to the other matters that came under her notice, and was fond of going to the Grange Market.

A person who was in the next stall to her has communicated to the author the following anecdote.

Counterfeit sovereigns and half sovereigns then were largely circulated throughout Ireland and England, and many people in the market had been cheated in that manner, but Bridget had escaped. Women as well as men were employed in this traffic, and some of the coins were so well executed that it was difficult to tell the true from the false.

Bridget went as usual to the market with her butter, and soon after, a well-dressed man, whom Bridget had noticed before dealing with one of the women near her, came up, and after cautiously looking round, examined her butter and purchased one pound, at the same time tendering a sovereign. Bridget had not noticed the glances, as she was otherwise engaged, but readily counted out the change and wrapped up the butter, and the stranger left her. But a suspicion rushed across her mind that all was not right ; and asking a neighbor to attend to her stall for a moment, she rushed after the man and found him.

" Well, my good woman, or rather girl, what can I do for you ?"

" I should like, sir, if you please," answered Bridget, respectfully, " to give you back that sovereign and get another for it."

" Why, that is good."

" That may be, sir, but meaning no offence, there is so much counterfeit money about that a body must be cautious."

Bridget had all her senses about her, and looked sharply at the man as she spoke. He hesitated and turned pale. Not a motion escaped the eye of his vigilant observer ; she saw her advantage and meant to keep it.

" Well, my good friend, I suppose that it is all right ; here is another."

That was also closely examined; but Bridget was not satisfied, and, followed by her friend, went into the nearest grocery. The coin was examined, tested, and pronounced good.

The man quitted the place at the top of his speed, and was seen no more in Grange. The same individual was afterward arrested in Scotland, and it was proved on his trial that he was one of the most dangerous men of an exceedingly dangerous class.

The Irish people are social and communicative, and lose no opportunity for meeting together. Weddings, wakes and funerals are largely attended, and there is a considerable intercourse of rustic gallantry between the youth of both sexes. As Bridget was by no means ill-looking, her society was courted by several of the other sex ; but although Bridget was civil to all, still she made no intimacies, and excepting a certain Belle Ross, who was destined to exercise an important influence over her destiny, was exceedingly reserved, and it passed into a proverb in the village that she was as hard as a rock, and that it was very difficult to make an impression upon her.  All the young men who met her at the different places of rustic resort tried, but vainly, to win her favor.

The son of her landlord met Bridget at a rustic ball, and was so pleased with her appearance that he called at the house and paid her some attention.  Here was a suitor after her own heart.  Bridget smiled on her new admirer, and it began to be hinted in the village that at last Bridget was caught.  But the news reached the ear of her swain's father, who called on old Dergan and asked him how much he was willing to give his daughter.  Not satisfied with his answer, he contrived a method of separating the lovers, much to Bridget's great indignation, but which however she was too prudent to express.  She did not care a straw about O'Brien (such was his name), but knew that if she married him she should be the first in the place, and that when the member of Parliament passed through he would dine or lunch with them ; and she knew that the O'Briens, who for five or six generations had always kept their property, entertained all the best company that came to the county.  But there was no time left for grief ; her mother was suddenly taken sick, and she was compelled to devote herself so closely to the duties of the dairy that she had no thoughts for love.  But it is very doubtful whether in the course of her life this singular woman ever did love.  That she was exceedingly ambitious, is beyond all manner of doubt ; and that she constantly endeavored to rise above her condition is equally certain.

Whisky is manufactured in large quantities in Ireland, and is despatched throughout the country in carts, and sold to the grocers and other places where it is retailed.  The drivers of these vehicles are frequently interested in the manufacture of this beverage and superintend its sale in person.

James Cunan, who served the county in which the Dergans resided, was passably good-looking, and had the reputation of being rich, which, as usual, report trebled.  His family was highly respectable, and he lived on a farm which he owned as large as O'Brien's, and, to crown the whole, at least three fourths of the girls in the county were longing to catch him in their nets.  This favored swain was captivated with Bridget, and made her some presents of fruit and flowers, which were not rejected ; and emboldened by her prompt conduct, Cunan asked her hand of her father, who replied " that he might take his daughter, in all welcome, but that he could not expect much till after his death."  Cunan replied, that he wanted the girl, and not his money ; and there the matter dropped.  The lover next Sunday asked Bridget to take a walk with him, and before they returned they were engaged—or, as the Irish term it, troth plighted—and the next week exchanged rings, as is the custom in that part of Ireland.

But her life was destined to prove the truth of the old adage, " that the course of true love does not sometimes run smooth."  Belle Ross, who was her constant friend and daily associate, won the heart of her brother, and this attachment was the commencement of all Bridget's future unhappiness.

The elder Dergan, who had now begun the descent of life, was exceedingly avaricious, and the love of money increased upon him.  Almost daily he grew more penurious.  Belle Ross, though pretty and smart, had only twenty pounds for her fortune, and depended on her needle for her subsistence.  The young people learned his opposition, and resolved to trust the whole matter to Bridget, who, as she could drive a sharp bargain, was rather a favorite with her father, and at times moulded him to her will. Three or four days elapsed before Bridget found an opportunity, and she thus opened the affair:

" I sold that butter well at the castle."

" You can drive a good bargain, and when you are Tim Cunan's wife, if ye want it now and again, I'll lend ye a little spare cash."

" Ye're very good I am sure, father."

" Has the Widow Mahone paid up yet?"

" No, but she promises to pay up to-morrow."

" Well, don't let her get behindhand."

" No, father."

There was a dead pause. Bridget disliked the whole business, but was determined to go through it, and at last, mustering up all her courage, said:

" Father, John is now pretty well grown !"

" Yes, he is a good bit of a lad, and I can tell ye what, Bridget, he is a mighty help to me in the store ; I could not do without him."

" Yes, I know that ; but, father dear, ye must know that ye can't always have John wid ye ; it's getting married may be he will some of these days !"

" It may be so."

" And, to tell you the truth, I think that he likes Belle Ross !"

" Belle Ross ?"

" Just that same !"

" Why, she is a pauper—she's next door to a beggar—she has not fifty pounds in the world that she can call her own !"

" But then, father, consither—"

" Consither what ?" exclaimed the old man savagely, with compressed lips and a lowering brow ; " I do consither one thing—that I have worked hard for what little I possess, and I know that when I go that it will be divided among yee's, but as long as I live I'll never consent that any child of mine shall ever marry a beggar."

" But then, I have not told ye that they were in love. I only said—"

" Ye're no fool, Bridget, and can see as far into matters as the next one, and I know that ye suspect that John is in love with this silly creature, who has nothing but her pretty face, and that'll soon fade ; and if ye choose, ye may tell him that if he pets that Belle Ross I'll never give him a penny ! And that you may tell him as soon as ye see fit. So that's my mind, and I'll not change it ; and ye can make what use ye see fit of it."

Bridget, who was not much surprised, sought the lovers, told them what had passed, and concluded with " I expected that it would be so !"

" Well, then, I'll tell you what can be done—we can go to America."

" Go to America ! where am I to get the money ? It takes a good round pinch of gold to get there."

" I think that ye'll contrive to get it," said Belle, with a significant smile.

The idea flashed on Bridget's mind, who was silent for a few moments, and then replied :

" Keep a still tongue in yere head and I'll get the money somehow ! But I am resolved to go to America and end this."

" And I'll go with ye," was the prompt answer.

The friends then separated. That night, when Bridget was in bed,

~he pondered over the whole matter and definitely settled her plans. She would go to America, and the means must be obtained. She well knew that in her father's present irritable mood it would be useless to even hint at such a thing, and that the demand in all probability would occasion an unpleasant scene. She ascertained where the cash was kept, but was silent on that point. She and Belle Ross again met, and spoke more about their plans of emigration ; but not even to her did Bridget say a word of the discovery, or the use to be made of it. No one should share her confidence, and then she would be perfectly safe. They parted ; and her companion, though she suspected Bridget's intentions, was silent. Three days were thus passed in the greatest anxiety, but as yet the propitious moment had not arrived. At last it came. Her mother had gone to watch with a sick friend, and her father, who had been drinking deeply, was wrapped in the slumber produced by intoxication. All her clothes had been gradually taken to the house of Belle Ross, whence they had been sent to Liverpool. Bridget entered the old man's chamber, went to his bedside, ascertained that he was unconscious, and, searching his garments, possessed herself of the keys, and softly creeping up stairs, noiselessly unlocked the door, took twenty pounds from the treasure there, and replacing the keys where she found them, joined Belle Ross, who had been watching for her a little out of the town ; and as the village clock struck eleven they commenced their journey, and bid an eternal farewell to the land of their birth. Both were doomed to end their existence violently.

Bridget and Belle walked rapidly, and at three in the morning stopped at an ale house, where they procured refreshments, and waited some hours. The journey was resumed ; and in three days they reached Liverpool, where Bridget met a young Englishman whom she formerly knew, who wrote at her dictation the following letter to her father :

"*Dear Father* :—Ere you receive this I shall be on the ocean, and on my way to America. I was tired of the old country, and think that there is a better chance for me in America than at home. Tell all the neighbors good-by for me—and believe me, ever your daughter,
"BRIDGET DERGAN."

Five pounds were enough to pay her passage, and the remainder she delivered to be sent to her father, to a man of the name of Patrick O'Brien—but who proved unfaithful to his trust, and never gave the money.

Bridget and her friend arrived in New York, and soon after she got a place in Brooklyn, where she received a letter from her father, a copy of which we lay before our readers :

" *Daughter Bridget* :—Although I did not approve of your going to America so sudden, you must do as you think best, and I hope that you will be happy in your new home. But if you don't succeed as well as you think, come back, and you will always find a home in your father's house.

" Your mother, little Pat, and the boys and girls, join with me in good wishes.               Your father,        PATRICK DERGAN."
"If you come back the past shall never be mentioned."

It does not appear that Bridget made any reply to this ; but after it was received, rarely mentioned either her home or her family. Her first place was with the Dorans, but it did not suit her, and she only remained about three weeks ; and then, for a time, enjoyed the hospitality of different friends. Her next place, at Bull's Ferry, was with Burrough Knapp, where she remained for three months ; but, as usual, something occurred. She had, when she quitted Ireland, been engaged, or, as the Irish term it, troth-plighted to Cunan ; but as she had not returned him his ring, was still considered as bound, and was reputed as almost married by all her acquaintances. In spite of all this, she allowed a young man in the neighborhood to sit with her for several successive Sunday evenings. The cook, who was older, bitterly reproved her, saying that if she were a decent girl she would never receive the visits of any young man and she an engaged woman. Bridget haughtily replied, that it was her business ; and the cook retorted, that when young girls were away from home they should behave like honest folks and not like —— ! The last epithet is too gross for our pages, but it completely overset what little reason Bridget had retained after the first part of the reproof. Without further delay, she knocked the cook down and belabored her with a small piece of wood. Mrs. Knapp, hearing the noise, came to the kitchen-door and asked what was the matter. The cook and Bridget both began to speak at once, but Mrs. Knapp imposed silence, and desired the oldest to speak ; then heard Bridget ; and after she had finished, paid her her wages and told her to leave on the following day. Bridget made no objection, returned to New York, and stopped for a while at Castle Garden. But still she was not satisfied, and was ever changing.

It is a curious fact in the history both of Belle Ross and Bridget Dergan, that they both suffered violent deaths—Bridget on the scaffold, and Belle on a steamer on the Ohio, where she was so severely scalded that she was known only by the marks on her clothing.

The facts above mentioned have been derived from a party who was well acquainted with Bridget in the old country, and who frequently visited her in prison.

For the closing scenes, and the incidents of her life, the reader is referred to the Confession.

**THE END.**

"Miss A. A. Bowlsby, from a portrait recently painted by Frankenstein," from the front cover of *The Great "Trunk Mystery" of New York
City* . . . (Philadelphia: Barclay & Company, 1871).

# LADY IN TROUBLE

THE CASE IN LATE AUGUST 1871 of "the body in the trunk" had everything that writers of nineteenth-century murder pamphlets cherished—mystery, a beautiful corpse, a resolute police department, and an alleged German-Jewish murderer.

*The Great "Trunk Mystery,"* somewhat abridged in this volume, incorporated the best (or the worst, depending on viewpoint) features of a murder pamphlet designed to sell. It included lurid drawings, blatant prejudices, and heavy overtones of illicit sex. It had such potential that it was printed in both English and German, as was the *Life, Trial, Execution and Dying Confession of John Erpenstein.* . . .

Naturally the publishers professed (in two languages) the purest of motives. The first paragraph read, "It becomes our duty to lay before the reader one of the most startling revelations of crime that was ever developed, even in this crime-saturated city of New York. The narration . . . must be given to the public, in a plain, comprehensible, and at the same time *modest* form."

Concisely and perhaps immodestly put, Alice Bowlsby, of Paterson, New Jersey, had become pregnant, visited a New York City abortionist, died, and was stuffed into a trunk that the abortionist sent off to a railroad station for shipment to Chicago.

Abortionists thrived in New York in those days, even advertising openly. One, Dr. Jacob Rosenzweig, alias Ascher, advertised in the New York *Herald:* "Ladies in trouble guaranteed immediate relief, sure and safe; no fees required until perfectly satisfied; elegant rooms and nursing provided."

Alice Bowlsby was a "lady in trouble." She left her aunt's home in Newark on August 23, 1871, presumably to go home to Paterson via

New York City. Apparently the father of the impending child, later revealed to be the son of a Paterson alderman and mill owner, had read the advertisement and supplied the money for the abortion.

Three days later, on August 26, Alice was seen again, by strangers. Her presence was detected when a horrible odor came from a trunk that a nervous lady had left in a New York railroad station. Police were called and they opened the trunk to discover the nude body of an unidentified young women.

A reporter called the corpse that of a "doubtless very beautiful" young woman, slight and delicate, and "as ethereal in form as Guido's Io."

The Great "Trunk Mystery" proceeded chronologically from the discovery, through some fine police investigative work, to the arrest of Dr. Rosenzweig, and finally to the body's identification.

Jacob Rosenzweig had most dubious medical credentials, including a $40 mail-order "diploma" from a Philadelphia "college." He spoke with a heavy accent, made to seem burlesque-stage comic by the reporter. The doctor was slowly enmeshed in a web of damning evidence.

The corpse was an immediate sensation. Although her body was badly decomposed—and the public was so notified—hundreds of persons filed by in the morgue to see if they knew her. None succeeded until a doctor and dentist from Paterson named her from their certain knowledge.

Back home, Mrs. Bowlsby and her family were stunned, but their grief was mingled with "a sense of disgrace and shame for one they had regarded as innocent and pure." Up at the mill, Alice's lover shot and killed himself. Obviously, he had never given much thought to relieving Alice's troubles by vows of marriage.

As for Alice's incredible beauty (reporter style), Mrs. Bowlsby said that actually her daughter was hardly "of full figure, well proportioned, and handsome," as described. Rather, said the mother, Alice was "delicate and frail . . . not what might be termed good looking."

The failed abortionist was sent to Sing Sing Prison for seven years, the maximum possible sentence for manslaughter. The judge despaired that Rosenzweig had escaped the gallows.

The body in the trunk and Rosenzweig's sentence did nothing to stop abortions, legal or illegal, although it sent abortion "doctors" scurrying temporarily into hiding. They returned, for there always would be "ladies in trouble."

# THE
# GREAT "TRUNK MYSTERY"

## OF

## NEW YORK CITY.

## MURDER OF THE BEAUTIFUL
# MISS ALICE A. BOWLSBY,

## OF PATERSON, N. J.

Her Body placed in a Trunk and Labelled for Chicago.

## MANY STRANGE INCIDENTS MADE PUBLIC.

BARCLAY & CO., PUBLISHERS,
21 NORTH SEVENTH STREET,
PHILADELPHIA, PA.

# GREAT "TRUNK MYSTERY."

## ATROCIOUS MURDER

### OF

## MISS ALICE BOWLSBY,

*A Resident of PATERSON, N. J.*

IT becomes our duty to lay before the reader one of the most startling revelations of crime that ever was developed, even in the crime-saturated city of New York. The narration of this most cruel and atrocious murder, for by no other name can it be known, and by that name alone should the perpetrator be summoned to answer, must be given to the public, in a plain, comprehensible, and at the same time *modest* form. This has been our task, and the reader may rest assured that we have performed it faithfully.

We will begin at the initial step in the disclosures, and unfold them in their chronological order. This will be most satisfactory to the reader, as well as in every way the truest. The story needs no embellishment to intensify its interest. The bare, naked, ghastly "*skeleton*" of facts is sufficiently sensational, without any gratuitous additions. Let us then turn to the first dire disclosures of that skeleton.

On the afternoon of Saturday, August 26th, a startling and frightful discovery was made in the baggage-room of the Hudson River Railroad Depot, New York City.

At about 2 o'clock, a common-looking furniture truck drove up to the entrance and deposited an ordinary travelling trunk. The driver, assisted by a boy, bore the trunk to the baggage-room, and at the same time a woman appeared, and exhibiting a ticket to Chicago, asked to have the trunk checked to that place. The woman was ill-dressed, and it was thought, belonged to the humbler walks of life. Mr. Dunning, the baggage agent, checked the trunk, and handed the woman the duplicate check. She then departed, seemingly to take the train. The trunk was placed among a number of others, and when an hour afterward, Dunning moved it out on the platform to have it placed in a baggage car, he noticed a disagreeable odor arising from it. This aroused his suspicions, and he at once informed Mr. Vandeward, the baggage master. That gentleman had the trunk removed to an outer building, and ordered it to be opened. To the indescribable horror of those who witnessed it, the object uncovered proved to be the body of a

### YOUNG AND BEAUTIFUL WOMAN.

The body was entirely nude, and had been shockingly distorted in the effort to pack it in so small a space. In the top of the trunk and covering the body were a comforter or heavy bed quilt, a piece of a blanket, a coarse chemise, and two or three other articles of common material. All these things, much soiled, emitted a very offensive odor.

Mr. Vandeward at once gave orders to close the trunk and summon officers Murphy and McCullough of the Twentieth Ward Police, who took charge of it. Captain McCaffrey was at once summoned, and messengers were dispatched in quest of a coroner.

At 9 o'clock Coroner Herrman arrived and gave a permit for the removal of the trunk and its ghastly contents to the Morgue, to await identification and inquest.

The scene at the depot after the discovery was an exciting one. Railway officials rushed up and down in the search for the woman who had brought the trunk, and policemen were active in their efforts to find some clue by which the persons engaged in what now seemed clearly a tragedy might be discovered. But few saw the woman or had their attention particularly called to her or her movements. One or two noticed that she exhibited nervousness when

### HAVING THE TRUNK CHECKED

and this in a marked degree when the baggage-man told her that the lid of the trunk was not secure, and advised her to buy a strap to go around it. Expense did not seem to her any object at all, although she did not appear to be a person likely to incur it heedlessly. This circumstance attracted one or two pairs of eyes to her, but only momentarily. The boy who assisted the carman to carry the trunk into the depot had a clearer recollection of the woman and her movements than any other person who saw her. His story as told to our reporter is as follows:

### THE STORY OF THE BOY.

My name is Alexander Potts; I am twelve years old, and live with my mother at Thirty-seventh street and Eighth avenue. I am around the Hudson River Railroad depot every day, where I sell candy and papers and carry light baggage from the carriages. On Saturday I was standing in front of the depot on Thirtieth street, about one o'clock, when I saw a one-horse cab coming toward the depot from the direction of Ninth avenue. The cab stopped in front of the ladies' entrance to the depot, and I ran and opened the door of the cab, when a lady got out. She wore a common calico dress with a thin alpaca shawl, and had on a small jockey hat without a veil. She wore no waterfall, but her hair was tied up in a small knot behind and enclosed in a net. She seemed to be about eighteen or nineteen years old, and her hands looked like those of a working girl. As she got out of the cab she handed the cabman a one-dollar bill and he drove off. She then turned to me and said, " Sonny, can you tell me where the ticket office is? " I asked her how far she was going, and she said she was

### GOING TO CHICAGO.

I then told her that if she went inside and got her ticket she could tnen get her baggage checked. She then went with me to the ticket office, and after inquiring the price of a ticket, she handed the ticket clerk two twenty-dollar bills, and he returned her the change, $18, and a ticket. The change he gave her was three five dollar bills, a two-dollar bill, and a one-dollar bill. She then stood talking with the ticket clerk about five minutes, but although I was standing near, I did not hear what was said, because I paid no attention. When she got through talking with the clerk, she turned to me and said that she had not intended to go to Chicago, but had

### CHANGED HER MIND,

and guessed she would on account of her baggage. I told her that unless she went her baggage couldn't go. She then asked me what she should do about her baggage, and said it would be there soon on Tripp's express wagon. We then went outside, and while standing in front of the depot she saw a wagon coming down the street from the direction of Ninth avenue. She then turned to me and said, " Here comes my man," and then beckoned with her finger to him as if to hurry him on. When the man with the wagon saw her beckon he seemed to drive faster. She then asked me if I would mind helping him in with the trunk, and said that she would pay me. When the wagon stopped in front of the baggage room, I stepped up to help the man to place the trunk on the sidewalk, but he wouldn't let me, saying he'd handle it himself. He

### LIFTED IT CAREFULLY,

and set it flat on the sidewalk. I then took one handle and he the other and we carried it into the baggage-room. I wanted to set the trunk o, its end, as they always do, when the woman and the man both stopped me, saying that the trunk contained glass, and it mustn't be handled roughly. I stepped up to the counter and told Frank, the baggage checker, that the lady wanted to get her baggage checked to Chicago. The truckman and I then took hold of the trunk to place it on the counter, when the lady placed her hands underneath the trunk and assisted us. She said that she would like to have an extra strap around the trunk, and I told Frank what she said. Frank then told her that the strap would cost her $1, and she answered, "I don't care for a dollar if you strap it good." Frank then put the strap around the trunk and drove three nails into it. She then gave Frank her ticket and $1. He punched the ticket and handed it back to the woman with a baggage check. She then turned to the truckman and said: "I'm much obliged to you for your trouble." They then

### SHOOK HANDS,

and the truckman drove off, wishing her good-bye. The woman and I then went into the street, and she handed me five cents. I told her that was not enough, and she gave me five cents more, and asked me to show her a good restaurant where she could get some dinner. I went with her to Keenan's saloon on Ninth avenue, between Twenty-ninth and Thirtieth streets. When we got there she would not go in, but said she guessed she would go to her friends, as she didn't have much time and very little money. She then left me and walked down Ninth avenue, and I went back to the depot.

### IN THE MORGUE.

The appearance of the body as it lay in the trunk was frightful. The trunk was but two feet eight inches in length, yet the young woman was over five feet in height, and had been literally crushed into it. Her head was forced over on her breast, and her limbs were drawn up to the very fullest tension of the ligatures in order to crowd the body into the narrowest compass possible. The rags which covered the body had evidently been selected for the purpose because of their worthlessness. Two pillow cases, which were among the number, had pieces torn out of the open ends, evidently to remove the name which had probably been written on them.

Our reporter viewed the remains as they lay in the dead-house at Bellevue. In life the young woman was doubtless very beautiful, although now sadly disfigured by death's terrible follower. She was apparently about twenty years of age, of slight and delicate figure, and as ethereal in form as Guido's Io. A tangled mass of the

### MOST BEAUTIFUL GOLDEN HAIR

fell in waves over her shoulders, which must have been as white as Parian marble, and eyes of blue, that even death's horrors cannot pale, look out in all their ghastliness from swollen and discolored lids. The limbs were white and shapely, and the feet tiny and delicate. The arms and hands were faultless in their symmetry, and every feature showed refinement and grace. The small exquisitely cut face was terribly discolored, and the mouth distorted by suffering. The teeth regular in

The "unknown" woman ordering the mysterious trunk to be lifted *carefully* from the truck.
(*Evidence of the boy Potts.*)

Die „unbekannte" Frau anordnend, den geheimnißvollen Koffer behutsam vom Wagen zu heben.
(Aussage des Knaben Potts.)

form and pearly in their whiteness. One of the knees was much bruised, and the skin had been peeled off. This shows what brutality the fiends must have practised in their efforts to force the delicate form into its narrow box. The trunk stood near the box enclosing the remains of the poor girl. In it were the mute witnesses to the terrible deed—the rags which accompanied the body. The trunk is an ordinary old shoe trunk. The hinges are loose, and the lock not secure. The inside of it is discolored with blood, but not a spot appears on the outside.

### THE POST MORTEM EXAMINATION.

Dr. Cushman, Deputy Coroner, went to the Morgue, and made a post mortem examination of the body. He found it, as it lay in the coffin, decently covered with a linen sheet. He says that the girl was about twenty years of age, and had been dead three days. The body Dr. Cushman found very much decomposed : the eyes were swollen and the mouth open. Decomposition had particularly far advanced in the head, neck, and trunk. There were no external marks of violence, but the lower part of the person was very much swollen and bloody. On opening the body the abdominal cavity was found to contain a large amount of fluid, and there were evidences of acute peritonitis. The examination of the womb showed marks of laceration, and there were found evidences of intense inflammation ; also of the placenta ; a small portion of the placenta still adhered to the posterior surface. All the other organs, the liver, kidney, heart, stomach, etc., were in a perfectly healthy condition. Dr. Cushman thought that death was caused by metroperitonitis—the result of malpractice, or criminal violation of nature's laws in the delivery of the unfortunate girl in childbirth. But up to the time here referred to, mystery had as yet veiled the whole.

### THE PHYSICIANS' THEORIES.

Physicians who examined the position of the body in the trunk were at a loss to understand how it could have been so distorted after death. When *rigor mortis* exists, the joints become as inflexible as iron bars, and this too five minutes after the breath leaves the body. This gives rise to the *dreadful suspicion* that the fair young victim was *crushed into the trunk while yet alive,* and several medical gentlemen give it as their opinion that this was actually the case. The joints were bent naturally, and when relieved from their confinement the limbs remained as they were bent, and it required force to straighten them out.

### THE SEARCH BY THE POLICE.

The police continued indefatigable in their efforts to fathom the mystery. Soon after the discovery, Captain Caffrey informed himself of all the facts that he could get, and then went to the Central Office and conferred with Inspector Walling. The result of the consultation was that the finding of the man who drove the truck should be the objective point. The boy Potts was sent for. He soon arrived at the Central Office in charge of Sergeant James. The boy said he did not notice the number of the truck, but was positive that the name of Tripp was painted on it. One of the cart inspectors and Ward Detective Freeman of the City Hall were then telegraphed for. Detectives Brice and McConnell soon arrived from the Thirty-seventh Street Station, and after a careful examinatio of the list of carmen and truckmen, the detectives started off at midnigh in search of any truckman who might bear the name of Tripp. At about one o'clock, officers Freeman and Carnoghan found, 231 Bowery, an old German carman, who gave his name as Medert Trapp. Trapp was

### MARCHED IN TRIUMPH

to the Central Office and confronted with Inspector Walling. He admitted that he had been applied to by a stranger to take a trunk for him from a house in Bond street to the depot, but said that he did not take the job.

Inspector Walling winked at Detective Tilly, as much as to say, " We've got the right man sure." Then it was suggested that the boy should see whether he could identify Trapp as the man. Young Potts was then brought in, and without hesitation he declared that Trapp was not the man. Trapp was thereupon allowed to depart. He seemed indignant at his detention, and vowed that he would have satisfaction.

The detectives were then started off with orders to search every part of the city, and not stop until they found Tripp. The search for Tripp was kept up unceasingly until about 8 o'clock on Tuesday morning, but no such man was found. At about 9 o'clock Detectives McConnell and Brice learned that

### A MR. LEE BRADY, OF THIRD AVENUE,

owned a truck which corresponded with the description of that which carried the trunk to the depot, and that he had taken some bagagge in it to the depot. The detectives hurried to Brady's house, taking the boy with them. On their arrival the boy failed to identify either Brady or his truck. Brady then told the detectives that a cabman by the name of Francis Cooper had driven a woman to the Hudson River Railroad depot on Saturday. They then ascertained that the cabman could be found at Seldon's livery stables, on Twenty-third street, near Third avenue. Thither the detectives bent their steps, and found Cooper. The boy recognized Cooper. He was the man. Cooper told the detectives that he was just in the act of leaving the stable with the coupé when a lady went into the office of the stable and told the clerk, a colored man, that she wanted to be driven to the depot, and inquired the price. When she was told that the price was $1.50, she said that she was poor and could not pay more than $1. The clerk receded from his demand, and the woman entered the cab by herself. Cooper took no particular notice of her, nor did he see her until they arrived at the depot. There the boy opened the door of the coupé and she paid him the dollar. He feels convinced, however, that he should know her if he ever saw her again. The police continued persistently in working on other clews as fast as they came up.

### THE SECOND DAY (MONDAY) AMID THE TRUNK MYSTERIES.

Early in the day, by order of Inspector Walling, the boy Alexander, Potts was taken in a carriage with officers Carnochan and Freeman, of the Twenty-sixth Precinct, to make a tour of the entire city, visiting every place where trucks stand for hire, with the hope that at some one of these he might identify the man or the vehicle concerned in the affair. Hours passed away, during which nothing was heard from this party, and it was presumed they were constantly engaged in carrying out the instructions they had received. Meantime the curious called in great numbers upon Inspector Walling, who remained at Police Headquarters, anxious to learn the latest developments. For all of these he had but one answer, that he had nothing new; but to the members of the Press he added that when he had the truckman, and that person had given him such information as would lead to the detection of the murderer, and he was so close upon the latter that escape would be impossible, he would give in full all the facts, but until then he should not give any whatever.

Not trusting to the inspection by the boy Potts, and anxious not to leave a single chance neglected, Inspector Walling issued orders which practically put every policeman in the force upon the case, and waited impatiently for something to turn up.

#### THE TRUCKMAN FOUND AT LAST.

At 3 o'clock a telegram was received from the Eighteenth Precinct that the truckman had been found, and was then in charge at that station, and in a few minutes Inspector Walling left Headquarters and went to the Eighteenth Precinct Station-house, in Twenty-second street, near First avenue. He there found a truckman named William Pickett, who lives at No. 471 First avenue, but who stands for hire at the corner of Third avenue and Twenty-ninth street. With Pickett was Warden Brennan, of Bellevue Hospital, and the statement of the latter has priority in this narrative of the startling events by which the abortionist was tracked to and dragged from his lair. He stated that he had known Pickett intimately for a long time, and that shortly after noon he came to the hospital greatly troubled to seek for advice. He had read the accounts of the mystery in the morning papers, and thought that he was the man who had taken the trunk to the depot. The Warden got Pickett to relate the circumstances, on hearing which he was convinced of the man's identity, and persuaded him to go around to Captain Cameron of the Eighteenth.

PICKETT'S STORY.

When they arrived there, Pickett told the captain that about 1 o'clock, P. M., on Saturday, a woman came to his stand on the corner of Twenty-ninth street and Third avenue, and asked him to go to the basement of No. 687 Second avenue and get a trunk of hers, which he would obtain by ringing the bell and telling the people what he wanted. Then he was to put it on his truck and bring it to the Hudson River Railroad Depot, whither she was going in a coupé. She paid him in advance, changing a five-dollar bill to do so, and they parted. He went to the house, rang the bell, and, the door opening, was ushered into the basement chamber. There was no hall. Here he observed several women and a tall man, whom the carman described so accurately, as to enable Acting Police Sergeant Rooney to identify him as Jacob Rosenzweig, whom he knew well.

ROSENZWEIG'S ARREST EFFECTED.

Without more ado, Captain Cameron, having ordered Sergeant Rooney to put on citizen's clothes, took the man to No. 687 Second avenue; went down the basement, and applied for admission. The door was opened, but the doctor was out. His wife and daughter only were in. The wife is in a delicate condition, having been confined but four weeks previous. Things looking unsatisfactory, Captain Cameron withdrew, taking care to put the house under strict surveillance, so that nobody could enter or leave without being seen. Sergeant Rooney, in his civilian disguise, watched for the doctor's arrival. He came at last, and was seen to enter a liquor store near his house. Rooney followed, and was about to arrest him, and Rosenzweig made a dash for liberty, because he recognized his captor. He was too late to escape, and fell into the officer's hands easily. Seeing that there was a struggle between the men, the police who had been quietly waiting on the other side of the way, dashed across, followed by a number of persons who quickly scented the game, and would have lynched the prisoner, but for the officers, some of whom were compelled to draw their revolvers while Sergeant Rooney got his man into a Second avenue car, and took him in safety to the Eighteenth Precinct.

When Captain Cameron returned with the truckman, earlier in the vening, from their unsuccessful attempt to find the doctor—or man who nad given him the trunk—they brought with them to the Station-house the servant girl from No. 687, and a Jew peddler boy, from whom he hoped to obtain some information.

THE TRUCKMAN MAKES A DETAILED STATEMENT.

Inspector Walling met the party, and immediately made the truckman recount the circumstances of Saturday. He told in addition to the manner of his engagement, as already described, and the delivery of the trunk, that he placed it on his cart and proceeded to the Hudson River Railroad depot, where he found the woman waiting for him, conversing with a boy whom she had engaged to help her with the trunk. He, the truckman, took hold of one end of the box to lift it off the wagon, and the boy attempted to raise the other end, and not being able to do it alone, was assisted by the woman. He and the boy then carried the trunk into the depot and put it on the counter to get it checked. While Frank Dunning, the baggage-master, was thus engaged, a bystander remarked that the lock was very weak. The woman asked for a rope to tie the lid down more firmly. Frank Dunning said he had nothing but a strap. She replied that it would do. "Do you know what it will cost you?" said he. "I don't care," she answered. "It is worth a dollar," the man remarked. She told him to put it on, and paid the money. The truckman then left.

When he heard this story, the Inspector, learning that the boy had arrived, called him in and made him relate his recollection of the facts in the man's presence. The latter, at the conclusion, said that every word was true, except the assertion that he shook hands with the woman when parting. This he strongly denied. Here was the only point of difference between them.

### ROSENZWEIG INTERROGATED.

Rooney brought his prisoner in at this juncture, and the Inspector confronted him with Pickett, and asked him if he knew anything about the trunk which he had given the man on Saturday. Rosenzweig appeared perfectly amazed at the question, and denied having ever before set eyes upon the truckman, and was totally in the dark about the trunk. "What trunk?" said he. Pickett said that he believed Rosenzweig to be the man who had given him the trunk, but he was not sure that he had ever seen the girl before. The wife, he thought, was in the basement at the time of its delivery, and asked him where he was going to take it. However, he was not very clear on these points. The inspector ordered the prisoner to be locked up, and the servant girl, truckman and Jew peddler to be set at liberty.

On further examination it was found that Mrs. Rosenzweig, who at first denied all knowledge of the trunk business, said very innocently that sh was too delicate to be down stairs on Saturday when the truckman called, but hastily correcting herself, she again professed total ignorance of any such affair having transpired. Inspector Walling found out afterward that the woman had been down to the basement four or five times since her confinement. Around this female's complicity in this affair, a great deal of doubt and uncertainty exists, and no light at all thus far has been thrown upon the woman who engaged the truck, went to the depot in the coupé, and was so diabolically cool in her efforts to have the evidence of the crime removed to a far distant city. She has thus far escaped: but not for long, if the fears of conviction are worth anything to unlock prisoners' lips.

### SEEKING TO IDENTIFY THE VICTIM.

Having disposed of these persons, Inspector Walling believing that some clue to the poor victim's identity might still exist in the shape of a valuable trinket, or article of wearing apparel, which the cupidity of the wretches into whose merciless hands she fell caused to keep, placed a close guard over the arrested man's premises, and afterward issued an order that they he thoroughly searched. He then returned to Police Headquarters. In brief then, although the task of relating these events has occupied so little space, the unravelling and pursuit of the matter, step by step, had to be carefully managed, not to alarm those whose arrest was desired, and the whole afternoon and evening were consumed in watching and investigating satisfactorily. No sooner had he reached his desk than two persons called upon him in the belief that they had recognized in deceased a friend whose fate and absence from home could not be accounted for. Their testimony was too indistinct and vague to be considered worthy of serious credence, especially when heard in connection with that of several others, who came to the Central Office during the early part of the day and claimed the dead girl as their friend. Yet each person was from widely-separated parts of the country and State. Late at night a gentleman waited upon Inspector Walling with a photograph, in the hope that by it some one who had seen the victim might relieve his anxious mind of the fear that she was the original of the carte. He had to leave in a state of uncertainty, as no one felt able to hazard anything like a just opinion.

About 10 o'clock Inspector Jameson, with several other officers, went to the house in Amity place, South Fifth avenue, occupied by the prisoner as an office, to find, if possible, the woman who had sent the trunk to the depot.

Not having any evidence by which to identify the woman, should she be on the premises, considerable caution was at first exercised to prevent alarming the inmates, or making an excitement in the neighborhood. The house was closely watched, and to the officers and the small band of reporters, it was for the time-being an object of intense interest. Several females were sitting on the stoop, apparently unconscious of the espionage on the house.

The rear window of a house on Amity street was taken as a place of observation by some of the reporters, and the movements of those in the house were watched with Argus eyes. A Saratoga trunk was seen on the porch looking out into the garden, that was thought to be one of the trunks used in the business.

The police finally entered the house, and Mrs. Ascher, the woman in charge, who is quite old, denied that the place was as it was represented

Dr. Rosenzweig, assisted by the Truckman, removing the trunk containing the body of
poor Alice Bowlsby.

Dr. Rofenzweig, unterſtützt von dem Fuhrmann bei Fortſchaffung des Koffers, der
die Leiche der armen Alice Bowlsby enthielt.

No proofs being at hand to show that it was, the police were obliged to
be satisfied with the statement that it was occupied by respectable people,
and that "Dr." Ascher only kept an office there. Subsequently Inspector
Walling sent the truckman and boy to Rosenzweig's, alias Ascher's,
house in Amity place with an officer. They saw all the females in the
building, but failed to recognize among them the woman who was at the
depot on Saturday.

### SKETCH OF THE PRISONER ROSENZWEIG, ALIAS ASCHER.

A.—Ladies in trouble guaranteed immediate relief, sure and safe; no fees required
until perfectly satisfied; elegant rooms and nursing provided. Dr. Ascher, Amity
place, etc.

This advertisement was clipped from a late issue of the *Herald*. The
following is an accurate description of the man now arrested:—

"Dr. Ascher," alias "Rosenzweig," of South Fifth avenue, below Amity
street, claims to be a Russian, but his voice has the twang of a German
Jew. He is very bulky in figure, about forty years of age, and is said to
know more of saloon business than of medicine. His diploma is said to
have cost $40. His house is a large three-story and basement one, and is
able to accommodate twelve patients. He does a large business. When
called upon he assures applicants, "These other fellows are all humpugsh;
they bromish to do something vot they don't do. I positively do all
operashunsh widout any danger, and as sheap as anybody." The corpse-
like faces to be seen peering through the bed-room blinds are enough to
horrify the stoutest-hearted passers-by.

### THE PROFESSIONAL ABORTIONIST'S BUSINESS VARIETY.

"Dr." Rosenzweig, besides the house in Amity place, of which more
hereafter, has another at No. 687 Second avenue, where he resides with
his family. How many more of these horrible dens he keeps in other
parts of the city may yet be discovered. From this house the body was
carried in the trunk to the depot. Those who know Rosenzweig say that
about two years ago he kept a lager beer saloon in this city, but probably
not finding it as profitable as he desired, he turned his attention to the
"practice" of medicine, which, in his hands, became the practice of murder. Hanging in his "office" is a diploma which he procured to give
him a licence to pursue his murderous calling. This diploma was obtained from an "institution" in Philadelphia, with eight principal profes-
sors and eight adjuncts. He told an acquaintance that he had paid $40
for that particular diploma, but, said he, I did not need it, for I have
got three or four of them. The "Dr." has a wife living, a daughter fourteen years of age, and a child of about a month old. He is a fat, coarse,
and sensual-looking fellow, without any traces of refinement in person or
manners, and does not bear the faintest appearance of the educated physician. None but the wretched creatures, who, driven to desperation by

their condition and the fear of discovery by friends, would place any confidence in his skill. Many of the misguided women that he has treated could not fail to have misgivings when they have placed themselves under his treatment, but probably preferred risking life rather than discovery in what they regarded as a misfortune. One of the friends of this monster is "Dr." Franklin, alias Jacoby.

Ronsenzweig is said to have boasted, some time ago, that he, with "Dr. Franklin, was in partnership in an abortion case. This Jacoby, until three or four years past, kept a barber-shop in Sixth avenue. Each of them, according to Rosenzweig, received an equal share in that transaction, and a gold watch was a part of the spoils.

Another case is related of a woman who was in excellent health when she first went under Rosenzweig's treatment, and after a few weeks of his "practice," she is described as being a piteous spectacle. The flesh hung to her bones, her eyes had lost their lustre, and she became as weak and decrepid as though old age had suddenly laid its hand upon her. She left him a complete wreck, and with her health probably blasted for life. He told a medical acquaintance that he produced a salivation by administering from fifteen to twenty grains of calomel, and said the medical gentleman referred to, "I never use more than two and one-half grains."

## DEVELOPMENTS OF TUESDAY, THE THIRD DAY.

Up to the period here suggested, all but one of the difficulties in the way of solving the bloody mystery had been overcome. That difficulty consisted in the identity of the outraged girl; a world of speculations were indulged in, identifying her with really innocent and living parties. By this reckless and merely sensational speculation much injustice was done, and we therefore suppress all reference to names thus wrongly published. Thus far (Tuesday) the body remained unidentified. In order, however, that no chance for identification might be lost, the body was placed upon ice, where it was continued for several days after.

Although the condition of the body had been fully published, and the stench, even outside the room where it was exposed in the dead-house of Bellevue Hospital, was almost unendurable, hundreds were drawn on Tuesday by a prurient curiosity to look upon the horrible mass. All of these made the pretence of desiring to see if they could identify the remains, but very few claimed to have friends or relatives missing, and none of these few saw anything that they could recognize. Warden Brennan, who still seemed to put faith in the Kelly story, thought it might be possible to recognize the body from the hair, the ears, and the forehead, which remained intact, and therefore permitted every one desiring to see the body to enter the room where it was exposed. The same was allowed on Wednesday, although decomposition was rapidly progressing, and the remains were becoming dangerous to the health of the hospital and vicinity.

### JUSTICE ON THE TRACK OF HER OWN

While the hope of ever identifying the murdered woman was almost dying out during Tuesday, that of bringing the murderer to justice was greatly strengthened. By order of Inspector Walling, Captain Cameron sent Sergeant Randall to the house of Rosenzweig early in the day to make a thorough search of the premises. It is a three-story and basement brick house, with a white marble stoop, and is one of two standing upon one lot. This makes it very narrow and causes the street doors to open directly into the rooms on the first floor and basement instead of into halls, as in full width houses. There are but two rooms on each floor, making eight in all, and none of them are of large size. The house is furnished comfortably, and even handsomely throughout, showing that the infamous practices of Rosenzweig yielded him an income sufficient to supply him with all the comforts of life. Sergeant Randall going to this house, which has been in constant possession of the police ever since it was pointed out by Pickett, made a systematic and thorough search of it with some important results. In the upper rooms nothing suspicious was found, nor was there any evidence anywhere that the house or any part of it had ever been used as a lying-in hospital. But in one of the drawers of the desk used by Rosenzweig were a number of papers, and in the cellar a most important discovery was made. In one corner under a pile of rubbish were found some bloody rags, portions of an old petticoat and the half of a chemise. This last was seized as a most valuable atom of evidence. It was of fine quality, and a determined effort had been made to destroy both its identity and the blood stains upon it. The latter had been attempted by partial washing with the usual result of spreading the stains evenly through the fabric, and the destruction of the identity had been sought by tearing the chemise into parts, only one of which had been left in this spot. This portion had been torn from the yoke, and had one of the arm-holes, but the sleeve had been wrenched out, as the ragged edges plainly showed, with sudden violence. With the bloody rags and petticoat, the chemise was wrapped up and taken to the station-house.

### A CRIMINAL ESTABLISHMENT AND ITS BRANCHES.

Nor did this bundle contain all the evidence carried away from the nouse. Among the papers in the drawer was a scrap on which was written, "Ladies cured with or without medicine, by Dr. Ascher, Amity Place," thus conclusively proving the identity of Rosenzweig with the remorseless abortionist exposed lately in the press. There was a certifi cate of death in the case of a still-born child, filled up on the regular blanks of the Board of Health, signed Dr. Rosenzweig, No. 15 Orchard street, and dated August 11, 1867, thus showing that he had pretended to practise medicine four years ago at least. There were receipts for rent, showing that he has rarely remained long in one place, and that he has lived or had an office at No. 105 First avenue, No. 33 Wooster street, No. 138 East Broadway, No. 5 Essex street, No. 79 Grand street, and at No. 15 Orchard street, as above stated. There were a dozen scraps of paper, on which were scrawled, scarcely legible, names and location which seemed to be memoranda of appointments in the practice of the pretender, and of no bearing upon the case. They were retained, however, and with the more valuable articles which had been secured, taken to the station-house. Before leaving the premises of Rosenzweig, Sergeant Randall made a discovery that for a time seemed to promise important results. This was in the fact, that in the cellar wall between his house and that next door, occupied by Dr. Sutlinski, there was a door, which was, however, closed, and fastened on the side of Dr. Sutlinski. The fact was, however, noted and reported to Inspector Walling.

### EVIDENCE OF AN UNDERTAKER.

While this search was being made, another and far more important link in the chain of circumstantial evidence against Rosenzweig was found. James F. Boyle, an undertaker at No. 658 Second avenue, which is only a few doors from the residence of Rosenzweig, called at the Eighteenth Precinct Station-house, and asked to see the prisoner, as he thought he could throw some light upon the case. He was taken out to the prison by Captain Cameron, and Rosenzweig having been called to the door of his cell, Boyle looked at him steadily for a moment and then said, "Yes, that's the man." His statement was then taken down by Captain Cameron, and is as follows:

On the morning of Saturday, the 26th inst., a man whom I recognize as Dr. Rosenzweig came to my store where I do business as an undertaker, and asked me how much it would cost to bury a woman, and then added that a servant girl of his had died; that she was very poor and only had $10, and that it did not matter to him how or when she was buried, so that it was done. I asked him what sort of a funeral he wanted. He said he only wanted a hearse. He then asked if I could take the body to the store, saying that it was not far off. I replied that I could only do this if he would furnish me with a certificate from the doctor who had ttended her, and then I could get a permit from the Board of Health. n further conversation, he said that the doctor who attended the deceased ived down town. He then went away.

In the afternoon the father of Boyle, who was present at the interview, called at the station-house and also recognized the prisoner as the man who had called.

### THE FELON'S CONFESSION.

Rosenzweig at last made his first confession, and without being asked to say anything on the subject, he astonished every one present by saying, in a quivering voice: "Yes, I wash dar, but I yust makes fun." Having thus, in police parlance, "given himself away," the grim countenance of Captain Cameron was lighted with a smile as he locked the door on his prisoner, and said, "I wonder if the fool knew what he was saying."

The next step in the case was to exhaust the possibility of the door in the cellar, and, by order of Inspector Walling, a visit was made late in the day by Captain Cameron and Sergeant Randall to the house of Dr Sutlinski, and thoroughly searched it. There was nothing found, however, to sustain the suspicion that there might be a connection between the two houses and the two doctors. Dr. Sutlinski was found to be, so far as the police could judge from appearances, a regular practitioner, and there was nothing irregular whatever about his house. There were several other failures during the day, among which was the arrest of two women suspected of hiring the truckman, but upon the truckman Pickett and the boy Potts being taken to the Sixth Precinct Station-house and confronted with the women, they declared without the least hesitation that neither bore any resemblance to the woman. Inspector Walling has as yet no clue to this woman, and has now but little hope that she will be found, but he considers that he has the principal in the case, and that he has evidence enough to convict him without the testimony of the woman who was an accessory to the crime. Enough has been done to thoroughly frighten the entire community of abortionists, and some of the most prominent of them seem to have fled from the city. Among these is Madame Van Buskirk, whose house at No. 8 St. Mark's place, was last Tuesday night for the first time entirely deserted.

The case is now ready for the final action of the coroner and district-attorney. Inspector Walling believes that all the evidence which it is possible to obtain is now in hand, and that it is sufficient to send Rosenzweig to Sing Sing. There are, of course, thousands of rumors floating about the case, as there always are in such affairs, and as many crude theories of amateur detectives as to the identity of the murdered woman, but they are unworthy of mention. The prisoner, who Tuesday night was furnished with a comfortable bed of blankets and pillows sent from his house, of course stoutly denied all knowledge of the crime, and his servant, Jane Thompson, who was up to this time still detained at the station-house, continued to profess entire ignorance of the affair. But with these denials, and with the identity of the girl yet unknown, th case is complete

A REPORTER'S MARVELLOUS STORY ABOUT DR. ASCHER, ALIAS ROSENZWEIG.

During the month of July last I was directed by the *Times* editor to investigate thoroughly the entire business carried on so extensively in this city by professional abortionists. In order to secure success, and to avoid suspicion, I was instructed to take a lady with me. After a long, tedious, and in many respects an unpleasant experience, we unearthed a mass of evidence that, if available in a court of law, would drive a score of villains to the refuge of the State prison.

Among others upon whom we called was "Dr. Ascher." at his office in South Fifth avenue, as advertised daily in the *Herald* for months previously. We rang the bell and were promptly ushered into the hall-way of an ordinary first-class house of the former period. It was of the kind of dwellings that would have been aristocratic ten years ago. A woman of, say, forty years of age opened the door and led us into the parlor. As we entered the room a young girl emerged therefrom. She seemed to be about twenty years of age, a little more than five feet in height, of slender build, having blue eyes, and a clear, alabaster complexion. Long blonde curls, tinted with gold, drooped upon her shoulders, and her face wore an expression of embarrassment at the presence of strangers. She retreated to the end of the hall, and stood there for a moment, and then ent to another part of the house. In a few moments the doctor made ..is appearance.

"Do you wish to see me?" he asked.

"Yes, sir. We have come to consult you professionally."

The room in which we were seated was nicely furnished. A fine tapestry carpet covered the floor; at the window was an elegant mahogany desk, against the wall was a long, easy sofa in the centre of the room was a marble-top table covered with books and pamphlets, and chairs were placed about in the usual manner. Folling-doors seemed to separate the rooms, and adjacent thereto was what seemed to be a piano, having a large cover of heavy damask. The man laid down the pipe from his mouth, for he had been smoking, and wheeling an easy chair in front of us, at once began the conversation.

### INTERVIEW DIRECT.

'I suppose you called for medical services?" he asked.

"We called for medical information," was the answer.

"Exactly; we probably understand each other. You wish to release a lady from difficulty."

"We came to inquire what you propose to do, and what your charges are for such work."

"Well, what are the symptoms—tell me exactly."

"We tell you nothing; but suppose that a lady is ——, and that ·—— are the symptoms. What can you do?"

"Well, you wish to save her and her family. I can lo it without danger. I will not fool you. You know what risk there is in this business. I want $200 down. If there is no trouble, I will see the lady safely through for that sum."

"But the *result*—what is to be done with that? Are we responsible?"

"No. I will take care of the 'result'" (with a significant look and motion of the hand to the lips). "You need not trouble yourself bout the

"But—a young lady and gentleman—what can they do to save their reputation?"

[Sotto voce.] "*I will give you marriage or burial certificates. I have facilities for both.* Is this the lady?"

"No, sir."

"Well, I must see the lady," he said, and bowed us out.

Next week I called alone. He was again beclouded in smoke.

"Well, sir," he began, "you have not brought the lady?"

"No; I have not."

"I cannot tell you anything without I see her."

"You told me you could attend to any case; in the far West, for instance."

"But I must know the person and her peculiarities."

"I want to know just what you could do in a certain case. Suppose it to be this——"

[Here an imaginary case was put.]

"Well. that is serious, but I have had lots of them. I can do the worst safely. If the first means fail I must go to the extreme."

"Dare you use instruments, and is it safe?"

"I do nothing but what is safe. I can do more than all these humbugs that pretend, yet cheat."

"But in case of the child's death, who is responsible in the eye of the law if a discovery is made?"

"Don't worry about that, my dear sir. I will take care of the *result.* A newspaper bundle, a basket, a pail, a resort to the sewer or the river at night. Who is the wiser?"

"But, doctor, if the mother dies?"

"If that should happen, of course you would stand the expense. *But you need never fear. The lady can be disposed of without trouble. I can get marriage or burial certificates without trouble. You know Madame Restell and all the others. I have the same facilities they have.* We can do the thing up handsomely, and I can save you lots of expense. All these other fellows are humbugs. But, why did you not bring the lady here?" he asked, with an evident suspicion of the visitor, and then turning the key in the lock and leaning his ponderous form against the door, he seemed to forbid our egress from the place.

"You seem to hang off," he continued. "What do you mean?"

"I don't bring you a case. I ask what would you do under the circumstances I have named?"

"You are a —— sneak and a liar!" he exclaimed, with flashing eyes and an excited manner. "You are a —— spy. I will split your head for you, you—you —— —— ——!"

The piano, or table, stood between me and the only means of exit, which his bulky form covered. The blinds, too, seemed to be fastened. He was a muscular man, at least three times the weight of myself, and appeared wrought up to the highest pitch of excitement.

"Let me see, sir," I exclaimed.

"You ——, I'll kill you —— (advancing), I'll give you all you want; you spy, you devil, you villain!"

Matters seemed desperate. I had not expected such a denouement. But I felt that there was but one thing to do—either to be conquered or o conquer, and leave the house I must, or else suffer violence at his hands.

Perceiving his desperation, I was at once upon my guard. A sudden movement of his hand to his breast pocket, startled me into the belief that he was about to draw forth a deadly weapon and possibly take my life as he had threatened. In an instant I drew a revolver, the sight of which intimidated him, and in his moment of terror and confusion I escaped.

"I will have you arrested," he screamed, as I slammed the door shut and hurried to the street. As I passed through the hall-way I saw the same girl who left the parlor when I made my first visit to the house. She was standing on the stairs, and it was the same face I saw afterward at the Morgue. I positively identify the features of the dead woman as those of the blonde beauty before described, and will testify to the fact, if called upon to do so, before a legal tribunal.

### AN IMPORTANT ITEM OF EVIDENCE.

Late Tuesday night, the servant of Rosenzweig, Jane Thompson, spoke to what may prove good purpose in a conversation with Warden Brennan, to whom she said that she had determined to tell everything she knew. With this preface, she again declared that she knew nothing whatever of the corpse in the trunk, that no one had died in the house within the past few days, and that she did not know of the trunk being in the house. She then made the important admission, that on the 7th of June a young woman died in the house just after her confinement, and was buried under the name of Mary Carrol, which was not her true name. The certificate gave dropsy as the cause of death, but the servant knew nothing as to what was the real cause. Thomas Carey, undertaker, No. 401 Third avenue, had buried the woman, and after the funeral the ser-vant and Mrs. Rosenzweig had taken the child, which, of course, had been born alive, to the Sisters of Charity at the Foundling Hospital and left it there. Inspector Walling was determined to get at the whole truth of this matter, as it is apparent only a part had been told.

### STARTLING ADDITIONAL DISCLOSURES—THE MURDERED GIRL'S IDENTITY ESTABLISHED.

At 7 o'clock Wednesday evening Warden Brennan reached Police Headquarters in great haste, and inquired for Inspector Walling. That officer was absent, as was supposed, at supper, but in fact had gone to the Eighteenth Precinct Station-house with a man who knew Ascher intimately, and by whom it was desired to identify him as the same person as the prisoner. Warden Brennan intimated that there had been important developments in the case, but he declined to state what they were until he had officially reported them to Inspector Walling. He, therefore, went at once with the three gentlemen who had accompanied him to the Eighteenth Precinct Station-house, where a long private consultation ensued between him, his companions and the Inspector. At its conclusion the three gentlemen went away, and some time afterward Inspector Walling stated that he was ready to give the important information that the body had been fully identified as that of the lady mentioned. He then read an official statement, made to him in writing, by Warden Brennan, saying that Dr. Theodore G. Kinne, of 162 Main street, Paterson, and Dr. Joseph F. Parker, a dentist, having his office in the same building, had identified the body. Having stated in brief terms the means of identification, he concluded with returning his thanks to the physician and dentist for the invaluable aid they had rendered in reaching this vital consummation in the case.

THE EVIDENCE IN DETAIL.

The facts connected with the identification are, however, entitled to be told in more detail than in the concise official statement of Warden Brennan. It appears that three days before, Dr. Kinne visited the dead-house, and, after attentively examining the remains, sought Warden Brennan in his private office, and told him that he thought he knew the identity of the deceased. The Warden had been told the same thing dozens of times before by all sorts of people, and paid at first no more attention to this statement than he had to the scores of others of like character which he had heard. In his incisive hasty way, he asked his visitor how he knew the identity. Dr. Kinne said briefly and calmly that he recognised a scar on the left arm, below the elbow, where he had vaccinated deceased. This was something more than the wild stories he had heard, and Brennan listened more attentively. He knew there was nothing more unusual than vaccination below the elbow, and that such a scar identified by the physician who had caused it was most important. But he was most anxious to have something more definite, and asked Dr. Kinne if he could not bring something more positive. Dr. Kinne reflected for a moment, and then saying decisively that he could, went away. It does not appear that anything more was heard of him until last Wednesday afternoon, and the hope raised by his first visit had nearly expired, when he returned with Dr. Parker, and both gentlemen desired an opportunity to make the fullest examination of the corpse possible under the circumstances.

### THE DEAD GIRL'S PHYSICIAN AND DENTIST.

Dr. Parker, before going to the dead-house, minutely described the work he had done in the mouth of Miss Bowlsby, which consisted in the extraction of one of the molars and the filling of two of the upper teeth, and stated that there was a scar on one of the jaws from an ulcerated tooth for which he had been consulted. The gentlemen then went to the dead-house with Warden Brennan, and the latter proceeded to get the body after it had been taken from the coffin, in a fit condition to handle, by drenching it with water from a hose. After this had been done, Dr. Parker made a thorough examination of the teeth, mouth and jaw of the deceased, and concluded by declaring his readiness to swear to the identity of the body as that of Miss Bowlsby. He recognized his work beyond the possibility of a mistake, and this ended the vexed question of identity. In addition, the gentlemen gave Warden Brennan details of the movements of the lady during the latter part of her life, and some facts which the Warden promised not to divulge, and he has kept his word. All that he was at liberty to say was, that Miss Bowlsby left the home of her aunt in Newark, to go to New York by the 9.15 A. M. train, on Wednesday last, saying she was going to her home in Paterson, and that since that time she has not been seen alive by any of her friends.

### THE HANDKERCHIEF! AY, THE HANDKERCHIEF OF THE GIRL-VICTIM!

But Inspector Walling, having at last a name for the victim, again ordered a search of the house of Rosenzweig, with the hope of finding somewhere about it some article of clothing belonging to her. If any such thing had been left about the premises it was certain that it was there yet, as a guard had been constantly on the house, and no one except the officers permitted to leave it since the arrest. By order of the inspector, Captain Cameron, with two of his sergeants, went to the house and searched it thoroughly from top to bottom, but no article belonging to the victim was found anywhere until they came to the kitchen. In the wash-tubs were the clothes which the girl, Jane Johnson, was engaged in washing, when she was arrested two days before. Picking these out, one by one, and examining them attentively, Captain Cameron came finally to a linen hem-stitched handkerchief, such as are usually carried by ladies. Holding it up to the gas-light, in one corner there seemed to be letters, but so faint, that they were not distinguishable. The searching was continued until the entire house was exhausted, but nothing further was found, and Captain Cameron returned to the station-house, where the hand-kercief was delivered to Inspector Walling. That officer placed the letters upon the handkerchief under a magnifying glass, and there in distinct characters, sentencing the monster Rosenzweig to the full penalty of his crime, were the letters, A. A. Bowlsby.

## THE DAY IN THE STATION-HOUSE.

Although Dr. Rosenzweig must have many acquaintances in this city, scarcely any paid him a visit of condolence last Wednesday. A few did call, but it would have been better for Dr. Rosenzweig, alias Ascher, if they had never taken it into their heads to see him at all. One person, a gentleman whose name was not ascertained, recognized in him a person whom he had engaged to attend his wife, then suffering from a feminine disorder. He almost killed the woman through ignorance, and was kicked down stairs and outdoors for his rascally assurance. Another person, a Jew, who had known the man formerly, waited on him in the hope of eliciting something like the truth; but he was greeted with doleful looks and flat denial. "These people," said Ascher, in whining tones, "know I am a Jew, and believe me to be rich, and want to extract it from me by prosecution. That is why I have been seized and incarcerated. I assure you, sir, I never met or saw the truckman in my life before. I am, in fact, perfectly innocent." His only other visitor was his counsel who administered what consolation he could. It was a dismal day for the wretched man, who sat in his cell listening to the pelting rain with a countenance as dark as the lowering heavens without. He was miserable and very nervous. Not so Jane Johnson, the servant girl, with whom our reporter had a very interesting conversation. She roamed about the station-house, and conversed freely, feeling no alarm at her position.

### WAS JANE JOHNSON A PATIENT?

The servant girl is apparently about twenty-seven years old. She is a brunette, and rather good looking. She entered the back room while the reporters were examing the captive, when going to the cooler, she took a drink of water. At this point a reporter called her and told her to sit down beside him. She did so, and fixing her black eyes steadily upon him, waited.

The remainder of the conversation would be uninteresting to the reader. Suffice it to say that the girl, after crying a good deal, "weakened somewhat," to use a police term, and acknowledged, in addition to the foregoing that "the trunk might have been taken out," but she would not say positively that it had; she never had observed anything wrong in the establishment and never knew of any blonde having been there as a patient. The result of this interview might have been summed up in a few words. Jane Johnson was a country girl, who, having been seduced, left her brother who she says, is worth some money, and came to New York, and to Rosenzweig's to destroy the evidence of her folly. The manner of doing so can only be inferred. Also she confessed that Mrs. Rosenzweig had been out much before the time she confessed to the authorities she had, and then, despite her point-blank assertions in the negative heretofore, she admits that a trunk may have been given to a carman on Saturday. It is probable that Rosenzweig will be in Sing Sing Prison ere many suns rol round, beginning the fullest term of service allotted by the law to his crime, which is manslaughter in the second degree under the law. There are several minor points yet to be solved, but the case is now complete in legal proof, and Inspector Walling does not consider it necessary to make any further effort.

FINAL DISAPPEARANCE OF MISS ALICE BOWLSBY FROM HER NEWARK FRIENDS.

On Monday Miss Bowlsby was reported at Police Headquarters to have disappeared from the house of her aunt in Newark the Wednesday before. No special importance, however, was at first attached to this circumstance in connection with the trunk mystery, and beyond the taking of an accurate description of the girl at the time of her disappearance, as is done in the cases of all missing persons who are reported at headquarters, no attention was paid to the matter. But on the following Thursday, this description of the girl as she left the residence of her aunt, Mrs. Harriet L. Williams, No. 80 Belmont avenue, Newark, had not only a sad interest, but in some of its parts is vitally important to the ends of justice.

She was a young girl whose life had apparently never been darkened, and upon whom the breath of suspicion had never fallen. Moving in respectable society, and having relatives in the highest circles, she was everywhere received as an ornament and a delight. Having a most amiable character, elegant in her manners, possessed of vivacity and good conversational powers, she was a favorite everywhere and especially among her male friends. Her rare beauty surrounded her with many devoted admirers. Her rarely regular features, clear complexion, blue eyes, profusion of light auburn hair, little figure and graceful carriage, made her marked among women for her personal attractions. When she left the home of Mrs. Williams on Wednesday these charms were heightned by the simple elegance of her costume. She had on a white lawn dress, tucked and ruffled, a blue sash and ribbon around the waist, a white straw hat trimmed with blue ribbons and flowers, a light shawl striped brown and red, a brown parasol, a black satchel or hand bag, such as ladies usually carry. She wore also a gold chain and locket, the latter containing a miniature of her mother, and she had in her pocket a portmonnaie, in which were several visiting cards. Saying to Mrs. Williams and her mother, who was also visiting that lady, that she was going home to Paterson by the way of New York, she gayly tripped away.

waving her adieu with her handkerchief which was to be the chief means of fastening the clutches of the law upon her murderer exactly one week later. She was never seen alive again by any of her relatives, and for a time her fate was a profound mystery. But even the fact of her disappearance was not known until after she had become the prey of the abortionist and, packed in the narrow compass of that trunk, her remains had been azed upon by thousands. Wednesday, Thursday, Friday, and Saturda he was not missed in the circle where she was so dearly prized. Her moth er, who remained with Mrs. Williams, supposed she was at home, and her relatives in Paterson, who had not heard of her departure from Newark, believed that she was still with her aunt.

## LITTLE ROSA.

On Thursday Captain Cameron arrested Rosa, the daughter, hoping to elicit something from her about the person who had transferred the trunk from the house to the depot. Soon Rosa was brought in as a kind of prisoner at large, and was permitted to occupy the captain's room, where she sat by the window reading most of the morning. The doctor was not quite as comfortable as he had been. He was much more irritable than he was the day before. He stared at anybody who approached him with a desire to chat. The Jew peddler was also among the unfortunates again. He had been released, but was rearrested on Thursday, by order of the Inspector, and lodged with his friends at the station-house all night

## DECEASED'S AUNT IDENTIFIES HER.

In the forenoon of Thursday, a lady drove up to the station-house in a close carriage. She was shown into the captain's private room, and had a long talk with him, in which she disclosed the fact that she was Mrs. Harriet L. Williams, of No. 80 Bellmont avenue, Newark, N. J., and the aunt of Alice Bowlsby, who had been staying at her house previous to her departure for New York last Wednesday. She said that she believed that from what she had gleaned concerning her niece's habits that Walter F. Conklin, of Paterson, was the seducer. She then drove to the Morgue and identified her niece. Thence she returned with a detective to the Central Office, and had an interview with the Inspector, to whom she repeated her story.

## JANE JOHNSON'S CONFESSION AT LAST.

At last the ends of justice seemed to be nearly attained. The servant girl confessed. She was removed to Bellevue Hospital on Wednesday night, as her condition demanded it, and the kindly offices of Warden Brennan were calculated to break down her obstinacy. On Thursday he was pre-eminently successful. Calling on her during the day, he obtained the following statement from her: On Wednesday, a young lady came in by the parlor door of No. 687 Second avenue, and went into the doctor's room. He took her up stairs to a private room on the second floor. Before she entered, the doctor had run in by the basement door, in a very great hurry, and met her as she entered. Before taking her up to the other room, he came to the kitchen and looked in at me. Then he retired, and shut the door after him. Immediately I opened it a little, and peeped out. There I saw the pair—doctor and young lady—going up the stairs. I remember the white lawn over-skirt looped up behind. She remained above during the evening, so far as I can judge, for, indeed, I never heard her go out. I asked Rosa, the doctor's daughter, who she was, and she said it was a patient who had called to see her father. I wanted to know if she had gone away the previous night, and Miss Rosa replied: "Oh! yes, she went away last night." "What," said I, "in all the rain?" "Yes," said Rosa, "her friends came with a coach, and, wrapping her up comfortably, took her away." "I should have thought there was danger of her taking cold." "Not at all," said Rosa. The first day that the lady was in the house Rosa went up stairs and remained there a long time. Her mother went up afterward, and came back to the kitchen in a short time to make a cup of tea, she said. This draught, made by herself, she handed to Rosa, who took it to the upper chamber. From what I could see, Miss Rosa and her mother waited on the lady. I did not mistrust anything, and, indeed, believed all was right, when Miss Rosa told me she had gone home with her friends. On Saturday Mrs. Rosenzweig told me to hurry up with my work, as she wanted me to get through by noon and take the children out to walk. This was such an unusual proceeding that I was delighted, and did my best to get ready. Miss Rosa went out at noon, and was absent about an hour and a half, returning at 1.30 o'clock. I remember nothing more of the circumstances until I recognized the comforter and baby's diaper, which were found in the trunk, as being the property of the Rosenzweig family. The other articles I never saw before.

### THE VICTIM'S PATERSON HOME AND HER PREVIOUS LIFE—SUICIDE OF HER ALLEGED SEDUCER.

The city of Paterson was intensely exiced last Thursday, first by the announcement in the morning papers that the victim was a Paterson girl, and later in the day by the report that the young man who had kept company with her before her disappearance had taken his own life, through fear of exposure and punishment.

At about 7 o'clock the news of the identification of Miss Bowlsby s remains was broken to her widowed mother by Drs. Parker and Kinne, who on the evening preceding had identified the body at the Morgue. The grief of the mother and the younger sisters was too terrible for words to express, a sense of disgrace and shame mingling with their sorrow for the loss of one whom they had loved as innocent and pure. For an entire week they had been in suspense, waiting for the news of Alice. Eight days previous she had left the house of her aunt, Mrs. Elizabeth L. Williams, in Newark, to return to her mother's house in Paterson. She did not arrive home on the day fixed, and inquiries were sent to Newark, for information of her. Word was returned that she had left Mrs. Williams' house, where she had been staying about three weeks, and ought to have arrived home on the preceding day. Then the search for the missing girl commenced. Her uncle, Mr. Charles E. Sandford, of Broadway, Paterson; her cousins, Henry Sandford and John Williams, of Newark; and Dr. Kinne, the family physician, gave nearly all their time for several days in endeavoring to trace her. A visit by young Sandford to the Morgue gave the first faint hope of success in finding her or learning her fate. He thought he recognized the body of the then unknown murdered girl, and the subsequent identification by Drs. Parker and Kinne, whom he induced to come to the Morgue, proved the correctness of his supposition.

### THE BEREAVED FRIENDS AND HOME.

The information was unexpected to Mrs. Bowlsby on Thursday morning, when she was informed of the identification of the body, for neither young Sandford nor the doctors had hinted their suspicions regarding the body at the Morgue to the bereaved mother. Friends and acquaintances dropped in to console her and the two young daughters in their terrible affliction. Occasionally a small crowd would gather in the street to look at the dwelling where the poor girl had spent the last years of her life. It is a small, two-story brick house, situated on West street, bearing the sign, " Mrs. Bowlsby, Dressmaking," in small, gilt letters. To this house the family removed ten years ago from Parsippany, upon the death of Mr. Bowlsby. Mrs. Bowlsby, with her three daughters, worked at dressmaking, Alice having been employed recently in an establishment at No. 163 Main street, over the office of Drs. Parker and Kinne. Alice and her sisters were esteemed by all who knew them, and not only Alice's mother, but all her acquaintances, believed her to be strictly virtuous. In answer to inquiries made on Thursday morning, the friends of the family stated that they could not say who was the seducer of Alice; they suspected a young man whose name would not be given until the inquest should be held. Dr. Parker was reluctant to give any information except that the murdered girl was well known to him as a pure, high-minded girl, whom he would never have suspected under any circumstances. He thought he could identify the man who had wronged her, but he believed that she had gone there alone, and that the man whom he suspected had nothing to do with the murder. The doctor exhibited a photograph of the deceased, a well-formed and intelligent looking blonde, with bright eyes, full lips and smiling face. The photograph agreed with the description given of her by the doctor and other friends of the deceased, and would

Opening of the MYSTERIOUS TRUNK, and horrible Discovery.

Deffnung des geheimnißvollen Koffers und schauerhafte Entdeckung.

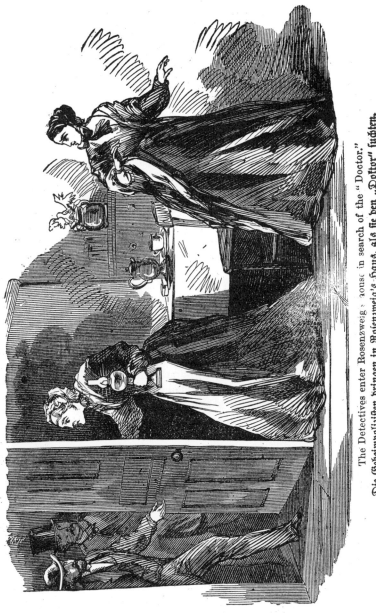

The Detectives enter Rosenzweig: iouse in search of the "Doctor."

Die Geheimpolizisten dringen in Rosenzweig's Haus, als sie den „Doktor" suchten.

indicate that she was what they pronounced her to be—a joyous good-natured girl, free of manner and fond of amusement, who had friends wherever she was known.

### THE GIRL'S DESTROYER.

Many stories were carried from one to another, giving the names of Miss Bowlsby's male friends. But it was, however, learned, by the statements of Mrs. Williams, of Newark, that Walter F. Conklin, the son of Alderman Conklin, had been very much attached to her, and had visited her at Mrs. Williams' house in Newark, three days before Alice left for New York. Mrs. Williams did not hesitate to say that he was responsible for Alice's misfortune. At 1 o'clock all the city was convinced that this supposition was correct. At that hour young Conklin committed suicide in Dale's Silk Mill, where he was employed. Conklin arrived at the mill early on Thursday morning, looking pale and nervous. He remained at his desk during the forenoon, conversing but little, and when spoken to concerning the absorbing sensation caused by the reports in the morning papers, he spoke of it as a matter of no consequence to him. At noon he did not go to dinner according to custom. While the other clerks were at dinner, one of the men employed in the mill heard the report of a pistol. He ran immediately to the office, but found no one, and continued his search, going into the large fire-proof room, where the most valuable silks were stored. On the floor he found Conklin's prostrate form. Blood was flowing from a wound back of the left ear, where the bullet entered. A revolver was found on the floor beside him. The man dragged the body out into the office and sent for physicians, at the same time sending information also to Alderman Conklin. When the physicians arrived they found that the wound was fatal, the ball having passed through to the temple, where it lodged. The dying man did not move. Within half an hour he was dead. Coroner Butterworth was immediately summoned and viewed the body. In one of the pockets was found the following note in young Conklin's handwriting:

I have long had a morbid idea of the worthlessness of life, and now to be obliged to testify in this affair and cause unpleasantness in my family is more than life is worth. Good by, dear father, mother, brother and sister.        WALT.

In his pocket a card was found on which was written, in his own hand "115 E. 24th st."

### INQUEST ON THE SUICIDE.

Coroner Butterworth immediately impanelled a jury and commenced an inquest. The testimony of the physician, the workmen at the mill, and others cognizant of facts connected with the shooting, was taken, after which the jury rendered a verdict that the deceased came to his death by his own hand.

## THE INQUEST AT BELLEVUE HOSPITAL.

The inquest on the body of Alice Augusta Bowlsby was held on Friday by Coroner Schirmer at Bellevue Hospital. The following jury was empanelled : Samuel W. Baldwin, No. 162 West Forty-fourth street; Charles McLacklin, No. 11 Park Row; Welcome Alexander, Bellevue Hospital; Adolph E. George, No. 118 Third avenue; Duncan C. Lee, Bellevue Hospital; Thomas C. Wilson, No. 107 King street; Peter G. Standish, No. 853 Third avenue. At about 10 A. M. Rosenzweig was brought in, accompanied by his counsel, Mr. Howe. He was a little paler than usual, and somewhat nervous in his behaviour. A large number of spectators were present, and others crowded around the doors to hear the testimony. Before beginning to hear the examination, Coroner Schirmer took out the jurors to view the body, which was then only a loathsome, putrid mass of flesh. The first witness called was Dr. Theodore Y. Kinne, a practising physician in Paterson, New Jersey.

### TESTIMONY OF DR. KINNE.

Q. Go on, doctor, and tell what you know about this case. A. My attention was first drawn to this case by seeing the reports in the Sunday and Monday papers of this city, coupled with the fact that a young lady patient of mine had mysteriously disappeared; the resemblance to this person in the account led me to suspect that the two were identical; I consulted with Dr. Parker, a dentist occupying rooms in the same building, No. 163 Main street, and, on Tuesday morning, the 29th, I came to Bellevue Hospital to view the body; the warden directed me to the room, where I found the corpse with only the face and head exposed; I found two marks upon the face which seemed to justify my suspicion, one being a scar upon the right side of the jaw, and the missing right eye tooth; I think I had with me the photographs of the young lady for whom I was searching, which I showed to the warden, to see if he could detect any similarity between them and the body the day it was found; he was not satisfied with the resemblance, and I returned to Paterson for further proof; in company with Dr. Parker, I visited Mrs. Bowlsby, the mother of the girl, and obtained other evidence which would be conclusive; Wednesday afternoon, the 30th, I visited Bellevue Hospital with Dr. Parker, and on presenting the proofs to Warden Brennan we were permitted to view the body, and identified it fully as Miss Alice Augusta Bowlsby.

### THE VERDICT.

We find that Alice Augusta Bowlsby came to her death by metroperitonitis, the result of an abortion produced, as we believe from the testimony, by Jacob Rosenzweig, between the 23d and 26th of August, 1871, at No. 687 Second avenue.

Coroner Schirmer (turning to the prisoner, who arose).—You will act your pleasure in answering the questions I am about to ask you.

Mr. Howe.—He will answer any question you may ask him.
Q. What is your name? A. Jacob Rosenzweig.
Q. How old are you? A. Thirty-nine years.
Q. Of what nationality are you? A. I am a Pole.
Q. Where do you live? A. At No. 687 Second avenue.
Q. What is your business? A. I am a physician.
Q. You have heard the verdict of the jury; have you any answer to make against the charge?

Mr. Howe.—The prisoner has a perfect answer to the accusation, and believes that before the calm deliberations of a legal tribunal he can make a perfect defence. He believes that a great deal of the testimony admitted here has been illegally admitted; but with that you have nothing to do. In regard to the atrocities and to this abortion charged upon him, he gives an emphatic denial, and declares that he is not guilty.

The prisoner was then committed to the Tombs to await the action of the Grand Jury.

The writ of *habeas corpus* in favor of Rosenzweig was not served on Friday, inasmuch as it was merely designed to procure his release on bail in case the coroner had seen fit to postpone the inquest. Another writ was obtained from Judge Jones with a view to secure the discharge of Rosa Rosenzweig, the doctor's daughter, but the coroner released her at the close of the investigation.

The police authorities endeavored to accumulate further evidence on Friday, but without material success. Professional pride dictated that the woman who so daringly guarded the trunk at the depot should be traced and arrested, but further effort in this direction was generally felt to be useless. Not a clue remained of the many that had been perseveringly followed to a disappointing conclusion. A long search was made among Rosenzweig's relatives, but none were found to resemble the woman described by the boy Potts.

The efforts to arrest Mrs. Rosenzweig were discontinued, it being very well determined that she would testify only in her husband's defence. The testimony of other witnesses was found to be needless, and the Jew peddler, arrested in the house, was therefore discharged from custody.

#### THE DESOLATED PATERSON HOMES.

Both the Bowlsby and Conklin houses were closed on Friday, and ew except sympathizing friends called upon the families. Walter F Conklin's body was placed in a coffin and removed on Thursday evening to his father's house at Water and North Main streets, after the remains had been viewed by a great number of the inhabitants of Paterson.

#### DISCOVERY OF FURTHER LINKS IN THE CHAIN OF EVIDENCE.

More evidence proving the identity of Alice Bowlsby, and establishing the guilt of the monster Rosenzweig, was discovered on Saturday. Ser-

-geant Rooney, in searching the house of Rosenzweig, at No. 687 Second avenue, found a false bosom, such as is used by women. Taking it, with other female wearing apparel, to the servant girl, Jane Johnson, now at Bellevue Hospital, he asked Jane if it belonged to her. Jane said that it did not, and was not in the house before the strange young lady came. The bosom was taken back to the Eighteenth Precinct Station-house, and Captain Cameron sent an officer to Paterson, to the home of the murdered girl, to ascertain if the bosom had been her property. Her mother, Mrs Bowlsby, identified it at once as having been made in her house, and worn by her daughter. It will be used as circumstantial evidence against Rosenzweig. Captain Cameron also sent the boy Potts, and the truckman William Pickett, to identify a fortune-teller, Mrs. Bailey, in Paterson, who was suspected to have been the one who accompanied the trunk to the depot, and exhibited so much coolness about the horrrible business. The suspected woman, however, could not be identified, and she has so far baffled every attempt at discovery.

## THE ABORTIONIST'S BAYARD STREET HOUSE.

The neighborhood of the house, at No. 98 Bayard street, was visited by a reporter last Saturday, and it being the Jewish Sabbath, the win-dows of the butcher were closed, though the door was open. About a dozen persons, male and female, were in front of the house, and through the open door of the shop the wife of Rosenzweig, his daughter Rosa, mother, and brothers, were seen moving about. Mrs. Rosenzweig had her bonnet on, as though she might have just come in; and the daughter Rosa was smiling and showing no outward signs of sorrow for the present rather uncomfortable position of her father. The drug-clerk, in the store opposite, told the reporter that "Dr." Rosenzweig had frequently got medicine there, always coming himself for it, but his employer being ab-sent, he could not tell what he got when he came. He said, also, that owing to the large number of Polish Jews living in the neighborhood, Rosenzweig did a large business in that vicinity.

## FUNERAL OF WALTER CONKLIN.

On Saturday the funeral of Walter Conklin took place at the resi-dence of his father, No. 8 North Main street, Paterson. Only a few of he friends of the family were present. Rev. Dr. Banvard, pastor of the First Baptist Church, to which the family belong, preached the funeral sermon. The remains were placed in the receiving vault of Cedar Lawn Cemetery.

## ROSENZWEIG'S GUILT

The chain of circumstantial evidence against "Dr." Jacob Rosenzweig, alias Ascher, is very strong, but the unfortunate failure of the police to secure the woman who engaged the truckman, Pickett, will leave the prosecution without any witness who can positively swear that the acoused performed the operation which resulted in Alice Bowlsby's death. The principal points thus far established are as follows:

*First.* The discovery of the dead body with unmistakable indications that an abortion had been committed.

*Second.* The removal of the trunk containing the remains from the house of Rosenzweig, on Second avenue.

*Third.* The identification of Rosenzweig by the truckman as his assistant in transferring the trunk from the basement to the truck.

*Fourth.* The identification of the remains by the Paterson physicians.

*Fifth.* The discovery of the sash and marked handkerchief in Rosenzweig's house.

*Sixth.* The identification of the clothes in the trunk by the servant.

*Seventh.* Rosenzweig's application to the undertaker on Saturday morning to bury a servant girl.

*Eighth.* Rosenzweig's bad character, suspicious practice, and numerous aliases.

The non-identification of the remains was to have been made the principal point in Rosenzweig's favor, but the appearance of the Paterson physicians demolished that defence.

It is expected that the defence will now be based upon the absence of witnesses to the abortion. Rosenzweig must have been instructed upon this point by his counsel, as whenever he is pressed he exclaims: " Who saw me kill her? no one saw me operate on her."

#### THE REMAINS OF ALICE AUGUSTA.

The body of Alice Augusta Bowlsby was quietly buried on Hart's Island at 5 o'clock Saturday-morning. Her friends sent word during the day asking that her remains be forwarded to Paterson for interment.

## THE SISTER AND MOTHER OF THE MURDERED GIRL IN COURT.—PRODUC-TION OF THE HORRIBLE TRUNK.

THE trial of Jacob Rosenzweig, for causing the leath of Alice Augusta Bowlsby, of Paterson, N. J., by means of an abortion, was commenced October 26, n the Court of General Sessions, before Recorder Hackett. Mr. William F. Howe, the prisoner's counsel, was early on hand. His junior associate sat beside him, while at the left hand side of both, the principal in the trial,

ROSENZWEIG,

surnamed the man with the colossal cranium, occupied a seat. District Attorney Garvin was in attendance, and sat composedly interweaving his fingers, while his able assistant, Algernon S. Sullivan, was leaning back on a chair, reflecting the light of his brilliant orbs on the frontispiece of his associate, Garvin.

Recorder Hackett surveyed the entire scene from the elevation of the bench, and listened attentively as the District Attorney prepared to deliver his opening address to the jury, who were in their places shortly after the Court room was opened. The horrible trunk, in which was packed for transportation the remains of the unfortunate Miss Bowlsby, was brought into Court, and kept to be put in as evidence against the accused. It is an ordinary-sized trunk, and apparently almost new. It was tied round with a rope, the same as when its contents were inspected at the depot of the Hudson River Railroad.

At a quarter past ten, ex-Judge Garvin arose and proceeded to address the twelve men sitting in judgment on the wretched prisoner. He briefly recapitulated the enormity of the crime charged, and stated to the jury what he expected to prove on the part of the people. The prosecution would prove that the deceased left her aunt's house in Newark on the 23d of August, 1871, and that she entered the dark, fearful den of the accused. They would also prove that she was never seen alive after entering this den. Her body was afterwards sent from the house in the trunk, then lying under the stenographer's desk, but none of her clothing was found upon it. They would be able to show by the medical testimony from what cause Miss Bowlsby died.

### TESTIMONY OF MRS. BOWLSBY.

Mrs. Bowlsby, the mother of the unfortunate Alice, was called as the first witness for the people. Witness briefly described the apparel of her daughter on the day she left to come to this city. After which she continued:—She also had a handkerchief with her, marked " A. Bowlsby," and a small basket containing some little trinkets; I never heard anything from or of my child after she left, until the body was recognized by Dr. Kenny at the Morgue; the deceased had a mole on the left side of her neck, and a vaccination on her left arm just above the elbow; on the left side of her jaw there was a scar caused from an ulcerated tooth which had broken off; there was also an eye tooth missing on the right side of her mouth.

At the conclusion of this testimony, the counsel for Rosenzweig proceeded to cross-examine
The Witness.—I did not see the handkerchief my daughter took away with her on the 23d of August. I knew all her handkerchiefs from the mark of " A. Bowlsby;" she wore a false bosom, or pads, at the time of leaving; the bosom was the same as very many ladies wear; Alice was the eldest of my children; her age was twenty-five.

In reply to the District Attorney.—There was a

young gentleman who used to keep company with my daughter; his name was Mr. Walter Conklin; he died on a Thursday; I don't remember the date; he committed suicide by shooting himself; he used to frequently visit the house; I do not know whether they were engaged or not.

### MISS CARRIE BOWLSBY,

the sister of the deceased, generally corroborated the testimony given by her mother. She recognized the pads shown as the ones made by her sister out of material belonging to a dress.

### JANE JOHNSON, THE SERVANT GIRL OF THE PRISONER,

was placed next on the stand.—Have lived with Dr. Rosenzweig; I was doing housework in the doctor's house; about the time of the trunk trouble, the parties living in the house were, the prisoner and his wife, her four children and myself; there was a young girl also; she was not living there, but she used to be there a great deal; her name was Nettie; I don't know her last name; the deceased came there with the prisoner on the 23d inst.; I saw her going up stairs; the Doctor, I think, went up with her; I never saw her after; I know that the woman called Nettie knew that the woman in white, the deceased, was in the house.

The trunk was here shown. The witness said she either saw that trunk, or one like it, in the kitchen previous to the visit of the deceased. I heard that the lady in white was a patient of the Doctor's; I heard it from Rosie, the prisoner's daughter; the trunk that looked like the one shown in Court belonged to the woman Nettie, who so often visited the house.

### WILLIAM PICKETT,

of No. 471 First Avenue, the carman who was hired to carry the trunk to the Hudson River depot, testified that on Saturday, the 26th of August, he took a trunk from the house of the prisoner; a young woman came to his stand and wanted him to take a trunk from Thirty-seventh street and Second Avenue to the Hudson River depot; he took the trunk from 687 Second Avenue; this same woman, accompanied by a boy, whose name he afterwards heard was Potts, met him at the depot when he arrived there with the trunk; a man opened the door, and I told him that I called for a trunk to take to Twenty-ninth street; the man then took hold of one end and helped to lift the trunk on the cart; that is the trunk (pointing to the one in court), and that man (pointing to the prisoner, Rosenzweig) is the man that helped me t carry the trunk; he is the man; he never spoke word; when we arrived at the depot, the boy assisted me to set the trunk on the counter to get it checked, afterwards the woman helped also; she looked at the lock on the trunk, and said she was afraid it would not hold; a strap was then put round it, for which the woman paid a dollar; I then went away. The witness recognized a boy shown him in Court as the one who helped him with the trunk at the depot.

The witness was cross-examined at considerable length, but it failed to shake his evidence.

### ALEXANDER POTTS,

the boy who assisted in carrying the trunk into the depot, was placed on the stand. He testified as follows:—I live at 429 Eighth Avenue; I carry baggage for a living, and remember being on Thirtieth street on Saturday, the 26th of August; I met a wo

man on that day; she came in a cab; I recognize the
carman; the woman asked me if I knew anything
about the trains; she came ten minutes before the
man with the truck; she bought a ticket for Chicago
at half-past four; I would know the trunk I helped
to carry to the depot if I saw it.

Q. Is that the trunk? (the trunk in[Court was here
shown the witness.) A. Yes, sir, that is the trunk I
saw; the baggage man checked the trunk for Chicago, and gave her a ticket for the same place; I afterwards saw the trunk opened, and saw a naked dead
ody; the body was squeezed in the trunk; the body
was lying on its side and doubled up.

PETER MURPHY,

a police officer, sworn:—The baggage master called
my attention to a trunk lying outside on the platform; we opened the trunk and found the body of a
woman wrapped in some blankets and .other things;
I reported at the station house, and then delivered the
body at Bellevue Hospital.

THOMAS S. BRENNAN.

Warden in Bellevue Hospital, identified the trunk as
the one that was brought to the dead house; Drs.
Henry and Parker examined the body twice; they
had a photograph of the deceased.

DR. JOSEPH F. PARKER

was the next witness. He said he was a dentist at
Paterson, knew Mrs. Bowlsby, and accompanied Dr.
Kenny to the Morgue, when they identified the body
as being that of Miss Bowlsby; he saw the mark of
vaccination, the mole and the cicatrix formed by an
ulcerated tooth on the right side of the lower jaw; he
found the eye tooth gone, broken off, which he had
seen about two months before in the mouth of Miss
Bowlsby, whose dentist the witness had been for five
years.

JAMES F. BOYD,

an undertaker, doing business at 336 East Thirty-fifth
street, testified that on the Saturday morning before
the body was found at the depot, the prisoner, Rosenzweig, came to him and said that a servant girl of his
had died, and asked how much it would cost to bury
her; witness asked him where she was, and the prisoner replied, "Not far away from here," but he did
not state where; he said she was very poor, and had
about $10; the prisoner asked him if he could take
the body of this girl to his store, and he told him
that he could not; that he (the prisoner) would first
have to get a certificate from the doctor; the prisoner
said the doctor lived away down town; he went out,
and said he would call again.

OFFICER LARUE

testified that he went with Pickett, the carman, to
Rosenzweig's house in search of the girl who had
charge of the trunk at the depot, but could not find
her; on Wednesday, the 30th of August, the officer
searched for clothing, and found in a stationary wash-
tub in the back basement of the prisoner's house, a
handkerchief marked "A. A. Bowlsby," with a lot of
children's clothing and ladies' wearing apparel; Sergeant Randall found a blue sash in a bureau drawer
up stairs, and also some jewelry—two ladies' watches,
chains, breastpins, and rings—which were returned
to Mrs. Rosenzweig.

OFFICER RANDALL

testified that he found a blue sash, and also the false
bosom, which he marked at the time; the bosom he
found in a barrel of old clothing in the kitchen; part
of a bloody chemise and a skirt were found in the cellar, covered over with dirt.

PIERRE C. RICHARDS,

a house agent, was sworn to establish the fact that

Rosenzweig had lived in the house 687 Second Avenue since the 1st of May.

DR. JOSEPH CUSHMAN

testified that he made a post-mortem examination of
the body of Alice Augusta Bowlsby, at the Morgue,
on Sunday, the 27th of August; the body was 5 feet
3 inches long, and well developed; the hair was
blonde and the eyes blue; there were no external
marks of violence. In the Doctor's opinion, death
resulted from metro-peritonitis, caused by abortion.

THE DEFENCE.

William F. Howe, the indefatigable counsel for
Rosenzweig, then proceeded in an able and exhaustive argument to open the case for the defence, and
in an argument of great length said that the crime
imputed to the prisoner was fiendish in the extreme,
and might well be hurled back against those who
had charged him with a fiendish crime—a crime so
full of revolting circumstances that humanity must
shrink at it aghast.

MEDICAL TESTIMONY.

Drs. Garrish and Parker were called for the defence, and gave testimony upon more technical questions on obstetrics, that served very little to elucidate
the main point at issue.

ANOTHER MRS. BOWLSBY.

The next witness called for the defence was a
demure-looking female, aged about thirty, who said
her name was Mrs. Cornelia Bowlsby; she lived in
Myrtle avenue, Brooklyn; I am married and have
six children; one of my children is named Anna
Martini Bowlsby; she is now married; she is sick
now and not here, but was here on Monday; she had

A POCKET HANDKERCHIEF

marked; I visited you (counsel) at your office recently, and afterwards went to the Districts Attorney's office to see the handkerchief marked "A. M.
Bowlsby;" I would know that handkerchief.

The handkerchief was here shown the witness,
who pronounced it the same as the one she had seen
in the District Attorney's office.

It is somewhat dirtier than when I first saw it; I
should say that

THE LETTERS ON THE CORNER OF THAT HANDKER-
CHIEF

were A. M., with the M partially rubbed out, also a
B, which is partially obscured; I don't know how
my daughter marked her handkerchiefs; we visited
Dr. Rosenzweig's on the 7th of August, the Thursday before my daughter was married; we had some
wine at the doctor's house; my daughter got some
wine on her gloves and took them off and wiped her
hand with her handkerchief; we read of the finding
of the handkerchief in the newspapers, and my
daughter then said

SHE WOULD BET

the handkerchief spoken of was hers.
Cross-examined—My husband's given name is
William Henry; we are not related to the Bowlsbys
of Jersey; we never heard of them previous to this
trial; I did not see my daughter marking her handkerchief; I did not make known what I knew about

THIS HANDKERCHIEF

until Mrs. Rosenzweig came to my house; that was,
I think, about three weeks ago; I did not give her
any satisfaction; I did not notice particularly, what
kind of a handkerchief my daughter had at the Rosenzweig's, only, that it was a very common one.
(Several questions were asked of the witness, and
the latter endeavored to equivocate. In fact she

persistently, wilfully affected to misunderstand the queries put to her.) A man came to our house in Brooklyn just before my daughter got married, and wanted to sell some steneil plates; he marked one handkerchief for my daughter—marked it A. M. Bowlsby; he marked it in the hall; I was in the basement at the time; I know he marked it; this was the only one that was marked.

### TESTIMONY OF JACOB COHEN.

Mr. Cohen examined :—I was sick on the Saturday the trunk was found at the railroad depot; I sent for Dr. Rosenzweig, who came to me at about half-past twelve; he sat two or three hours with me, as I was very sick.

Cross-examined :—I do not recollect what date it was, but I know two or three days afterwards the doctor was arrested; I am a cigar and cigarette manufacturer; I was sick at my house, which is some distance from Mr. Rosenzweig's house; the doctor was with me nearly all the time he staid, with the exception of going back and forth to the store in front.

After some unimportant testimony as to the reputation and character of the prisoner,

### ROSENZWEIG WAS PUT UPON THE STAND.

He testified as follows :—I am a physician; I reside at 687 Second avenue; I graduated in Warsaw; I came to this country in 1865; I established my business in this country at 33 Bayard street; I know the Bowlsbys of Brooklyn; I have known them about six or seven months; I never did know the Bowlsbys of Paterson; I have heard all the testimony that has been given in this Court; my wife and daughter are in Court; never saw the girl Nellie Willis now in Court, at No. 3 Amity place, within a year or two, and never performed an abortion upon her; he also emphatically stated that the undertaker's testimony was all false; that he never said anything about a servant girl being dead near by; he did not know a woman named Nettie staying in his house on Friday or Saturday nights, and when Jane Johnson swore to that she testified to what was not true. Before he left the stand Rosenzweig said, he never performed an abortion at any place in the city of New York, nor did he know of any woman being brought to his house, dead or alive, during the week of the alleged occurrence who had any operation performed upon her.

The counsel, at a quarter past ten, proceeded to address the jury on behalf of the accused. He (the counsel) would show, when he came to direct the attention of the jury to the evidence, that the District Attorney had failed completely to prove anything against his client. They (the defence) contended, first,

### THE BODY TAKEN TO THE MORGUE

was not that of Alice Augusta Bowlsby. The jury must have in their minds some doubt as to the identity of the body found in the trunk with that of the missing girl, the murdered Alice A. Bowlsby. The jury must have a doubt of this, because the mother of the deceased herself had. The counsel continued at considerable length, endeavoring to interpret the testimony in a favorable light for the wretched man who was his client, but the effort was a total failure. He

### CONCLUDED

with a Tombs Police Court appeal to the jury to have pity on the wife and children of the prisoner, whom the jury would deprive of a natural protector, etc., if they concluded to convict. He concluded at a quarter to twelve, at which time District Attorney Garvin arose to argue the case on behalf of the people.

### AFTERNOON PROCEEDINGS.

District Attorney Garvin commenced his address by depicting in elegant language the enormity of the crime with which the prisoner stood charged. After this he ably recapitulated the bits of evidence that together made so conclusive the guilt of Rosenzweig. He explained to the jury the temptations to which young girls, who have an inheritance of beauty which is more

### DANGEROUS TO THEIR PEACE OF MIND

afterward than anything else they may possess, are subjected day by day until they arrive at womanhood, and after they arrive at that period, they meet one whom they love. They are importuned, caressed, and in a moment of thoughtlessness they fall—their ruin is consummated. The vile seducer has no responsibility, his victim

### DARE NOT DENOUNCE HIM

because by so doing she lays herself open to the cold criticism and sarcasm of an unsympathetic world. She dare not talk to her father. She cannot to her mother. She will not divulge the secret grief that is gnawing at her heart to her sister, and her brother, if she has one, is not approachable. Her seducer has forsaken her, and walks erect among his fellow men in comparative security. What then is

### THE POOR VICTIM

to do? To whom will she fly for relief? She takes up a newspaper, runs her eyes up one column and down another. The advertisements of such fiends as the prisoner arrest her attention, stating that his business is the relieving girls of their troubles in this way. She goes to him in a moment of desperation, and is lost! Her cold corpse is the result. How many

### SLEEPLESS NIGHTS

testify to the agony of mind of the seduced girl previous to taking the fatal determination of consulting these hell-hounds called abortionists; when she knows and calculates with horror that every day brings her nearer shame? O, what a fate is this! How many unfortunate, erring women have died lingering agonizing deaths at the hands of these Dr. Aschers, who sticks a sign out in

### A DARK ALLEY,

and allures the miserable into his lair? This man practices abortions in Amity place as Dr. Ascher; he keeps a place in Second avenue as Dr. Rosenzweig for a respectable business. If he is discovered in his vile doings, it is Dr. Ascher that is arrested, and not Dr. Rosenzweig. Does not this speak for itself? The learned gentleman then

### WENT ON TO ANALYZE THE EVIDENCE,

and draw deductions applicable to the points of the case.

When Judge Garvin concluded, Recorder Hackett charged the jury. The counsel for Rosenzweig read several points which he requested the Recorder to incorporate in his charge, which was done with three exceptions.

### THE CHARGE

of his Honor was an elaborte and lengthy one, and thoroughly exhaustive. The case was given to the jury at precisely nine minutes after two o'clock, who retired to deliberate, and did not return up to three o'clock.

### THE VERDICT.

The jury returned at twenty minutes to four, with a verdict of guilty of manslaughter in the second degree. Recorder Hackett then sentenced him to the State Prison at hard labor for seven years. He regretted that the penalty was not death.

Charles K. Landis, the developer of Vineland and a leading citizen of
Cumberland County, enraged at being excoriated weekly by Uri Carruth in the *Vineland Independent*, stormed into the newspaper's com-
posing room and shot its editor on March 19, 1875. Carruth died a year
later due to complications resulting from his head wound, and Landis
was brought to trial for murder. But after a protracted trial, Landis was
found innocent by reason of temporary insanity. Above is a view of the
shooting, from the New York *Daily Graphic*, March 27, 1875.

# ,MURDERS IN PRINT

PRIMARILY THIS IS A BIBLIOGRAPHY of separate publications (1692–1901) relating to murders in or associated with New Jersey. Its boundaries, however, have been stretched to include a few later accounts, and also one near-murder in 1878. Not covered are a couple of manslaughter cases and two pamphlets about a Cooperstown, New York, killing, which bear New Jersey imprints of 1805 and 1806.

The introductory narratives and nearly all of the bibliographical entries have been prepared directly from the murder publications, or copies. For a few that have not been examined, the descriptions are based (with due note) on those in the *National Union Catalog* or Thomas McDade's *The Annals of Murder*. For this and many other reasons the compiler is much indebted to McDade and his *Annals*.

The libraries holding copies of these publications are identified by *National Union Catalog* designations:

Henry E. Huntington Library (CSmH), Connecticut Historical Society (CtHi), Yale University (CtY), Georgetown University (DGU), Library of Congress (DLC), National Library of Medicine (DNLM), University of Georgia (GU), Northwestern University (IEN), Kansas State University (KMK), Boston Athenaeum (MBAt or MBA), Harvard University (MH), Massachusetts Historical Society (MHi), American Antiquarian Society (MWA), University or Minnesota (MnU), University of Missouri (MoU), New York State Library (N), New-York Historical Society (NHi), Cornell University (NIC), New York Public Library (NN), Schomburg Collection (NN-Sc), Association of the Bar, New York (NNB), Fordham University (NNF), New York University (NNU), Duke University (NcD), New Jersey State Library (Nj), New Jersey Historical Society (NjHi), Jersey City Free Public Library (NjJ), Joint Free Public Library of Morristown and Morris Township (NjMo), Washington Headquarters Association, Morristown (HjMoW), Newark Public

Library (NjN), Princeton University (NjP), Rutgers University (NjR), Fairleigh Dickinson University, Rutherford (NjRuF), Historical Society of Pennsylvania (PHi), Free Library of Philadelphia (PP), Library Company of Philadelphia (PPL), Brown University (RPB), University of Virginia (ViU), University of Washington (WaU). An appended "L" means Law Library.

## GEORGE ACKER

With its intermittent lecturing on the evils of drink, this pamphlet is virtually a temperance tract. Its message is based on Isaac H. Gordon's murder near Montville, where the local folk, it seems, spent much of their time at the bar. Among the drinkers crowding Provost's hotel on the afternoon of October 18, 1859, were two canal workers, both well into their cups—George Acker and Isaac H. Gordon, the latter boasting drunkenly that he had considerable cash. On the road later, Acker, bent on robbery, hit him with a rock, dragged him into the brush, and cut his throat, returning at night to bury the body in a sandpit. There it was found on October 26, and Acker was soon arrested. He confessed between his trial and March 1860 hanging.

> Acker, George, 1826-60.
> Life and confession of Geo. Acker, the murderer of Isaac H. Gordon. The trial, sentence, and an appeal to young men; to which also is added the astounding disclosures of the celebrated chemist, Dr. Cox, on the adulteration of liquors, their poisonous compounds, the tests, etc. . . . [New York: Baker & Godwin, printers, 1860]
> cover-title, 51, [1]p. 23cm. DLC MH NHi
> Copyrighted 1860 by Frederick Stone (cf. p. 49).
> Letterpress (incl. port., map) on covers.
> "From my lonely cell I submit these, my sober second-thoughts, to the public, hoping that it may avail something for the support of a wife and four children left in poverty. . . ."

## JESSE AND STEPHEN BOORN

Notwithstanding the lack of a *corpus delicti*, it was believed around Manchester, Vermont, that Jesse and Stephen Boorn had killed their brother-in-law, Russell Colvin, who disappeared in 1812, "a man of weak intellect, and . . . at times insane." Pressure on the Boorns (themselves apparently rather weak-minded) produced confused statements, inconsistent confessions, and a trial in November 1819. The guilty verdict "gave unqualified satisfaction to the crowds in attendance," but one doubter advertised for news of Colvin, who soon was found working on a farm in Dover Township, N.J. While "so com-

pletely insane as not to be able to give a satisfactory account of himself," he was identified properly and the Boorn brothers' ordeal ended.

**Sargeant, Leonard, 1793-1880.**
The trial, confessions, and conviction of Jesse and Stephen Boorn, for
the murder of Russell Colvin, and the return of the man supposed to
have been murdered. By Hon. Leonard Sargeant. Ex-lieut governor of
Vermont. Manchester, Vt.: Journal book and job office, 1873.
48p. 23cm. MH-L MWA NHi NNB NjR

Appendix (p.[27]-48) contains indictment and evidence.
There are several earlier publications on the case, all from 1820. Sargeant was
defense counsel at the 1819 trial.


# WILLIAM BRIGSTOCK

In a mutiny led by boatswain's mate William Brigstock aboard the
British armed frigate *Hermione* near Puerto Rico, September 20,
1797, an officer died. The mutineers stole a few things, then delivered
the ship to officers of the Spanish king, "now at war with his . . .Bri-
tannic Majesty." Six months later Brigstock and two of the others appeared on a ship lying at Perth Amboy. They were arrested and jailed
in New Brunswick, Brigstock indicted for murder and all three for
piracy. On June 28, "in obedience to the special command of the President of the United States," Brigstock (an American) was released, his
charges dropped. This pamphlet contains all the pertinent 1798 docu-
ments, in copies certified March 1, 1800. Its purpose is not stated.

**Brigstock, William, defendant.**
. . . The United States, (a.) William Brigstock, otherwise called John
Johnston. Indictment for murder. [New Brunswick, N.J.: Printed by
Abraham Blauvelt? 1800]
8,[7]p. 23cm. DLC MWA NN NjP NjR (copy) PPL

Caption title.
At head of title: Circuit Court of the United States, Middle Circuit of the
New-Jersey District.


# JOEL CLOUGH

Mrs. Elizabeth Longstreth kept the public-house in Bordentown
where Joel Clough, a stonemason, had lived since June 1831. He was a
sober, gentlemanly young man whose misfortune was to fall in love
with the landlady's daughter, Mary Hamilton. The latter, widowed
about the time of Clough's arrival, turned the proverbial deaf ear to
him. Already she had refused to marry him, but on April 6, 1833, he

proposed a second time. Again she turned him down, whereupon Clough produced an ivory-handled dagger, stabbed her repeatedly, then attempted to kill himself by taking poison. No more successful was his brief escape from jail shortly before the hanging. That public event, on July 26, entertained an unusually large body of spectators.

Clough, Joel, 1804–33.
   The authentic confession of Joel Clough, the murderer of Mrs. Mary W. Hamilton. With an extract of a letter to his mother. Chief Justice Hornblowers charge to the jury, sentence of death, &c. Also an account of his escape from prison, his recapture, and execution. Philadelphia: Copy-righted, and published by order of the sheriff of Burlington County. And for sale . . . by Robert P. Desilver, 1833.
   22p., 1 leaf. 20½cm. NHi NjHi NjR PHi PPL

————.
   Confession, of Joel Clough, who was executed at Mount Holly N.J. July 26, 1833, for the murder of Mrs. Mary W. Hamilton, with his life, written by one that knew him; also his last speech at the gallows, taken in short hand by a spectator, with likeness, and verse on the death of Mrs. Hamilton. New-York: Printed and sold wholesale and retail, No. 5, Chatham square, upstairs, and at J. Scarlets, No. 8, Market street, Philadelphia, also by W. Applegate, 257 Hudson Street, 1833.
   2p.l.,3-6[1]p. illus. (incl. port.) 22cm. DLC NHi NjR (copy)
   Text begins on verso of title-leaf.

————.
   Last words and dying speech of Joel Clough, executed at Mount-Holy [sic], July 26th 1833. For the murder of Mary W. Hamilton, together with the trial. Philadelphia: Published by W. Johnson, 1833.
   8p. illus. 24½cm. NjR (copy) PHi

————.
   The only true and authentic life and confession of Joel Clough; containing his life and confession, from 14 years of age, anecdotes, letters, escape, capture, &c. Written by himself . . . Philadelphia: Robert Desilver [1833]
   24p. illus. 21½cm. MH-L
   McDade 187.

————.
   Report of the trial of Joel Clough, on an indictment for the murder of Mrs. Mary W. Hamilton, before Chief Justice Hornblower, and four associate judges, at Mount Holly, New Jersey, in June 1833. Counsel for the state.—John Moore White, esq. Attorney General; Hon. Samuel L. Southard; and Joseph Warren Scott, esq. For the defendant.—David Paul Brown, esq. of Philadelphia; Isaac Hazelhurst, and George Cambloss, esq'rs. Boston: Published by Beals, Homer & Co., 1833.
   48p. 21cm. DLC MHi MoU-L NNB HjHi NjJ NjR (copy)

————.

The trial and sentence of Joel Clough; who was executed on the 26th July, 1833, for the murder of Mary W. Hamilton, of Bordentown, N.J. Philadelphia: Sold wholesale and retail by J. Scarlet, No. 8 Market Street; New-York: and No. 5 Chatham Square [1833]
17p. incl. port. 21cm. NNB NjR (copy)

————.

Trial of Joel Clough, on indictment for the murder of Mary W. Hamilton, before the Burlington Oyer & Terminer and Circuit. Chief-Justice Hornblower, presiding, and four associate judges. New-York: Published by William Stodart, 1833.
70p. 16½cm. MH-L NHi NjHi NjR (copy) PP PPL

————.

Trial, sentence, confession and execution of Joel Clough, who was executed on the 26th July, for the wilful murder of Mrs. Mary Hamilton, at Bordentown, N. Jerse [sic] on the 6th of April, 1833. Also an account of his escape from prison a few days previous to his execution. New-York: Printed and sold . . . by Christian Brown [1833]
27,[1]p. illus. 20cm. MWA
McDade 191.

————.

Lippincott, Joseph P.
A history of the famous Joel Clough murder case, tried in Burlington County courts in June, 1833. Compiled from data in possession of Joseph P. Lippincott, esq., of Mount Holly . . . Mount Holly, N.J.: Dispatch Press [1894]
cover-title, 20p. 21cm. NjR
Errata slip inserted.

Courtroom scene, from *Harper's Weekly* (March 26, 1870).

## MARY COLE

The quiet of a cold winter's night in rural Lafayette Township was broken, just days before Christmas 1811, when Mary Cole slashed the throat of her mother, Agnes Thuers. Mary's husband, roused by the noise, took no part in the killing but did help bury the victim. In the cellar was a previously dug hole. Mrs. Theurs's corpse remained there for two months before renters of the Cole house found her putrefying body. Cornelius and Mary Cole were arrested "in a retired place" and tried. She was hanged for committing the crime; he was imprisoned for concealing it. It was revealed that Agnes Thuers, among other offenses, had insisted for a year on sharing their bed.

Cole, Mary (Thuers) 1790–1812.
The confession of Mary Cole, who was executed on Friday, 26th June; at Newton, Sussex County, N.J., for the murder of Agnes Teaurs, her mother. New-York: Printed for the purchasers [1812]
12p. illus. 20cm. NHi NjR (copy)
The spelling "Teaurs" used throughout.

——————.
[Same title] [n.p.] 1812.
8p. illus. 19½cm. DLC NjR (copy)
Text is same as in the preceding, but from a different typesetting.

Kirn, John W.
A genuine sketch of the trial of Mary Cole, for the wilful murder of her mother, Agnes Thuers; who was tried, found guilty, condemned, and executed on the 26th of June, 1812, at Newton, in the county of Sussex, and state of New-Jersey; together with a short account of her life, her farewell letter to her husband, and her dying speech: to which are added some serious remarks by John W. Kirn, by whom this compilation is made, at her request. New-Jersey: Printed for the purchaser, 1812.
16p. 22cm. NjR
"New-Jersey" (part of the imprint) is in gothic type, as is "New-Brunswick" in Sketch of the Trial (following entry)—a style commonly used by New Brunswick printer Lewis Deare. This pamphlet has the same text (although from a different typesetting) as the other, except for two initial words added to the title, and a poem (plus two preceding lines) added on page 16: "A Penitent Pleading for Pardon."

——————.
Sketch of the trial of Mary Cole, for the wilful murder of her mother, Agnes Thuers; who was tried, found guilty, condemned, and executed on the 26th of June, 1812, at Newton, in the county of Sussex, and state of New-Jersey; together with a short account of her life, her farewell letter to her husband, and her dying speech: to which are added, some serious remarks by John W. Kirn, by whom this compilation is made, at her request. New-Brunswick [N.J.] Printed [by Lewis Deare?] for the publisher, 1812.
16p. 21½cm. DLC NjR (copy)

—————.
[*Same title*] Norwich [Conn.] Printed for Israel Brumley, Jr., 1813.
16p. 20cm. CtHi (p. 9-16 lacking) MWA
McDade 203.


## PETER B. DAVIS

In what is now Mountainside lived Baltus Roll and his wife, alone,
reputedly prosperous. Near midnight on February 22, 1831, two men
reached their house by sleigh, dragged the old man from bed, beat
him, and left him outside in an icy puddle to die. A week later Peter B.
Davis, a wayward Camptown (Irvington) tavern keeper, was arrested. His accomplice disappeared after confessing to a friend his part
in the crime and shortly killed himself. Davis, a heavy drinker, in debt
and demonstrably interested in Roll's money, was tried (one witness
was "old and blind and seemed to believe in witches") and acquitted of
the murder charge, the accomplice's hearsay confession being inad-
missable. But Davis was sentenced to a prison term for forgery.

**Davis, Peter B., b.1783?**
  Trial of Peter B. Davis, for the murder of Baltus Roll. Held before a
special term of the Court of Oyer and Terminer and General Jail Deliv-
ery for Essex County, June 28, 1831, Chief-Justice Ewing presiding.
Newark [N.J.] Printed and published at the office of the New-Jersey
Eagle, 1831.
  28p. 20½cm. CSmH NjHi NjR
  For some added details see Elizabeth Van Loan, "The Murder of Baltus Roll,"
*Proceedings of the New Jersey Historical Society*, 80 (1962): [111]-15.


—————.
  [*Same title*] Newark, N.J.: Daily Journal printing establishment,
1883.
  32p. 21½cm. NHi NN NjR


## BRIDGET DERGAN

Bridget Dergan or Durgan (depending on the pamphlet in question)
was born Bridget Deignan. See above, pp. 85-86.

**Brendan, ———.**
  Life, crimes, and confession of Bridget Durgan, the fiendish mur-
deress of Mrs. Coriel. For which she was executed at New Brunswick,
N.J. By Rev. Mr. Brendan. Philadelphia: C. W. Alexander [1867]
  1p.1.,19-46,[2]p. illus. (incl. plates, ports.) 23½cm. DLC
  Entry from DLC.

————.

Life, crimes, and confession of Bridget Durgan, the fiendish murderess of Mrs. Coriel; whom she butchered, hoping to take her place in
the affections of the husband of her innocent and lovely victim. The
only authentic, and hitherto unpublished, history of her whole life; and
the hideous crime for which she was executed at New Brunswick, N.J.
By Rev. Mr. Brendan. Philadelphia: C. W. Alexander, publisher,
c1867.

1p.l.,19-46,[2]p. front., illus. (incl. plate, ports.) 23½cm. NHi PPL

PPL (photocopy in NjR) lacks unnumbered leaf at end, possibly a variant
form.

————.

[*Same: German edition*] Leben, Verbrechen und Geständnisse der
Bridget Durgan, der Mörderin der Mrs. Coriel . . . Die einzige authen-
tische und bis jetzt nocht veröffentlichte Geschichte ihres ganzen
Lebens . . . Von Rev. Mr. Brendan. Philadelphia: C. W. Alexander
[1867]

1p.l.,19-46,[2]p. illus. (incl. ports.) 23½cm. DLC

Entry from DLC.

President James A. Garfield was shot by Charles J. Guiteau in Washington, D.C., on July 2, 1881, but died more than two months later in
his summer cottage (seen above as depicted in *The Illustrated London
News*) in what was then the fashionable Elberon section of Long
Branch. Guiteau was tried and convicted in the District of Columbia
but appealed to the United States Supreme Court that he should have
been tried in New Jersey where the murder was technically committed.
The appeal was denied and the convicted assassin executed on June 30,
1882.

The life and confession of Bridget Dergan, who murdered Mrs. Ellen Coriell, the lovely wife of Dr. Coriell, of New Market, N.J. To which is added her full confession, and an account of her execution at New Brunswick. Philadelphia: Published by Barclay & Co. [1867]
1p.1.,21-49p. illus. (incl. ports.) 23½cm. DLC IEN-L MH-L MnU NHi NN NjR PP

"My name is Bridget Deignan and not Dergan, as I am called. . . ." (p. 37).
McDade (275) notes also an edition of 1881 with fourteen additional pages dealing with other murders. No location indicated.

## JAMES P. DONNELLY

Donnelly was as "beautiful as an Absalom." Although newly certified as a physician, he was the bookkeeper of a Highlands resort hotel in July 1857. Albert S. Moses, a "shrewd and doubtless fast young man," arrived on the July 30. Next evening he won five dollars from Donnelly, playing cards at the bar. When the game resumed upstairs, Donnelly took a guest's money from the hotel safe. Before the play ended, near morning, he had lost over half. To repair the loss, he entered Moses's room and stabbed him. But he failed to recover the money or silence the victim, who died after naming his attacker. Permitted the customary last words on hanging day, January 8, 1858, Donnelly orated for more than two hours on his innocence.

Donnelly, James P., 1833–58.
. . . James P. Donnelly versus the state of New Jersey. Jos. P. Bradley, Wm. Pennington and J. W. Scott, counsel for plaintiff in error. Wm. L. Dayton, attorney general, counsel for the defendant. New York: Wynkoop, Hallenbeck & Thomas, law printers, 1857.
cover-title,150p. 25½cm. NjR

At head of title: Supreme Court, in error.
Proceedings, of Donnelly's trial in the Monmouth County Court of Oyer and Terminer for the murder.

————.

The trial of James P. Donnelly, for the murder of Albert S. Moses, on the first of August, 1857, at the "Sea View House," Navisink, New Jersey. Reported expressly for the Monmouth Inquirer. Freehold [N.J.] Printed at the office of the Monmouth Inquirer, 1857.
38,[2]p. 25cm. CtY-L DLC MH-L NHi NNB NNU-L NjR (copy) PHi PP

Letterpress on covers.
Advertising matter: p. [39-40] and back cover.

**Morris, Abraham Havens, 1828–1913?**
The Highland mystery. Trial and execution of James P. Donnelly, for the murder of Albert S. Moses, at the Sea View House, Highlands, N.J., by A. H. Morris, a member of the jury. Freehold [N.J.] Inquirer print, 1887.
cover-title, 1 leaf, [5]-32p. incl. port. 18cm. NjHi (photo) NjR

————.
The Highland tragedy. Trial and execution of James P. Donnelly, for the murder of Albert S. Moses, at the Sea View House, Highlands, N.J., by A. H. Morris, a member of the jury. Freehold [N.J.] Inquirer print, 1887.
cover-title, 1 leaf, [5]-32p. incl. port. 17cm. NHi NjR (p.27-32 lacking)
Same as the preceding except for variant title.


## CYRUS EMLAY

As the noose dangled nearby, Emlay regretted his last misdeed and many of its predecessors. Except for a short period at sea, he lived always in Burlington County where, while working for his first employer, he "became addicted to strong drink, dances and frolics," and "continued [his] sinful course." From time to time he stole—once in league with his employer Humphrey Wall, a constable—and spent time in jail as a result. "I was offended with him for several circumstances in this affair." Later, he confessed, "I drank hard, and resolved to murder him." On the night of March 14, 1801, Emlay stole a few things, slipped through the window, and struck the sleeping Constable Wall with an ax. A tree served as the gallows.

**Emlay, Cyrus, 1766?–1801, defendant.**
A short account of the trial of Cyrus Emlay, a black man, who was convicted of robbery, arson and murder, on Thursday, May 28th, 1801—received his sentence on Friday the 29th, and was executed, agreeably to said sentence, on Friday, June 12th, 1801. Aged about 35. With his confession, taken from his own mouth a short time before his execution. And a number of interesting letters which passed between him and his connections previous to his exit. To which is added an account of his execution, and conduct at the tree, &c. Second edition. Burlington [N.J.]
Printed by S. C. Ustick, 1801.
16p. 20cm. NHi NjR (copy)
"The following is the substance of the Address delivered on the occasion by Judge Boudinot": p. 7-9.
Although this pamphlet is identified as "second edition," no other publication concerning the Wall murder has been discovered.

# JOHN ERPENSTEIN

See above, pp. 59-60.

Erpenstein, John, 1812-52.
  Lebensgeschichte, Prozess, und Hinrichtung, zu gleich mit dem letz-
ten Bekenntniss des Johann Erpenstein, zum Tode verurteilt wegen
Vergiftung seiner Frau und hingerichtet in Newark, N.J., am 30. März
1852. Geschrieben von ihm selbst . . . Newark, N.J.: Herausgegeben
von Pastor Wm. Winnes; Gedruckt bei D. Fanshaw, New-York, 1852.
  42p. 19cm. NjHi NjR (copy)

————.
  Life and dying confession of John Erpenstein. Convicted of poisoning
his wife, and executed in Newark, N.J., March 30, 1852. Written by
himself, and translated from the German. ⟨Published for the benefit
of his children.⟩   Newark: Printed at the Daily Advertiser office, 1852.
  18p. 24½cm. DLC NjR (copy)

————.
  . . . Life, trial, execution and dying confession of John Erpenstein.
Convicted of poisoning his wife, and executed in Newark, N.J., March
30, 1852. Written by himself, and translated from the German. ⟨Pub-
lished for the Benefit of his children.⟩   Newark: Printed at the Daily
Advertiser office, 1852.
  vii(i.e.,viii),[3]-17,[1]p. 22cm. DLC MH-L NHi NNU-L NjHi NjN
NjR
  At head of title: Second edition.
  Copyright by Rev. William Winnis [i.e., Winnes]

# JOHN FOX

On December 26, 1855, John Henry, about seventeen, and John
Fox, a few years older, arrived in New Brunswick on the afternoon
train. They found quarters for the night, Henry registering under a
false name. In the morning they were seen walking together. Later
Fox appeared alone, dishevelled, muddied, and bloodied, due (he
said) to "one of the damnedest falls he ever had in all his life." Henry's
dead body was found near town on December 30, and Fox was arrested at Elizabeth. Hanged on July 25, 1856, he denied the murder
but admitted to a less than saintly past. John Henry, son of a New York
politician, was more mysterious. In his pockets were a mask, false
moustache, and burglary tools. Fox's words: "I thought more of him
than any other man except one."

**Fox, John, 1835?–56, defendant.**
Trial of John Fox, for the murder of John Henry, at the special term of Middlesex Oyer and Terminer, at New-Brunswick, N.J., May, 1856. Containing the testimony of the witnesses, the speeches of the counsel, the charge to the jury by Judge Vredenbergh [i.e., Vredenburgh], the verdict, and the sentence of the prisoner. New-Brunswick [N.J.] Published at the Fredonian and Daily New-Brunswicker office, 1856.

1p.1.,52,16,[2]p. 25cm. CtY-L DLC GU MH-L MWA NHi NNB NNF NNU-L NjHi NjR PP ViU-L

"Entered . . . in the year 1856, by John F. Babcock."
Printed in double columns.

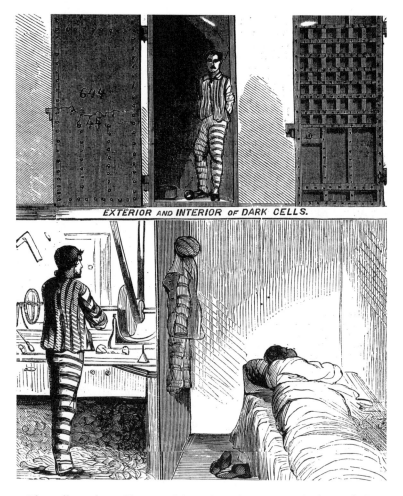

The cells and workhouse of Sing Sing Prison, to which Jacob Rosenzweig was condemned, from *Harper's Weekly* (June 22, 1867).

## MARGARET GARRITY

In July 1851, Margaret Garrity had a spot of news for Edward Drum: she was *enceinte*. Their scheduled August wedding would have made the news less dire, but now Edward refused to marry her, soiled and pregnant. On the wedding day he was there—with Ann McGuire, who had shared him for nearly a year, unbeknownst to Margaret. The latter cornered faithless Edward the next evening, on the street, and shoved a carving knife into him. Thinking his death well earned, the citizens of Newark took Margaret to their hearts at once and later cheered the "not guilty" verdict. A poet-of-sorts wrote extravagantly that "few her virtue can surpass." But few considered the possibility that Margaret had willingly participated in the goings-on that led to her pregnancy.

Eames, John Costin.
    Innocence rewarded, or The successful triumph of Margaret Garrity, who was tried for the murder of a false lover, at Newark, New-Jersey, United States of America, in the month of October, 1851. Composed by John Costin Eames. [Newark? 1851]
    Broadside. 26 x 16½cm. NjR
    Poetry.

## MATTHIAS GOTTLIEB

Prussian-born Matthias Gottlieb (they called him "Cutlip") reputedly deserted from one of the German mercenary regiments during the Revolution. After several prior moves, he was living at Newton in 1795. On December 19, having been "about the village as usual," he returned home drunk. At his wife's nagging, he took up a knife, whetted it carefully, stabbed her three times—she died on December 24— and was jailed shortly. He had a long wait before the trial but a very short one before the hanging. For the latter event the Reverend Hunt preached lengthily on sin, working his way through the gamut of iniquities. Not least of these was slaying one's wife, "a bosom companion . . . the partner of our joys—the soother of our miseries."

Hunt, Holloway Whitefield, 1769-1858.
    A sermon, preached at the execution of Matthias Gotleib [i.e., Gottlieb], for murder; at Newton, October 28, 1796. By Holloway Whitfield [*sic*] Hunt, A.B. & V.D.M. Printed [by Edward Hopkins and William Hurtin?] in Newton, New-Jersey: Nov. 11, 1796.
    8p. 21cm. MWA NjR (copy)

## JAMES GRAVES

The insanity plea was not unknown in the nineteenth century, and its abuses already stirred a good deal of public disfavor. At Newark on December 20, 1881, James Graves sought out and killed his landlord's teenage son. The following month he was tried and condemned despite vigorous efforts to have him treated as insane rather than criminal. For two years a few men struggled in vain to prevent the execution, with unsuccessful appeals to the courts and governor. Among those who examined Graves, Dr. Edward Charles Spitzka found him completely demented and deplored the general lack of sympathy for his condition. "I have never, in an extensive experience with insane criminals, seen as wretched a spectacle as this." He was hanged nonetheless on January 3, 1884.

Spitzka, Edward Charles, 1852–1914.
   The case of James Graves, the insane murderer executed at Newark. Being a paper read before the Society of Medical Jurisprudence and State Medicine. By E. C. Spitzka, M.D., professor of neuro-anatomy and pathology at the New York Post-Graduate Medical School. Together with the discussion by counsellors-at-law Kalisch, Kitchell, ex-judge Hull, and Doctors Young and Gray . . . New York: Steam press of Industrial Printing Company; Stettiner, Lambert & Co., 1884.
   cover-title, 38p. 22½cm. NjN NjR (copy)
   "Reprinted from the American Journal of Neurology and Psychiatry for April, 1884."

## JACOB S. HARDEN

Even men of the cloth have been driven to desperate ends. Among them was Jacob Harden, a Methodist minister appointed in 1856 to a pulpit in Mount Lebanon. The Dorland family soon appeared at his services and fixed upon him as a matrimonial prospect for their daughter Dora. Harden was encouraged to visit Dora at their home, finally spending the night with her. Next morning the talk was of holy matrimony, a topic unwelcome to the young minister. An irregular liaison followed, however, and the Dorlands eventually forced him to marry Dora late in 1858. A few months after, he poisoned her and was free again—briefly. His plaintive last words on the gallows were: "I did not know that poisoning was considered murder."

**Harden, Jacob S., 1837–60.**
Life, confession, and letters of courtship of Rev. Jacob S. Harden, of
the M.E. Church, Mount Lebanon, Hunterdon Co., N.J. Executed for
the murder of his wife, on the 6th of July, 1860. At Belvidere, Warren
Co., N.J. Hackettstown, Warren Co., N.J.: E. Winton, printer, 1860.
1p.1.,[v]-vi, 7-48p. front. (port.) 25cm. DLC MH-L NHi NN NNB
NNU-L Nj NjHi NjR

Introduction signed (p. vi) by E. W. (i.e., Eben Winton).

"Entered according to Act of Congress, in the year 1860, by John Flock," noted
on p. vi as "One of the publishers of this book."

Letterpress (incl. port.) on covers.

# BENJAMIN F. HUNTER

Benjamin F. Hunter and John M. Armstrong, two Philadelphians,
stepped off the Camden ferry one night in January 1878. They headed
toward the house of Ford W. Davis, who owed money to Armstrong,
who in turn owed money to Hunter, who coincidentally held an insurance policy on Armstrong's life. Armstrong hoped to collect Davis's
debt. Hunter hoped to collect Armstrong's insurance. At a signal
Hunter's accomplice, Tom Graham, skulking nearby, leapt from the
shadows, attacked Armstrong with a hammer and fled in panic.
Hunter's ax blows also failed. Visiting next day as a supposed friend,
Hunter finally brought about Armstrong's death by tampering with
the bandages. When his faint-hearted accomplice revealed the plot,
Hunter was arrested and eventually hanged.

Hunter-Armstrong tragedy. The great trial. Conviction of Benj. F.
Hunter, for the murder of John M. Armstrong. Hunter secures insurance policies on the life of Armstrong amounting to $26,000, and lays a
plot to murder him. His tool, Tom Graham, weakens after striking the
first blow, and the chief instigator finishes the awful work . . . Philadelphia: Barclay & Company, 1878.

1p.1.,19-63,[1]p. illus. (incl. ports.) 24cm. DLC MH-L NHi NNB
NjR

Cover-title: The great Hunter-Armstrong tragedy.
Other letterpress on covers.

[*Same*] Philadelphia: Barclay & Company, 1878 [c1879]
1p.1.,19-91p. illus. (incl. plates, ports.) plates. 23½cm. DLC NN

Entry from DLC. McDade (494) notes also editions of 69, 70, and 86 pages,
copies apparently in DLC.

## GEORGE B. JARMAN

Jarman was the classic loser. A man of good family, he first failed in a business venture that cost him most of his inheritance. Thereafter he moved around, working as a peddler, store clerk, physician, and "in the New Brunswick area principally as a schoolmaster." At forty-seven he had become "a confirmed drunkard: frequenting the lowest company." One day in April 1828, while traveling along Georges Road, Jarman was "persuaded in an unfortunate hour" to stop at a wayside tavern. Baited by some loutish fellow drinkers, he drew a Spanish dagger and stabbed one of them to death. While awaiting the hangman's services (on August 8) he was converted by local Methodists and died a fervent believer.

> The life and confession of George B. Jarman; who was executed for murder in New-Brunswick, N.J., on Friday the 8th of August, 1828. Together with original pieces in prose and poetry, composed by him while in prison . . . New-Brunswick [N.J.] Published by Jacob Edmonds, William Packer, & Aaron Slack [1828]
> 8p. 21cm. DLC NjHi NjR
> Rev. George G. Cookman's address: p. 5-6.

## ABRAHAM JOHNSTONE

It was a "singularly uncommon and peculiar case . . . the proof being founded entirely on presumption." This pamphlet—probably ghostwritten (by a clergyman?) for Johnstone—was published to give information on the case "independent of the malignant assertions, and innumerable falsehoods . . . propagated . . . by prejudiced persons." Largely, it is an antislavery and religious tract. Born a slave in Delaware, Johnstone has served five masters and escaped two would-be abductors from Georgia before settling near Woodbury, New Jersey, in 1792. Unfriendly neighbors suspected him of stealing, and finally of murdering Thomas Read, "a Guinea Negro" who had sued him. He denied the killing but admitted "a too great lust after strange women."

> Johnstone, Abraham, d. 1797.
> The address of Abraham Johnstone, a black man, who was hanged at Woodbury, in the county of Glocester [sic], and state of New Jersey, on Saturday the the [sic] 8th day of July last; to the people of colour. To which is added his dying confession or declaration, also, a copy of a letter to his wife, written the day previous to his execution. Philadelphia: Printed for the purchasers, 1797.
> 47p. 20½cm. DLC MBAt MH MWA NHi NN-Sc NcD NjHi NjR
> "My real name is Benjamin Johnstone. But when I came to Jersey changed it, took my brothers viz. Abraham Johnstone." (p. [32])

# WILLIAM JONES

Is there life after hanging? Here a surviver tells all. Some time before his execution, the condemned man was visited by a doctor. The latter had a seductive thought for him, "that there was a moral possibility of recovering persons who had been hanged . . . provided the vertibre [sic] of the neck was not broken; and gave . . . the necessary precautions: how to act in the dreadful day of trial." On that dreadful day, while the experience was unpleasant at best, Jones did manage to avoid a broken neck, and the doctor did manage to revive him after the event. Notwithstanding aches and pains, Jones was back in proper fettle within three or four days, planning to leave at once for happier surroundings. (A hoax perhaps?)

Jones, William.
    The wonderful and surprising resurrection of William Jones, who was executed the 6th of May, at Newark, for the murder of Samuel Shotwell. In a letter from him to E—— W——, in New-York, dated M——— T——, May 13, 1791 . . . [Signed] William Jones. [New York? 1791]
    Broadside. 32 x 26cm. NHi NjR (copy)
    Recorded in both Evans (no. 23475) and Morsch (no. 142) as a possible Newark imprint.


# MARTIN KENKOWSKY, ALIAS LOUIS KETTLER

A footnote to the history of the German-American community in New Jersey and its environs. Philomina Müller was found near Weehawken on May 13, 1881, dead for some days. Leaving her husband four months earlier, Mina had been consorting with Louis Kettler—his real name was Martin Kenkowsky. Her lawful spouse notwithstanding, Mrs. Müller married Kettler on May 3, expecting to sail the next day for a new home in the "old country." Kettler, however, was not ready for this denouement, having already a wife, two children, and a well-exercised taste for philandry. Not long after the wedding, and a few drinks at Schützen Park, he steered Mina into the countryside and brutally slayed her.

    Wedded and murdered within an hour! The cruel murder of Mina Miller by Kenkouwsky, alias "Kettler." The Guttenberg-Hoboken tragedy. A thrilling and remarkable case, which recalls the murder of Mary Rodgers, "the segar girl," which took place on the same spot, the scene of other murders of a like character. The only life of Mina Miller published. Philadelphia, Pa.: Barclay & Co., publishers [1881]
    1p.1.,19-46p. incl. plates, ports. 23½cm. NIC-L NjR (copy) 45.

# ANTOINE LE BLANC

See above, pp. 7-10.

Le Blanc, Antoine, 1802–33, defendant.
S. P. Hull's report of the trial and conviction of Antoine Le Blanc, for the murder of the Sayre family, at Morristown, N.J., on the night of the eleventh of May, 1833 . . . With his confession, as given to Mr. A. Boisaubin, the interpreter. New York: Lewis Nichols, printer [1833] 48p. illus. (port) 19cm. NHi HjHi NjMo NjR

————.

Trial of Le Blanc. Special Oyer and Terminer for Morris Co., Morristown, N.J. 13 of August, A.D. 1833. Before his honour Judge Ford . . . [Morristown? 1833]
34p. 18cm. NjMo (missing)

Caption title (from p.3). The only copy known to this compiler lacks the title-leaf (p.[1-2]), according to George C. Rockefeller's notes in NjR.

The above entry (i.e., caption title) is from that in J. H. Fraser, *Early Printing in Morristown, New Jersey* . . . (Morristown, N.J.: Joint Free Public Library of Morristown and Morris Township, 1970), no. 53, which, however, fails to note the missing title-leaf.

————.

The trial, sentence and confession of Antoine Le Blanc, who was executed at Morristown, N.J. on Friday the 6th Sept. 1833. For the murder of Mr. Sayre and family. The execution took place on the green in the presence of a crowd of spectators. It was calculated that no less thae [sic] twelve thousand persons were present, of which the majority were females.    This will be found one of the most interesting works of the kind.    Second edition. Morriston, N.Y. [sic] printed, 1833.
20p. illus. 24½cm. CtY DLC MH-L N-L NHi NNB NNF NjHi NjMo NjR (copy) PHi

"Never before published but in part."

Morris County, N.J. Sheriff's Office.
The execution of Antoine Le Blanc, will take place on Morristown green, about noon this day. All persons except those belonging to the troop, going on horse-back or in wagons, or carriages of any kind, are notified and requested to leave their horses and carriages at some convenient place out of town, and to go [to] the place of execution on foot. This arrangement becomes necessary, and all well-disposed persons will yield to it, when it is known, that the horses, wagons &c., would create confusion, if not danger; and would greatly interfere with the spectators on that occasion. Friday, Sept. 6th 1833. George H. Ludlow, sheriff. Morristown, N.J.: Printed at the Jerseyman office [1833]
Broadside. 19x36cm. NjR (copy) NjMoW

Copy in NjMoW has manuscript notation: "B Howell Frank Howell & M Howell went to see him hung by the Neck."

## CHARLES LEWIS

He was newly arrived in Princeton, a bewhiskered man of about fifty, large and well dressed. When a local jeweler named James Rowand was clubbed to death and robbed one evening in November 1862, suspicion fell upon the stranger, who called himself Charles Lewis. He was arrested, tried, convicted on circumstantial evidence, and hanged in April. The defense attorneys, well known and able, unaccountably rested their case without presenting testimony—perhaps to avoid revelations of Lewis's past, which he had kept well hidden. Newspapers identified him as a professional criminal, formerly of Massachusetts and New York, with a collection of aliases and a fancied connection with the unsolved New York murder of Dr. Harvey Burdell in 1857.

**Lewis, Charles, d.1863, defendant.**
Trial of Charles Lewis for the murder of James Rowand, of Princeton, N.J. Princeton, N.J.: Published at the Standard office, 1863.
cover-title, 55p. 22cm. DLC MH-L NNB NNU-L NjHi NjP NjR (copy)

"In preparing the foregoing account . . . we have used the evidence as reported in the True American and Gazette, but have had it corrected from other notes." (p. 55.)

——————.
The Burdell mystery unravelled. New York: National Police Gazette office, 1863.
31,[1]p. illus. (incl. ports.) 24cm. DLC NHi NN NjHi (copy) NjR

Caption title (p.3): The Princeton murder. The Burdell mystery unravelled! Confessions of Charles Lewis, alias Symonds, alias Jones, alias Davis, alias Gibbons, alias Gibson, His intimacy with Dr. Burdell. He becomes jealous of him! Suspects the Doctor of being intimate with his paramour during his absence. Supposed to have personated Dr. Burdell in the mock marriage with Mrs. Cunningham. He marries a respectable young lady, attempts to kill her, saves herself by stabbing him with a fork. Graphic scenes in his cell. His execution!

**Mercer County, N.J. Coroner's Jury.**
Full proceedings of the inquest relative to the murder of the late James Rowand. [Princeton, N.J., 1862]
Broadside. 62x48½cm. NjHi NjR (copy)

The jury was called by John Fenning, justice of the peace, in the absence of a coroner. The sessions covered November 14-18, 1862.
In seven columns.

**Thomson, Peter**
Life and adventures of George W. Symonds, the Burdell murderer. By Peter Thomson, official reporter of Special Sessions. New York: National Police Gazette office [1863]
1p.1.,4-28(i.e. 30)p. illus., plates. 23½cm. DLC NHi NjR (copy)

Deals entirely with the life and criminal career of George W. Symonds, "alias Lewis," with scant reference to the Rowand murder at Princeton.

## THOMAS LUTHERLAND

One of England's lesser gifts to the New World was Thomas Lutherland. At the end of a rascally life he declared: "I have . . . committed more sins than man could almost commit, for Drunkenness, Whoring, Swearing, Tempting Young Women to Debauchery, and then leave them." Indeed he had. Housed with a bigamous second wife and children in Salem, he committed his last sin in November 1691, robbing and murdering a Philadelphia merchant, John Clark, who traded in West Jersey. When Clark's unattended boat and later his body were found, townspeople pointed the accusing finger at Lutherland, who was seized and tried. Unpracticed in such cases, "the Court was very cautious in passing Sentence of Death"—endorsed, however, by "the best Yeomandry in the Country."

Lutherland, Thomas, 1653?–92.
    Blood will out, or, An example of justice in the tryal, condemnation, confession and execution of Thomas Lutherland, who barbarously murthered the body of John Clark of Philadelphia, and was executed at Salem in West-Jarsey the 23d of February, 169½. Philadelphia: Printed and sold by Will. Bradford, 1692.
        8p., 9-12 leaves, 13-19p. 20cm. NN

————.
    Rex et regina vs Lutherland. Being a facsimile of a pamphlet printed & sold by Will. Bradford in Philadelphia in the year 1692 on the tryal, condemnation, confession and execution of Thomas Lutherland. With an introduction and comments on the ancient law of the bier, by Joseph S. Sickler. Woodstown, N.J.: The Seven Stars Press [1949 (c1948)]
    cover-title, [28]p. 23cm. DLC NN NNU-L Nj NjP NjR
    Includes complete facsimile (19p.) of the original 1692 publication. The same facsimile, reproduced from the 1949 reprint, appears also in *The Way It Used to Be*, 1, no. 10 (November 1976): 1, 16-32.
    See also Sickler's article, "Blood Will Out: Rex et Regina versus Lutherland," *Proceedings of the New Jersey Historical Society*, 53 (1935): 108-110.

## WALTER C. MCALISTER AND OTHERS

Four young Paterson men (Walter C. McAlister, George J. Kerr, William A. Death, and Andrew J. Campbell) got together at a local saloon on the night of October 19, 1900. They plied a seventeen-year-old Dutch girl, Jennie Bosschieter, with drugged liquor, took the stupefied girl by cab to a roadside spot in nearby Hawthorne, and raped her one by one—they offered the waiting cabbie a like opportunity, which he declined. Finding her now unconscious, they returned to Paterson where a doctor, roused from bed, discovered that she had died in the interim. The four then abandoned Jennie's body some distance away. Three were tried (Kerr pleaded *non vult*) and convicted of second-degree murder, and all four received prison sentences.

**McAlister, Walter C., defendant.**
. . . Trial of Walter C. McAlister, Andrew J. Campbell and William A. Death for the murder of Jennie Bosschieter, giving in full all the testimony, the rulings of the court and the arguments of counsel as taken from the transcript of the official stenographer. Paterson, N.J.: The Paterson Publishing Company, 1901.
1p.l.,412p. 23cm. DLC Nj NjJ NjRuF NIC NN NNB WaU-L
At head of title: . . . Passaic County Oyer and Terminer, state of New Jersey.

A view of the library of Sing Sing Prison, from *Harper's Weekly* (June 22, 1867). One wonders if its users were "jailhouse lawyers" or avid readers of murder pamphlets.

# JOHN MCKINNEY

Demon Rum claimed another victim on August 7, 1855. In Newark a party of young men had been on the town for a number of hours, drinking here and there. Somewhat under the influence, they made their way near midnight to Putnam House, where a dance was in progress, with a bar for its patrons. Fancying a few quaffs of lager beer, perhaps a little dancing, the young men were taken aback when the proprietor, Conrad Bauer, asked them to pay for admission, whereupon "a clinch ensued." They started to withdraw. When Bauer turned to regain his seat on the landing, John McKinney thrust a dagger into Bauer's buttock, cutting an artery from which he died of bleeding. McKinney fled, was arrested in New Orleans, tried for murder, but convicted of manslaughter.

> McKinney, John, defendant.
> Report of the trial of John McKinney for the murder of Conrad Bauer, at the Essex County Court of Oyer & Terminer, January term, 1856. [Newark, N.J.? 1856]
> 14p. 30½cm. MH-L NHi
> Printed in triple columns.

# SINGLETON MERCER

Whatever its advantages, seduction is not without risk. Mahlon Hutchinson Heberton learned this on February 10, 1843, from "one of Colt's revolving pistols." He was "handsome and well made—wore whiskers, moustache and imperial," a wolf among the lambs. He had met Sarah Mercer (sixteen) on the street and eventually had his evil way with her. The Mercers were duly enraged, especially the girl's brother. Heberton, knowing the latter had violent plans for him, started across the river (all parties were Philadelphians) but was killed as the ferryboat reached Camden. Singleton Mercer was tried and, to the joy of all, acquitted, as mentally unstable. One medical witness noted that he was afflicted with constipation, "which leads directly to insanity."

> A full and complete account of the Heberton tragedy: to which is added Beauchamp, or The Kentucky tragedy. New York: Published for the trade [ca.1849]
> 68p. front. 15cm. MH-L MWA NHi
> From McDade 677, which notes twenty-seven leaves at the end, advertising books of John B. Perry (Philadelphia). KyHi records a copy or variant with 64p. and 1843 imprint date.

Mercer, Singleton, b. 1823, defendant.
The Philadelphia tragedy. With six fine engravings of the principal
characters and scenes. Drawn by R. Browne, esq. Full and complete
details of the seduction of Miss Sarah Gardner Mercer, by Mahlon Hutchinson Heberton, together with an account of the murder of young
Heberton by Singleton Mercer, the brother of the unfortunate young
girl. To which is added, the trial and acquittal of Mercer for the murder. New York: The Sun, 1843.
   12p. illus.(incl.ports.) 28cm. (The Sun extra—New York, April 8,
1843) NHi NjR (copy)
   Caption title.

——————.
The trial of Singleton Mercer for the murder of M. Hutchinson He-
berton, at Camden, N.J. on Friday 10th February 1843. New York:
The Herald office [1843]
   [8]p. (folded)
   Description supplied by Thomas McDade (letter, April 20, 1978).

## JAMES MUNKS

Notwithstanding publication of the 1847 edition in Newark, these
accounts reveal no connection with New Jersey, although a New Jersey banknote was carried by the victim, Reuben Guild (possibly the
Reuben Guild of Whitehouse, New Jersey). One Sunday in November
1817, James Munks was on his way home in central Pennsylvania.
Stopping for several hours at a roadside tavern, he drunkenly resumed
his journey, soon to meet another traveler. A sudden thought: "I must
kill this man!" He shot the hapless stranger and stole everything, even
clothes. But he dropped a songbook, which led to his conviction and
hanging. The 25-year-old father of two, Munks had sinned early and
"grew viler and viler.'"

Munks, James, 1793-1819.
The confession of James Munks, who was executed at Bellefonte,
Centre Co. Pennsylvania, Saturday, January 23, 1819, for the murder
of Reuben Guild. New York: Printed and sold . . . at No. 139 Cherry-
street, 1819.
   8p. illus. 21cm. DLC
   Text begins on verso of title-page.
   McDade 707.

——————.
Confession of James Munks, who was executed on Saturday, January
23, 1819. For the murder of Reuben Guild. Written by himself. Newark, N.J.: Aaron Guest, printer, 1847.
   8p. 21½cm. NjP NjR (copy)

## PETER W. PARKE AND JOSEPH CARTER

In most of these cases the killer was identified acceptably. Not so the killer of John B. Parke and three others in his household at Changewater on May 1, 1843. For two years the aroused yeomanry bumbled around in search of someone to hang. A few officials and many neighborly volunteers collected allegations and rumors, chased suspicious characters in every direction, and arrested haphazardly a number of startled citizens, producing thereby not one solid clue. Virtually without reason, Joseph Carter and Peter W. Parke became the chosen ones and were hanged. No hindrance to these proceedings were the lawyers and judges, who did their required tasks at six trials, of which Carter had two.

Farrow, Ruth Trask.
Murder along the Musconetcong: a tale of Jersey justice . . . By Ruth Trask Farrow . . . [Hong Kong: Manufactured by T.F.H. Publications, inc., 1973]
3p.1.,174p. 22cm. NjHi NjR
Bibliography: p. 172-74.

Parke, Peter W., d.1845.
Protest of Peter W. Parke, who was executed on Friday, Aug. 22d, 1845, in which he declares his innocence to the last moment of his life, also his opinion concerning the Changewater murder, with a brief examination of the character and testimony of some of the principal witnesses for the state. Published for the benefit of his widow and three orphan children. New-York: For sale at all the periodical stores, 1845.
24p. 22cm. NNU-L NjR PPL
"Entered . . . in the year 1845, by John F. Hunter, Jr."

## PETER ROBINSON

A New Brunswick carpenter, "sober, steady, and industrious," Peter Robinson was in debt to Abraham Suydam, who had sold him a lot and lent money for house-building. On December 3, 1840, Suydam went to visit Robinson and forthwith disappeared. Suspicious citizens searched the house and found Suydam's body, which was exposed then at the courthouse "for a short time to the view of such persons as were desirous of seeing it." Robinson, arrested (with his wife and brothers), confessed the crime: He has struck Suydam with a mallet and later with a spade before burying him in the cellar—a premeditated act. Due to Peter's "great horror of surgeons and phrenologists," his body was not dissected after the "strictly private" execution.

Life and confessions of Peter Robinson, the murderer of A. Suydam, New Brunswick, with his last letter and declaration, in his own language and hand writing. [New York: Published at the office of the New York Herald, 1841]

[2]p. incl. port. 60x41cm. NjR

Caption title.

Printed in five columns.

The supplied imprint is based on Robinson's portrait, which is printed from the same plate used in *The Trial of Peter Robinson, for the Murder of Abraham Suydam* (below).

The life and confessions, together with historical reminiscences, last moments, dying statements, and execution of Peter Robinson, who murdered Abraham Suydam, president of the Farmers' and Mechanics' Bank in New Brunswick, on the 4th of December, 1840, at New Brunswick; and was hung in front of the jail there on the 16th of April, 1841. The whole carefully taken down from the prisoner's own lips, revised and corrected, and reported exclusively for the "New-York Herald," by William H. Attree. New York: Published at the Herald office, 1841.

16p. incl. port., facsim. 25cm. NjHi NjR (copy)

Printed in double columns.

**McConaghy, Robert, d.1840, defendant.**

Trial, confession, and execution of Robert M'Conaghy, for the murder of Mrs. Brown and her five children [in Huntington County, Pa.] . . . To which is added the confession of Peter Robinson, the murderer of Mr. Suydam, of New Brunswick . . . Philadelphia, 1841.

16p. 21cm. MH-L

McDade 648.

Ein neues Trauer Lied, auf die Hinrichtung von Peter Robinson, der am 16ten April, 1841, in der Stadt Neu Braunschweig, im Staat Neu Jersey, hingerichtet wurde, für die Ermordung von Abraham Suydam, Präsident der Farmers' und Mechaniks' Bank, in selbiger Stadt, im December, 1840. [n.p., 1841]

Broadside. 37½ x 20cm. NjR

A narrative of the case in verse.

**Robinson, Peter, 1808–41, defendant.**

Trial and extraordinary confessions, sketches and anecdotes of the life of Peter Robinson, who was executed at New Brunswick, N.J., on the 16th of April, 1841, for the murder of Abraham Suydam, on the 3d of December, 1840; giving a particular account of his parentage, his conduct through life, the causes which led him to murder Mr. Suydam, the minute details of the murder, letters to his wife while in prison, his last will and testament, &c., as he gave it to the Rev. H. J. Leacock, a few days previous to his execution. To which is added an account of many interesting incidents which took place during the last 24 hours of his life, and in particular during the last night previous to his execution, when his wife, father, and 2 brothers visited him for the last time, and remained with him through the night, and during which time he gave

an account of the mysterious disapearance [sic] of his sister Susan, whom he has been accused of murdering. New York, 1841.
24p. illus. (incl. port.) 21½cm. NHi NjR (copy)

———————.

Trial, confession, and execution of Peter Robinson, for the murder of Abraham Suydam, esq., of New Brunswick, N.J. Executed April 16th, 1841. ae 32 years. New York: Published by the reporter, April 16, 1841.
16p. illus. 22½cm. MH-L NHi NN NNU-L NjHi (copy) NjR

———————.

Trial of Peter Robinson for the murder of Abraham Suydam; as reported for the Newark Daily Advertiser, by Daniel Dodd, Jr. esq. Newark: Printed and published by Aaron Guest, 1841.
47p. 20½cm. NjHi NjR (copy)

———————.

The trial of Peter Robinson, for the murder of Abraham Suydam, esq., president of the Farmers' and Mechanics' Bank, of New Brunswick. Containing a very full and accurate account of all the testimony adduced on the trial—the whole having been carefully taken down as it was delivered: also, the very eloquent and impressive charge of Chief Justice Hornblower, to the jury, and his final most affecting address to the wretched criminal on pronouncing upon him the sentence of death: together with a full account of all the strange and horrid confessions of Robinson as made to different persons before his trial, and to his counsel and others since his conviction. Sentenced to be hung on the 16th day of April next. The whole reported for the New-York Herald, by William H. Attree. New York: Published at the office of the New York Herald [1841]
32p. illus. (port.) 26cm. DLC MH-L N-L NHi NN NNB NNU-L NjHi NjR PP PPL

Last page numbered only "2," the type for the preceding number (3) apparently having fallen out of the form.

———————.

[Same title] New Brunswick, N.J.: Published and for sale by S. G. Deeth, bookseller, March 30, 1841.
32p. illus. (port.) 26½cm. DLC NjR

Except for different imprint, this is identical with the preceding, even to the imperfect numbering of page 32.

———————.

A true account of the murder of Abraham Suydam, late of New-Brunswick, together with an accurate outline of the testimony, elicited on the examination of witnesses. [New Brunswick, N.J.] Printed at the Times office, and sold at S. G. Deeth's bookstore [1840]
8p. 24½cm. DLC MH-L NjR RPB

Caption title.
"The investigation . . . was made by the Police Court . . ." (p. 3.)
Manuscript inscription in NjR copy: "Mr. Vanderbilt Spader 1840"; in DLC copy: "Peter Force Esq. from the reporter, S. G. Deeth."

A race riot and brutal killings shocked Patenburg, Hunterdon County, in 1872. Involved were several hundred feuding Irish and black workers who were building a railroad tunnel through the Musconetcong Mountain. On the night of September 21, Irish workers attacked blacks in cabins near the work site. One of the blacks slain in the melee was Denis Powell, as depicted above in *Harper's Weekly* (October 12, 1872). Inquests were held on the bodies of the victims, but local magistrates did not prosecute the case.

## JACOB ROSENZWEIG

See above, pp. 117-18.

The great "trunk mystery" of New York City. Murder of the beautiful Miss Alice A. Bowlsby, of Paterson, N.J. Her body placed in a trunk and labelled for Chicago. Many strange incidents made public. Philadelphia, Pa.: Barclay & Co., publishers [1871]

1p.l.,19-102p. incl. plates, ports. fold. front., illus. (plan) 24cm.
CtY-L DLC DNLM KMK MBA MH-L MWA NN NNB PPL

Includes (p. 70-77) an account of the suicide inquest of Walter F. Conklin, Alice's "seducer."

Listed, improperly it would seem, in L. H. Wright, *American Fiction, 1851–1875: Contribution toward a Bibliography (San Marino, Calif.: Huntington Library, 1957), no. 1018.*

There are several variants, all with "The Trial of Rosenzweig" added on p. 102-4: one published 1871 (NjR); others copyrighted 1872 (CtY MH-L NN NjP NjR), 1873 (CLU), and 1875 (ViU), otherwise unchanged.

[*Same, German edition*] Das grosse Geheimniss des Koffers in N.Y. City. Ermordung der schönen Miss A. Bowlsby von Paterson, N.J. Phila.: Barclay and Co. [1872]

1p.l.,19-104p. PHi
Entry from George C. Rockefeller notes in NjR.

The trunk tragedy; or, The late mysterious murder in New York of the young and lovely Miss Alice A. Bowlsby, of Patterson, N.J., in the vile den of a New York abortionist . . . Suicide of the alleged seducer, Conklin . . . Philadelphia, Pa.: C. W. Alexander [1871]

60,[2]p. incl. plates. 23cm. CtY DLC MH-L NcD NcD-L
Entry from DLC.

## MATILDA C. SHANN

Throughout her trial Mrs. Shann, "a rather handsome woman of commanding figure," sat among loyal relatives. She was a Princeton boarding-house keeper who, toward the end of 1892, insured the life of her son John for $2,000. Soon he began to fail and died miserably on April 18. Poisoning was suspected. By the next day his mother (and beneficiary) had learned that an inquest was planned. An insurance detective prowled around the town. That night, intestines and other items disappeared from the corpse, still lying in the bedroom that John had shared, oddly, with a sister—the work, Mrs. Shann said, of three mysterious strangers. The bereaved mother was tried and acquitted.

Beasley, Chauncy Haven, 1857–1913.
Closing argument on the part of the defense in the case of the State vs. Mattie C. Shann, under indictment of murder. By Chauncy H. Beasley, esq., of the Mercer County bar of New Jersey. Trenton, N.J.: MacCrellish & Quigley, printers, 1893.
32p. 20cm. MoU-L NjR (copy)

# JOHN SHIELS, ALIAS JAMES KEASE, AND OTHERS

In Philadelphia, August 1787, two rascals found each other: John Shiels (alias James Kease) and John Watson (alias Campbell). After a stealing expedition in West Jersey they met Patrick Kennon, fresh from the city jail. Together they planned another larcenous foray— delayed a few days by Shiels's unexpected confinement in the work-house. Setting out at last, they reached Mrs. Jenkins's house in Evesham Township on the night of September 1, quite intoxicated. Kennon burst inside, to find the widow Jenkins and her daughter set for battle, in which the former was mortally injured. As she dashed down the lane "roaring aloud," the three fled. Pursuers found them the next day asleep, and they were hanged three weeks later. "Jersey justice" indeed!

> **Shiels, John, d.1787, defendant.**
> The trial of James Kease, Patrick Kennon, and John Campbell, for burglary and murder. Before the Honorable Isaac Smith, esquire, second justice of the Supreme Court of New Jersey; Joshua Maddox Wallace, George Anderson, Thomas Fennimore, and Israel Shrieve, Esquires, associates and commissioners. At a Court of Oyer and Ter-miner, and General Gaol Delivery, of the state of New-Jersey, for the county of Burlington, holden at the city of Burlington, on Tuesday the 18th of September, 1787, by virtue of a commission under the great seal of the state, for holding said courts, dated at Burlington, the 22d day of May, 1787 . . . By a person present at the trial. Philadelphia: Printed in the year 1787.
> 24p. 21cm. DGU DLC NjR (copy)
> "Published by desire."
> Kease's true name was John Shiels; Campbell's was Watson.
> This description is of the DGU copy. Since the McDade entry, from DLC, differs in two details—"John" Kease and Patrick "Kinnon"—there is an uncon-firmed possibility that the two copies are variants.

## WILLIAM SMART

William Smart did not live up to his name. In England he "began very early in sin and wickedness." In Maryland he was inclined to "roving about and other vices." In Philadelphia, where dissipation flourished, he "soon got acquainted with many bad houses and evil company." In Burlington County he behaved no better, at one point amusing himself, with two cronies, by terrorizing an old lady. To-ward the end of May 1772, Smart was at Elizabeth Knight's public-house in Evesham Township, drinking beer, when a thought struck: Why not rob the tavern? He crept up to the door that night, crashed through it, and clubbed Mrs. Knight to death. His "dying words" on the gallows included pious exhortations against sin.

Smart, William, 1749–72.
The dying words and confession of William Smart, who was tried for and found guilty of burglary. He was executed at Burlington, pursuant to his sentence, on Saturday the 4th of July, 1772. Containing the history of his life, and a particular account of the murder of Elizabeth Knight. To which is added the judgment hymn. [Philadelphia?] Printed in the year 1772.
8p. 19cm. NjHi NjR (copy)

## ELIPHALET M. S. SPENCER

"In her person she was as fair a temple, as was ever erected by the great architect of the universe." This paragon was Adaline Dobbin, unfaithful to four husbands. With the first (1837) she went to Ohio, where they parted after three years. She and the second (1842)—first "captivated with her personal appearance in the street"—were divorced in eleven months. The third (1843) died unaccountably in a year. Number four (1845) was Eliphalet M. S. Spencer, with whom she moved to Jersey City. There he shot her, in July 1846, only to be acquitted of murder later by reason of insanity. In her many extramarital adventures Adaline was supported by an obnoxious mother, who hated her daughter's husbands—and her own.

Parish, Daniel.
Late murder in Jersey City: or, A brief sketch of career of Mrs. Spencer, the victim: a woman of four husbands at the age of twenty-four, the most extraordinary female character of the present generation. The writer's defence to the charges of the mother of this depraved woman, re-published in a sheet called "The Cleveland Plain Dealer." Truth sometimes stranger than fiction, always stronger . . . By D. Parish. Cleveland: Printed for the author, 1846.
20p. 20½cm. N-L NHi NjR (copy)

Mrs. Dobbin's statements to the press idealized her late daughter and smeared the four husbands. Daniel Parish was number two of the latter.

## SAMUEL STODDARD

No copy of Samuel Stoddard's narrative, "written with his own Hand," has been located. The title below is derived from Andrew Steuart's advertisement of the pamphlet ("This day . . . published") in the *Pennsylvania Gazette* of December 16, 1762, copied in *New Jersey Archives*, 1st ser. 24, p. 114–15. The narrative, in Steuart's words, "lays before you a Series of unheard-of Villanies, and most atrocious Crimes . . . It appears, by his own Confession, that he was a crafty, subtle Fellow, and carried on his sinful Practices of Art and Dissimulation, especially with the Women." Besides an account of the trial, and a "most surprising Dream of Vision," it includes Stoddard's "last Speech and dying Words, which he spoke to the People."

**Stoddard, Samuel, d. 1762.**
A narrative of the unhappy life and miserable end of Samuel Stoddard, late of Egg Harbour, in the county of Burlington, and province of West-New-Jersey; who was tried at a Supreme Court, held at Burlington aforesaid, on Saturday, the sixth of November, 1762, for the barbarous, cruel and inhuman murder of Jacob Gale, late of Egg-Harbour aforesaid; of which crime he was found guilty, and, according to sentence, was executed at the city of Burlington, on Tuesday, the 23d of the same month. Philadelphia: Printed and published by Andrew Steuart, 1762.

The title in Evans (no. 9197) differs somewhat—e.g., victim's name is Jacob "Cole"; references to "Egg Harbour" are absent.

## PETER STOUT

What is fitting response to "some abusive language"? Peter Stout pondered this question for a few days and had his answer. On the morning of November 19, 1802, he set out with ax in hand, soon meeting his teenage abuser. They walked together, chatting, until Stout dropped back suddenly and struck his companion to the ground, a couple of added blows completing the enterprise. Arrested three days later, after serving (curiously enough) on the coroner's jury, he confessed. At first unrepentant, he turned to religion during the months in jail, regretting "a long and continued course of licentious conduct and crimes." For the killing he had been "urged on by the devil." The murder was in Dover Township, the hanging in Freehold.

An account of the murder of Thomas Williams, the apprehension and conviction of Peter Stout, who committed the murder: together with the sentence of the court, the confession of the criminal, his behaviour before and after condemnation, and his execution . . . Trenton [N.J.] Printed by Sherman & Mershon, 1803.
12p. 18½cm. NHi NjR

**Stout, Peter, 1776?–1803.**
The last speech, confession, and dying words of Peter Stout, who was executed at Monmouth Court-House, New-Jersey, on the 13th of May last, for the horrid and unprovoked murder of Thomas Wiliams [sic], a youth of about fourteen years of age: together with the sentence of the court, and the criminal's behavior before and after condemnation. Morris-Town [N.J.] Printed for every purchaser, July 1803.
12p. 18cm. NjR

Text is almost identical to that of the preceding, although from a different setting of type.

## HOWARD SULLIVAN

One day in mid-August 1884 Ella Watson, a budding girl of fifteen, was selling eggs and chickens to merchants in the South Jersey community of Yorktown. That night she was found nearby—clubbed, strangled, robbed, and raped. Two local blacks were promptly arrested—on speculation, it seems—but released soon. A reward was offered for discovery of the stump from which the killer had cut his club. Howard Sullivan, a stout black teenager, found it speedily. During the girl's funeral, before a "profoundly attentive throng," he and two others were seized. A black detective posing as a fellow prisoner induced Sullivan's confession. The death sentence was a shock, for he had expected a short jail term.

Borton, Benjamin, 1841–1912.
   The Yorketown tragedy; Ella Watson's tragic death. Sullivan's arrest, trial and confession . . . Salem, N.J.: Press of South Jerseyman, 1884.
   cover-title, 16p. illus. (incl. ports.) 22½cm. DLC NHi NjR (copy)
   Copy in NHi is inscribed: "Compliments of the Author, Benj. Borton, Harrisonville, N.J."
   The former spelling, "Yorketown," is used throughout.

## UNKNOWN

The parties to this case are anonymous at both ends. A woman of about twenty-five, her throat cut, was found at the edge of Rahway on Saturday morning, March 26, 1887. There were signs of a struggle (clothing disarrayed, scattered bruises and bloodstains, her face stamped-upon) but not of rape. In the vicinity were a basket of eggs, a small, bloody knife, a satchel containing female garments, and a man's shirt. For weeks the police and a coroner's inquest explored a flood of clues and allegations from far and wide. Several thousand people viewed the body, after which a local church took it for funeral and burial. Despite every exertion, the mystery remained: undetermined were the motive and the identities of both victim and assailant.

National Police Gazette.
   $250 reward. [*Engraving.*] The above is an accurate portrait, published only in the . . . National Police Gazette . . . of the young woman mysteriously murdered at Rahway, New Jersey, on March 25, 1887. It represents her with every article of dress worn by her, and as she appeared the day before the murder. To any person or persons, who from this clue, may discover the murderer and secure his or her conviction, I will, on proper proof, pay the above reward. (Signed.) Richard K. Fox.
New York: "Police Gazette" Publishing House [1887]
   Broadside. 39 x 16½cm. NjHi NjR (copy)

## WILHELMUS VAN AUKEN

At the Sussex County jail in mid-January 1821 he wrote sentimentally of his wife: "I loved her unspeakably, for our hearts were knit with pure love and compassion." Yet he had killed her brutally on New Year's Day. Clearly Van Auken was deranged, a condition of six years' duration which expressed itself in morbid anxiety about his ultimate salvation. "I thought probably I had fell from grace and could have no repentence." An uncle "had often heard him say he had committed the unpardonable sin." The sin is not identified but neighbors, suspecting it was the unsolved murder and robbery of a peddler a half dozen years earlier, welcomed Van Auken's hanging on January 25, 1822.

Van Auken, Wilhelmus, 1784–1822, defendant.
A succinct account of the trial of Wilhelmus Van Auken, who was indicted, tried and found guilty of the murder of his wife, Leah Van Auken, and sentenced to be executed on the 25th day of January, 1822, at Newton, Sussex County, N.J. Together with a short narrative of his life, written by himself, a few days before his execution. Newton: Printed for the publisher, January 1822.
12p. 20cm. Nj NjR (copy)

————.
The trial of Wilhelmus Van Auken, who was indicted, tried and found guilty of the murder of his wife, Leah Van Auken, and sentenced to be executed on the 25th day of January, 1822. At Newton, Sussex County, N.J. Together with a short narrative of his life, written by himself, a few days before his execution. Kingston [N.Y.] Printed at the Plebian office, 1822.
15p,[1]p. illus. 21cm. DLC
Entry from DLC catalog.

## GEORGE B. VOSBURGH

On January 1, 1877, the Reverend Vosburgh moved to Jersey City. His wife fell ill in November and by February 1878 was near death. Arriving to await the event, her relatives watched his strange behavior, decided the good parson was poisoning his wife, and sent specimens for analysis, which confirmed the presence of poison. They now contrived to substitute, in place of the husband's offerings, meals they themselves had prepared. Thereupon Hattie's condition improved. Vosburgh was cleared of attempted murder after a long trial with extensive medical testimony. An incident to the proceedings was his allegation that Hattie had induced abortions on two occasions, with the help of her mother.

Vosburgh, George Bedell, b.1849, defendant.
The trial of Rev. Geo. B. Vosburgh, pastor of the Bergen Baptist
Church, Jersey City, N.J., for alleged wife poisoning. Revised and corrected from the reports published by the Jersey City Evening Journal,
C. H. Benson reporter. Jersey City: The Evening Journal Association,
1878.
122p. 23cm. NN NjJ NjR (copy)

# JOHN WARE

The Wares were a Kallikak-type family of Gloucester Township,
near Berlin. The father was an irrascible old man who regularly badg-
ered his wife about past infidelities (nine, to be exact). With them
lived a daughter and her family, a son John, and a disreputable older
woman. John was illiterate, an attempted suicide, married but separated, and once arrested in a cow-stealing plot. Agitated by a bitter
family argument on the morning of August 16, 1870, he aimed a
loaded Springfield at his father and shot him dead. Despite a general
realization that evil circumstances and bad heredity had a part in the
crime, the young man was hanged, unrepenting, "and . . . six women
looked upon the terrible scene."

Ware, John, 1847–71, defendant.
Life, trial, confession and conviction of John Ware, for the murder of
his father, near Berlin, Camden County, New Jersey. Photographs by
T. Brooks. Designs by George Nutting. Engravings by Harmon H.
Smith. Philadelphia: Barclay Publishing House, 1871.
1p.1.,19-55p. plates, port. 23½cm. CtY-L MH-L NHi NNB
Published shortly after March 13, 1871.

[Same] 1p.1,19-72p. plates, port. 23½cm. DLC NjR (copy)
Includes addendum (p. 57-72) printed after the December 15 execution.

# WESLEY WARNER

Not among the elite of Mount Holly was the Peak family, which
included one son imprisoned for murder and several loose daughters.
Lizzie Peak was a kept woman when Wesley Warner discovered her in
1890. Abandoning his wife and children, Wesley Warner and Lizzie
removed to Brooklyn, where finally a bar-room brawl put him in jail
for awhile. In 1892 they settled in with the Peaks, and Warner found a
job at the county fair. Lizzie and two sisters—"a 'fly' crowd and sus-
ceptible to more than idle flirtation"—spent long hours at the fair with

male companions. At the Peak house one night, when the girls returned with three young men, Warner stabbed Lizzie (in a state of delirium tremens, it was claimed). Hanging day was September 6, 1894.

A history of Wesley Warner's crime! The murder of Lizzie Peak. Illustrated. Mount Holly, N.J., 1894.
26p. illus. (incl. ports., facsim.) 25cm. NjR (copy)

Letterpress (advertising matter) on covers.
"Previous executions" (in Burlington County): p. 23-24.

[*Same: facsimile reprint*] [Burlington, N.J.: Republished by Henry H. Bisbee, 1972] NjHi NjR